The Stepfamily Puzzle: Intergenerational Influences

ALL HAWORTH BOOKS & JOURNALS
ARE PRINTED ON CERTIFIED
ACID-FREE PAPER

The Stepfamily Puzzle: Intergenerational Influences

Craig A. Everett, PhD
Editor

The Haworth Press, Inc.
New York • London • Norwood (Australia)

The Stepfamily Puzzle: Intergenerational Influences has also been published as *Journal of Divorce & Remarriage*, Volume 19, Numbers 3/4 1993.

The Haworth Press, Inc., 10 Alice Street, Binghamton, NY 13904-1580 USA

Library of Congress Cataloging-in-Publication Data

The stepfamily puzzle : intergenerational influences / Craig A. Everett, editor.
p. cm.
Includes bibliographical references.
ISBN 1-56024-518-2 (alk. paper)
1. Stepfamilies. 2. Intergenerational relations. I. Everett, Craig A.
HQ759.92.S729 1993
306.874–dc20 93-11502
CIP

INDEXING & ABSTRACTING

Contributions to this publication are selectively indexed or abstracted in print, electronic, online, or CD-ROM version(s) of the reference tools and information services listed below. This list is current as of the copyright date of this publication. See the end of this section for additional notes.

- ***Abstracts of Research in Pastoral Care & Counseling***, Loyola College, 7135 Minstrel Way, Suite 101, Columbia, MD 21045
- ***Applied Social Sciences Index & Abstracts (ASSIA),*** Bowker-Saur Limited, 60 Grosvenor Street, London W1X 9DA, England
- ***Bulletin Signaletique***, INIST/CNRS-Service Gestion des Documents Primaires, 2, allee du Parc de Brabois, F-54514 Vandoeuvre-les-Nancy, Cedex, France
- ***Current Contents/Social & Behavioral Sciences***, Institute for Scientific Information, 3501 Market Street, Philadelphia, PA 19104-3302
- ***Family Life Educator "Abstracts Section,"*** ETR Associates, P.O. Box 1830, Santa Cruz, CA 95061-1830
- ***Guide to Social Science & Religion in Periodical Literature***, National Periodical Library, P.O. Box 3278, Clearwater, FL 34630
- ***Index to Periodical Articles Related to Law***, University of Texas, 727 East 26th Street, Austin, TX 78705

(continued)

- ***Inventory of Marriage and Family Literature (online and hard copy)***, National Council on Family Relations, 3989 Central Avenue NE, Suite 550, Minneapolis, MN 55421
- ***Mental Health Abstracts (online through DIALOG)***, IFI/Plenum Data Company, 3202 Kirkwood Highway, Wilmington, DE 19808
- ***Periodical Abstracts, Research 2***, UMI Data Courier, P.O. Box 32770, Lousiville, KY 40232-2770
- ***Psychological Abstracts (PsycINFO)***, American Psychological Association, P.O. Box 91600, Washington, DC 20090-1600
- ***RIC-CERDIC (Religious & Social Sciences Index)***, Palais Universitaire, 9, place de l'Universite, 67084 Strasbourg, Cedex, France
- ***Sage Family Studies Abstracts***, Sage Publications, Inc., 2455 Teller Road, Newbury Park, CA 91320
- ***Social Planning/Policy & Development Abstracts (SOPODA)***, Sociological Abstracts, Inc., P.O. Box 22206, San Diego, CA 92192-0206
- ***Social Sciences Citation Index***, Institute for Scientific Information, 3501 Market Street, Philadelphia, PA 19104
- ***Social Work Research & Abstracts***, National Association of Social Workers, 750 First Street NW, 8th Floor, Washington, DC 20002
- ***Sociological Abstracts (SA)***, Sociological Abstracts, Inc., P.O. Box 22206, San Diego, CA 92192-0206
- ***Studies on Women Abstracts***, Carfax Publishing Company, P.O. Box 25, Abingdon, Oxfordshire OX14 3UE, England

(continued)

SPECIAL BIBLIOGRAPHIC NOTES

related to indexing, abstracting, and library access services

- ❑ indexing/abstracting services in this list will also cover material in the "separate" that is co-published simultaneously with Haworth's special thematic journal issue or DocuSerial. Indexing/abstracting usually covers material at the article/chapter level.
- ❑ monographic co-editions are intended for either non-subscribers or libraries which intend to purchase a second copy for their circulating collections.
- ❑ monographic co-editions are reported to all jobbers/wholesalers/approval plans. The source journal is listed as the "series" to assist the prevention of duplicate purchasing in the same manner utilized for books-in-series.
- ❑ to facilitate user/access services all indexing/abstracting services are encouraged to utilize the co-indexing entry note indicated at the bottom of the first page of each article/chapter/contribution.
- ❑ this is intended to assist a library user of any reference tool (whether print, electronic, online, or CD-ROM) to locate the monographic version if the library has purchased this version but not a subscription to the source journal.
- ❑ individual articles/chapters in any Haworth publication are also available through the Haworth Document Delivery Services (HDDS).

ABOUT THE EDITOR

Craig A. Everett, PhD, is a marriage and family therapist in private practice in Tucson, Arizona, and Director of the Arizona Institute of Family Therapy. In addition to his 20 years of experience in clinical practice, he was formerly President of the American Association for Marriage and Family Therapy. Dr. Everett's previous positions include Director of Family Therapy Training and Associate Professor at both Florida State University and Auburn University. He has been the editor of the *Journal of Divorce & Remarriage* (formerly the *Journal of Divorce*) since 1983 and is an editorial board member of six professional journals.

The Stepfamily Puzzle: Intergenerational Influences

CONTENTS

Introduction

The public interest in understanding the difficulties of blending family systems through remarriage has grown significantly over the past decade and is evidenced now in the availability of numerous therapeutic and psychoeducational programs, as well as self-help groups and trade literature. Unfortunately, the pursuit of research and theory regarding stepfamilies has not evolved at the same pace as the public's interest and concern. As a matter of fact, it has taken me over two years to assemble this collection of articles which address the broad intergenerational picture of the stepfamily's experience.

In many respects–for therapists, educators, researchers, and the families themselves–the behavior and expectable functioning of stepfamilies still have the uncertain qualities of a "puzzle." Part of the reason for this is that the amazing variety and complexity of variables and dynamics that become operationalized in a blended family system have not been charted completely.

The articles in this work are intended to set some of these variables into an intergenerational framework which includes the roles of grandparents, parent-child interactions, the struggles to define boundaries and achieve marital intimacy, and the underlying effects of financial support. The reader will observe that there is not one article that attempts to integrate and pull together all of these variables. Perhaps the absence of such a contribution defines the cutting edge for the field.

Craig A. Everett, PhD
Tucson, Arizona

[Haworth co-indexing entry note]: "Introduction," Everett, Craig A., Co-published simultaneously in the *Journal of Divorce & Remarriage* (The Haworth Press, Inc.) Vol. 19, No. 3/4, 1993, p. 1; and: *The Stepfamily Puzzle: Intergenerational Influences* (ed: Craig A. Everett), The Haworth Press, Inc., 1993, p. 1. Multiple copies of this article/chapter may be purchased from The Haworth Document Delivery Center [1-800-3-HAWORTH; 9:00 a.m. - 5:00 p.m. (EST)].

Stressors, Manifestations of Stress, and First-Family/Stepfamily Group Membership

Alan Zeppa
Rosalie Huisinga Norem

SUMMARY. A multiple analysis of covariance (MANCOVA) design is utilized to test the generally accepted propositions that stepfamilies experience more stressors and negative manifestations of stress than do first families. Results do not support either of these propositions, possibly indicating that lingering sociocultural bias against stepfamilies continues to prejudice first-family/stepfamily comparisons.

INTRODUCTION

For many years, scholarly interest in "blended families" lagged far behind the growth rates of this increasingly common family form. Only in this decade have we witnessed a veritable explosion of consideration, after years of slow but steady growth initially

---

Alan Zeppa, PhD, is Lecturer in the Department of Child and Family Development, University of Minnesota, Duluth, MN 55812-2496. Rosalie Huisinga Norem, PhD, is Professor in the Department of Family Environment, Iowa State University, Ames IA 50011-1120.

Journal Paper No. J-13433 of the Iowa Agriculture and Home Economics Experiment Station, Ames, Iowa, Project No. 2543, a contributing project to North Central Regional Project NC-164.

[Haworth co-indexing entry note]: "Stressors, Manifestations of Stress, and First-Family/Stepfamily Group Membership," Zeppa, Alan, and Rosalie Huisinga Norem. Co-published simultaneously in the *Journal of Divorce & Remarriage* (The Haworth Press, Inc.) Vol. 19, No. 3/4, 1993, pp. 3-23; and: *The Stepfamily Puzzle: Intergenerational Influences* (ed: Craig A. Everett), The Haworth Press, Inc., 1993, pp. 3-23. Multiple copies of this article/chapter may be purchased from The Haworth Document Delivery Center [1-800-3-HAWORTH; 9:00 a.m. - 5:00 p.m. (EST)].

fueled by the accelerating divorce rates in the 1960s and 1970s (Lagoni and Cook, 1985). By contrast, stress in families has received considerable theoretical attention in the family studies literature ever since Rueben Hill's seminal study (1949) on family adjustment to the crises of war-induced separation and reunion (McCubbin et al., 1980). In spite of the attention in both areas, however, very little has been done to specify ways in which the manifestation of stress in stepfamilies might differ from that of intact biological families (Pasley and Ihinger-Tallman, 1982). The major purpose of this paper, therefore, is to compare and contrast the manifestations of stress in "first-marriage" families with "remarried" families. Specifically, data from a random sample of first families and stepfamilies are analyzed to address the research questions:

Do stepfamilies experience greater levels of stressors than first families? Also, do stepfamilies experience more negative manifestations of stress than first families?

PREVIOUS RESEARCH

Stepfamily Development

The incredible proliferation of stepfamilies makes questions such as those posed above increasingly significant in today's rapidly changing society. As recently as 1976, for example, it was estimated that as few as 10% of all U.S. children under 18 lived in stepparent households (Nelson and Nelson, 1982); by 1980, that figure had conservatively risen to 16% (Cherlin and McCarthy, 1985). It has been suggested that, given current trends, the stepfamily is likely to become the most prevalent family form of the not-too-distant future (Duberman, 1975; Visher and Visher, 1979).

A more compelling rationale underlying the current study pertains to what Spanier and Furstenberg (1987) refer to as a lack of accurate data with which to facilitate our understanding of remarriage and stepfamily life. To be sure, most prior empirical findings and theoretical perspectives have tended to support the notion that life in remarried families is "more problematic" or "less healthy" than life in nuclear families. One influential early paper posited, for example, that stepfamilies were especially vulnerable to interpersonal disturbances and malfunctioning because of the poorly articulated role definition of stepparents, which implied many contradictory functions (Fast and Cain 1966). Extending these ideas, Cherlin (1978) argued that higher divorce rates for second marriages were due to the "incomplete institutionalization" of remarriage in this country. According to Cherlin, since the problems faced by remarried families were intrinsically different from those faced by first families, any solutions to those problems based upon first-family norms were inherently inappropriate.

Researchers have also sought to integrate some of these empirical findings into various theoretical frameworks. Citing studies that indicate a greater incidence of psychological and physical abuse in stepfamilies, sociobiologists Daly and Wilson (1980) and Lightcap et al. (1982), implied that stepparents would tend to be more neglectful and/or abusive because their perceived relatedness to their stepchildren would be relatively low when compared with that of biological parents. Noting empirical evidence linking stress and physical abuse of children (Strauss et al., 1980), stress theorists Martin and Walters (1982) reasoned that, if excessive stress in families leads to abuse and there was more stress in families where step relationships occur, then abuse was more likely to occur in these families.

Recently, a few investigators have seriously questioned the nature of the evidence that stepfamily life in general is less healthy than first-family life. Although stepchildren, for example, have been routinely viewed by professionals and lay people alike as being emotionally "poorer" than children of intact nuclear families, as well as being at greater risk of physical and psychological abuse, no conclusive evidence exists indicating that children brought up in stepfamilies perform psychosocially or behaviorally less competently than do offspring of intact biological unions (Robinson, 1984).

Instead, an early study by Burchinal (1964) indicated that neither personality characteristics nor social relationships of adolescents were related to marital status of the parents. Other researchers found no significant differences between high school students brought up in stepfather families and those raised in natural-parent households (Wilson et al., 1975). A third large investigation by Bohannon and Erickson (1978) concluded that children living with stepfathers do just as well on all the behavioral characteristics studied as do children living with natural fathers. Another analysis indicated that children in stepfather families might be receiving more competent parenting than children in intact families (Santrock et al., 1982).

Robinson (1984) stated that such seemingly contradictory findings might be due in large part to methodological shortcomings and contended that outcomes are frequently contingent upon the methodology that researchers choose. Others have concurred. Although Ganong and Coleman (1984) found little empirical support for the presumption of significant differences between stepchildren and children from intact nuclear families, they also reasoned that the dominant atheoretical "deficit comparison" approaches to stepfamily research have contributed to the commonly perceived negative stereotypes of stepfamilies and stepfamily members (Ganong and Coleman, 1986; Coleman et al., 1985). Underlying all these approaches is an unchallenged premise that variations from the intact nuclear family are dysfunctional and inadequate. It is this deficit comparison model that has formed the basis of most of the research central to the field.

Quite likely this has been the case with stepfamilies and stress. Whereas all varieties of stepfamilies are presumed to be subject to most or all of the stressors common to first families, investigators have also posited the existence of a plethora of stressors evidently unique to stepfamilies.

Visher and Visher (1978), for instance, stated that intrafamilial sexual attraction is a source of greater tension in stepfamilies than in nuclear families, owing primarily to a weakened incest taboo resulting from the nonbiological relationships of the stepfamily members. These same authors (1985) also suggested that other sources of stressors for stepfamilies might stem from stepfamily life cycles seldom following the "biological pattern"; a previously childless stepparent might enter into a household containing children of various ages, for example. Similarly, Goetting (1982) asserted that an important task in the process of remarriage is the changing of one's individual identity into a conjoint one–emotionally, psychically, parentally, and economically–and that this process is more complicated for remarried families than for first-married ones. Whiteside (1982) and Papernow (1984) stressed the importance of establishing "stepfamily boundaries" independent of any previous biological family ones. The Vishers (1985) also implied a potential for disruption latent in the relationship with the ex-spouse and quasi-kin. McGoldrick and Carter (1980) inferred that an adequate "emotional divorce" from the previous marriage is critical in the process of committing to the possibilities of the remarried household. Because there is initially no consensus on the roles and expectations of stepparents and stepchildren, Ransom et al. (1979) suggested that a major source of stressors in stepfamilies arises out of the need to restructure and clarify these roles. The list goes on.

Given the chorus of investigators expounding upon the belief that stepfamily life is fraught with a greater variety of stressors than is first-family life, it is perhaps unsurprising that the few papers that have examined the question of stress in stepfamilies in any depth have pointed to this untested body of work as a general indicator of elevated levels of stress in second families (Pasley and Ihinger-Tallman, 1982). Under scrutiny, however, such findings appear increasingly inadequate, based more on "whoozle effects" than upon rigorous examination of the facts. Gelles (1980) describes a whoozle effect as a phenomenon that occurs when a particular finding reported in one study is accepted by others without consideration of the possible limitations of the study. Over time, the original findings become treated as facts that form the basis for more studies, more findings, more facts, etc. What is needed, obviously, are studies aimed at challenging the notion that stepfamilies are prima facie more stress-ridden than intact biological families.

Family Stress

In its present form, family stress and coping theory is largely an outgrowth of Hill's seminal study (1949) on family adjustment to the crises of war-induced separation and reunion. Essentially a two-part theoretical model of families under stress, a descriptive section posited a "roller coaster" course of adjustment to stressor events, which were disruptive of a family's preexisting sense of balance;

once disrupted, that homeostatic state was thought to be followed by a disorganized interval superseded, in turn, by a period of trial-and-error crisis resolution (the "angle of recovery"), which subsequently led to a new level of organization or homeostasis (Walker, 1986).

Hill's original model basically posited that a family's response to stressors was a function of the interaction between several variables, each composed, in turn, of several component parts. Recently, articles have begun to appear that argue that any complete understanding of the process of families under stress is unlikely to occur unless researchers make attempts to integrate all of the interdependent levels of the social system into their models (Walker, 1986). According to Walker, existing work has tended to focus on only one or two of the various levels of the social system, obscuring vital differences between individuals and families and ignoring levels of which the family is but a single part. Partial confirmation of this idea has been provided by Norem and Blundell (1988), who pointed out, in their study of farm families and marital disruption, that stressors from a variety of sources affect not only interpersonal relationships, but also economic well-being and overall life style as well.

Walker (1986) posited multiple interdependent levels of the social system in her conceptualization of a contextual model: individual, dyadic, familial, social network, community, and cultural/historical. Boss (1987) suggested that the end result of the stress process is partly shaped by the broad contexts external to the family. Her contextual model of family stress supposes an external context that largely shapes the family's internal context. Crucial to her conceptualization is the notion that perception of any stressor event is mediated by the internal and external contexts and that the resultant meaning given the stressor event by the family involved determines whether the family will cope or fall into crisis. Inasmuch as the process of stepfamily development is largely one of merging multiple "family cultures and identities" (Pasley and Ihinger-Tallman, 1982), it logically follows that the stress process in these families is unusually complex. Importantly, family stress research has predominantly focused on analyzing data without disaggregating by group differences (Malia et al., 1988).

METHODOLOGY

Description of the Sample

This research examines data from the nine-state North Central Regional Project on Stress in Families in their Middle Years, with support provided by respective state agricultural experiment stations. The sample is about evenly divided between urban and rural and was designed to target families with two parents and at least one adolescent living at home, with wives between 35 and 54 years of age. The data reported here were gathered in the spring of 1983.

Data were received from 1,945 families across the project area, resulting in an overall response rate of approximately 32%. Questions in the survey focused on stressors such as major life events and daily irritations; resources of family integration and adaptability, social networks, and socioeconomic status; and outcomes of individual symptomatology, general health, and satisfaction with aspects of individual and personal life.

Although the age of respondents ranged from 24 to 72, almost 80% fell within the targeted age parameter of 35 to 55. All but 5% reported at least one child in the home. The average education of both husbands and wives is about 13 years. Almost half of both men and women have education beyond high school. Mean family income is $32,600, and over 30% of the wives are employed full time, with an additional 20% employed part time outside the home. Family size averaged 4.8. Only instances in which both the husband and wife responded were included in the population from which the final sample was drawn.

One complication of the current study arose from the data set's failure to elicit information pertaining to family type. Thus, further data reduction was necessary to determine the number of stepfamilies vis-à-vis first families in the overall sample. Acting on the certainty that at least some of the children within stepfamilies would have had to have been born before the couple's remarital date, stepfamilies were ultimately disaggregated from the total sample through the expedient of comparing the current couple's wedding date with the birth dates of every child. Although it is certainly possible that some of the families accordingly grouped in this fashion might not, in fact, be stepfamilies, it was assumed that the margin for error was relatively low.

A first step in this process was to ensure that complete data existed regarding the target criteria (i.e., the couple's marriage date and childrens' birth dates), which had the effect of paring the overall sample to just under 923 of the 1,470 families for whom data for both husband and wife were obtained. Ninety-one of these families met the criteria for designation as stepfamilies. A random sample of an equal number of the remaining 832 first families was drawn to begin the comparison of the two groups on the selected target variables. Final cleaning of the data further pared the final sample to 85 first families and 87 stepfamilies.

Hypotheses and Variables Used in the Study

The major purpose of this paper is to test hypotheses based on empirical and/or clinical findings that overwhelmingly imply a positive relationship between stepfamilies and (1) increased levels of stressors and (2) negative manifestations of stress. The literature, although untested, is clear upon these points: The stepfamily structure is more complex than an intact nuclear family structure, and the greater the structural complexity of a family, the greater is the level of stressors and negative manifestations of stress relative to other families (Pasley and Ihinger-Tallman, 1982). Thus, two general hypotheses related to the overall research questions are:

Hypothesis 1.
Spouses in stepfamilies will report more stressors than spouses in first families.

Hypothesis 2.
Spouses in stepfamilies will report more negative manifestations of stress than spouses in first families.

Stressors. Two indicators of stressors (Hypothesis 1) were utilized from the project questionnaire–family life events and daily stressors. Drawing partly upon McCubbin, Wilson, and Patterson's (1979) Family Inventory of Life Events (FILE), a family life events scale of 48 items was administered to both spouses to assess the total number of stressor events that had occurred in the year before the survey. Regarding the total number of stressors as reported by husbands and wives, it is hypothesized that:

> Hypothesis 1a.
> Spouses in stepfamilies will report a greater number of family life events than spouses in first families.

An 18-item inventory (Norem and Brown, 1983) of everyday situations (e.g., work, leisure) and relationships (e.g., children, neighbors) and their effects upon husbands and wives was used as a second measure of stressors. Husbands and wives were asked to indicate, on a 5-point Likert scale, the effect each of the items had had upon their lives. Concerning the effect of commonplace daily interactions upon a family, it is hypothesized that:

> Hypothesis 1b.
> Spouses in stepfamilies will report more negative impact from a variety of daily stressors than spouses in first families.

Manifestations of Stress. Multiple indicators were also utilized to assess the manifestations of stress (Hypothesis 2)–the degree of disturbance caused by various family life events, individual symptomatology, and global and specific measures of individual satisfaction.

The first of these measures was derived from the family life events scale already described. In addition to being asked whether or not the particular event had occurred to the family in the last 3 years, husbands and wives were also asked to report how disturbing this event was to them on a 5-point Likert scale. With respect to the level of disruption caused by various family life events, it is hypothesized that:

> Hypothesis 2a.
> Spouses in stepfamilies will report being more disturbed by family life events than spouses in first families.

To assess individual symptomatology, a theoretically valid 5-item subset of an individual and family health status inventory scale developed by Norem and Brown (1983) was used to measure depression-related behaviors for the individual spouses. Ratings on a 5-point scale ranging from "never" to "almost always" for items like "had trouble sleeping" and "found it difficult to relax" were included. It is hypothesized that:

Hypothesis 2b.
Spouses in stepfamilies will report more individual symptoms than spouses in first families.

Five single-item Likert scale indicators of various aspects of individual satisfaction were used as final measures of manifestations of stress. Olson et al. (1983) suggested that global measures of life satisfaction are appropriate measures of manifestations of stress because they indicate the degree of discrepancy between expectations and present conditions. More specific measures indicative of one's satisfaction with current family life, relationship with spouse, relationship with children, and with childrens' relationship with each other were also included in the current analysis to ascertain whether differences in patterns of satisfaction exist between stepfamilies and first families. Therefore, it is finally hypothesized that:

Hypothesis 2c.
Spouses in stepfamilies will report less individual satisfaction with their life as a whole, with their current family life, with their spousal relationship, with their relationship with their children, and with their childrens' relationship with each other than spouses in first families.

In addition to the independent variable determining family group membership and the multiple dependent measures for level of stressors and manifestations of stress, eleven demographic covariates were utilized throughout the analysis: age of husband, age of wife, husband's education, wife's education, family size (as reported by husband), family size (as reported by wife), family income, husband's income, wife's income, years married, and community size. The demographic characteristics of stepfamilies and first families are summarized in Table 1.

Analysis Strategies

Because a major goal of this study is to specify how much of the differences on multiple measures of family functioning between

TABLE 1. Sample characteristics--covariate means/standard deviations for first families and stepfamilies

	Means		Standard deviations	
	First families (n=85)	Step-families (n=87)	First families (n=85)	Step-families (n=87)
COVARIATES				
Age, wife	45.30	43.00	7.11	5.95
Age, husband	47.40	46.40	7.59	8.12
Education, wife	13.06	12.75	2.34	2.01
Education, husband	13.71	12.82	2.92	3.08
Years Married	23.73	14.31	7.10	6.36
Income, family	39737.02	33997.45	19778.13	20089.62
Income, wife	10309.82	8677.23	8900.79	8430.31
Income, husband	28138.74	26394.16	16678.40	16574.67
Family size:				
Wife reporting	5.11	5.31	1.21	1.53
Husband reporting	5.05	5.33	1.23	1.56
Community size		First families	Step-families	
Percentage residing in:				
Less than 2,500		37.6%	43.7%	
Between 2,500-50,000		21.2%	25.3%	
More than 50,000		41.2%	31.0%	

intact biological families and stepfamilies is attributable to group membership and how much might be due to other factors, multiple analysis of covariance (MANCOVA) was chosen as the primary means for specifying the significance of any variation between the groups on the multiple dependent measures.

In MANCOVA, the linear combination of dependent variables is statistically adjusted for differences in the covariates. The adjusted linear combination of dependent variables represents the combination that would have been obtained if all participants had started out with the same scores on all the covariates. In this way, an accurate assessment can be made of whether differences in the dependent variables can be attributed to family group membership rather than to chance. Thus, MANCOVA affords a more precise look at the relationship between group membership and multiple dependent variables with the effect of the chosen covariates partialled out (Tabachnick and Fidell, 1983). A subset of commands from SPSS^x MANOVA were utilized to complete the analysis (SPSS^x, 1983).

RESULTS

Stressors Variables

The two hypotheses associated with the first research question posit that husbands and wives in stepfamilies will report a greater number of family life events and more negative impact from a variety of daily stressors than will spouses in first families. Results of the omnibus MANOVA summarized in Table 2 do not support these hypotheses.

Multivariate analysis of the relationship of family group membership to the set of dependent variables with the effect of the covariates partialled out results in extremely low F-values for the criterion statistic. These results demonstrate no significant relationships between the independent variable of family form and (a) the number of stressor events reported by husbands or wives and (b) the impact of daily stressors on husbands and wives. After the effects of a variety of demographic covariates are controlled, the data strongly suggest that stepfamilies and first families do not significantly differ in the amount of stressors as reported by either spouse.

TABLE 2. Means and F values of family form, covariates and stressors variables--multivariate and univariate analyses

	Means		F values	
	First families (n=85)	Step- families (n=87)	Covar- iates	Family form
MULTIVARIATE	-	-	1.527*	.082
UNIVARIATE				
Stressors variables				
Family events:				
Wife reporting	5.69	6.48	1.614	.072
Husband reporting	4.08	5.10	.885	.265
Daily stressors:				
Wife reporting	39.14	39.10	1.577	.025
Husband reporting	38.52	39.87	2.574**	.019

**Significant at .01 level.

*Significant at .05 level.

Instead, examination of the equivalent analysis of the set of covariates and the set of dependent variables with family form effects eliminated demonstrates a multivariate relationship significant between the .05 and .01 levels. Univariate findings summarizing results of independent multiple regressions for the covariate group and the four dependent variables taken separately (also Table 2) reveal that the most significant single relationship is between the covariate group and the individual dependent variable corresponding to the perceived negative impact of the husband's daily stressors. Indeed, this last is the only one of the univariate relationships significant at the .05 level or above, although two of the others lie just outside our decision criterion.

Analysis of multiple regressions for each dependent variable in turn, with covariates acting as multiple continuous independent variables, clarifies the data further (see Table 3). A wife's reported number of events for 3 years is significantly related to only two of the individual covariates, family size (as reported by the wife) and husband's educational level. The wife's daily stressors are likewise significantly related to only two of the covariates, family size (reported by wife) and husband's income. None of the individual covariates are related to either of the other two dependent variables. For stressors, demographic factors acting together rather than individually clearly account for more of the reported variance in the dependent variables measuring stressors than does either first-family or stepfamily group membership.

Stress Manifestation Variables

As for the second research question, results from the omnibus MANOVA for manifestations of stress (Table 4) do not support the hypotheses that first families and stepfamilies differ significantly in (a) the level of disturbance caused by family life events, (b) the individual symptom levels of spouses, or (c) the global/specific satisfaction levels of spouses.

TABLE 3. Significant individual covariate predictors of stressors variables

Stressors variables<>Covariates	t value
Wife's reported events<>	
Family size (Wife reporting)	2.39*
Husband's education	-2.41*
Daily stressors for wife<>	
Family size (wife reporting)	2.03*
Husband's income	-2.03*

*Significant at .05 level.

TABLE 4. Means and F values of family form, covariates and outcome variables--multivariate and univariate analyses[a]

	Means		F values	
	First families (n=85)	Step-families (n=87)	Covar-iates	Family form
MULTIVARIATE	-	-	.895	.661
UNIVARIATE				
Outcome variables				
How disturbing family events:				
Wife reporting	25.84	27.62	.911	.048
Husband reporting	18.06	20.91	.663	.485
Symptoms of depression:				
Wife reporting	8.95	9.26	.786	.034
Husband reporting	8.29	7.70	.620	1.402
Satisfaction with life as whole:				
Wife reporting	4.98	5.07	.982	.158
Husband reporting	5.14	5.05	1.563	.287
Satisfaction with family life:				
Wife reporting	4.98	5.27	1.008	3.099
Husband reporting	5.36	5.32	.774	.117
Satisfaction with spousal relationship:				
Wife reporting	5.29	5.38	.934	.533
Husband reporting	5.69	5.54	1.437	.831
Satisfaction with own relationship to children:				
Wife reporting	5.47	5.58	1.501	.073
Husband reporting	5.45	5.15	.900	.053

TABLE 4 (continued)

TABLE 4. Means and F values of family form, covariates and outcome variables--multivariate and univariate analyses [a]

	Means		F values	
	First families (n=85)	Step-families (n=87)	Covar-iates	Family form
Satisfaction with children's relationship with each other:				
Wife reporting	4.81	5.13	.856	.626
Husband reporting	4.96	4.96	.872	.003

[a] No relationships significant at .05 level or greater.

As with the previous set of hypotheses, multivariate analysis of the relationship between family form and the set of stress outcome variables with the effects of the covariates eliminated results in insignificant values of F. As before, the data strongly imply that, after control for demographic factors, stepfamilies do not differ significantly from first families in negative manifestations of stress.

With the effects of biological or stepfamily group membership partialled out, the multivariate findings do not demonstrate any significant relationship between the set of covariates and the dependent variables considered as a group (Table 4). Either no group differences in manifestations of stress exist between stepfamilies and first families, or whatever differences do exist can be attributed to variables not included in the analysis. Only five of the outcome variables demonstrated significant relationships to any of the covariates analyzed individually (Table 5).

TABLE 5. Significant individual covariate predictors of outcome variables

Outcome variables<>Covariates	t value
Wife's satisfaction with family life<>	
Wife's age	-2.05*
Wife's satisfaction with relationship with children<>	
Community size	-2.65**
Wife's satisfaction with children's relationship<>	
Community size	-2.12*
Husband's satisfaction with wife<>	
Husband's age	2.44*
Husband's satisfaction with children's relationship<>	
Husband's age	2.25*

*Significant at .05 level.

**Significant at .01 level.

CONCLUSIONS AND RECOMMENDATIONS

Certainly, the current study was never intended to be definitive, and is admittedly limited in several regards. We note but cannot explain, for example, the inflated figures for family income in both the first-family and stepfamily samples utilized in the study. Identified through the use of a commercial mailing list, it is evident that the sample might systematically exclude many low income families. Similarly, we offer no cogent explanations for the high family sizes reported for both groups, especially for first families. Both of the foregoing could indicate that the sample might not be truly representative of the general population.

Also, the data do not offer much insight into several critical questions currently being considered in the literature on remarried life. Given the failure to elicit information relating to family type, the data do not address those questions pertaining to the relative diversity of the stepfamily structure when compared to the intact family form. And, since it was primarily intended to study families in their middle years, the data say nothing about the initial stages of stepfamily formation. If spouses in stepfamilies were married an average of 14 years, it is questionable whether they would be expected to differ very much on the dimensions of the dependent variables. It is entirely possible that the present study has tapped that subgroup of stepfamilies that have been successful in solving the many problems associated with remarriage to form lasting and stable unions.

Even acknowledging these caveats, we still believe the current study has much to offer. The results do not support the commonly accepted notion that stepfamilies in general experience more stressors and negative manifestations of stress than do first families. Clearly, they provide a sharp challenge to the deficit comparison model that has dominated thinking regarding stepfamilies for decades and lend overt support to the proposition that it is the conditions rather than the nature of some stepfamilies that most distinguish them from first families.

These findings have several implications for researchers and theoreticians, raising serious questions regarding the broadly accepted theoretical givens concerning stepfamily life. It is hoped that this study and others like it will give renewed impetus to studies that subject such chains of assumption and, ultimately, conjecture, to a much needed dose of scrutiny.

Ideally, the findings of this study will also prove useful to those providing direct services to stepfamilies. Taken as part of a body of recent work that indicates significantly fewer differences between first families and stepfamilies than had previously been thought (Robinson, 1984; Santrock et al., 1982; Ganong and Coleman, 1984), such studies indirectly contribute to updating the "common sense" regarding stepfamily development. More directly, one implication to be drawn from the current study is that perceived stepfamily deficits vis-à-vis first families are perhaps attributable more to socioeconomic effects or to unconscious bias than they are to the fact of living in a stepfamily per se. It is far too easy simply to aver that stepfamilies fare better or worse when compared with first families, when what goes into making such statements involves value judgments at the deepest and most subconscious levels. Stepfamilies are only different from first families, perhaps not in the ways in which we have been conditioned to believe, but different nevertheless. We have only begun to explore the nature of these differences, much less to understand them.

LITERATURE CITED

Bohannon, P., and Erickson, R. (1978). Stepping in. Psychology Today, 11, 53-59.

Boss, P. G. (1987). Family Stress. Pp. 695-714 in M. B. Sussman and S. K. Steinmetz (Eds.) Handbook of Marriage and the Family. New York: Plenum Press.

Burchinal, L. (1964). Characteristics of adolescents from unbroken, broken, and reconstituted families. Journal of Marriage and the Family, 26, 44-51.

Cherlin, A. (1978). Remarriage as an incomplete institution. American Journal of Sociology, 84(3), 634-650.

Cherlin, A., and McCarthy, J. (1985). Remarried couple households: Data from the June 1980 current population survey. Journal of Marriage and the Family, 47(1), 23-30.

Coleman, M., Ganong, L. H., and Gingrich, R. (1985). Stepfamily strengths: A review of popular literature. Family Relations, 34, 583-589.

Daly, M., and Wilson, M. (1980). Discriminative parental solicitude: A biological perspective. Journal of Marriage and the Family, 42(2), 277-288.

Duberman, L. (1975). The reconstituted family: A study of remarried couples and their children. Chicago: Nelson-Hall Publishers.

Fast, I., and Cain, A. (1966). The step-parent role: Potential for disturbances in family functioning. American Journal of Orthopsychiatry, 36(3), 485-491.

Ganong, L. H., and Coleman, M. (1984). Effects of remarriage on children: A review of the empirical literature. Family Relations, 33, 389-406.

Ganong, L. H., and Coleman, M. (1986). Clinical and empirical literature on stepchildren. Journal of Marriage and the Family, 46(2), 309-318.

Gelles, R. (1980). Violence in the family: A review of research in the seventies. Journal of Marriage and the Family, 42(4), 143-155.

Goetting, A. (1982). The six stages of remarriage: Developmental tasks of remarriage after divorce. Family Relations, 31, 213-222.

Hill, R. (1949). Families under Stress. New York: Harper and Row.

Lagoni, L., and Cook, A. S. (1985). Stepfamilies: A content analysis of the popular literature. Family Relations, 34(4), 521-526.

Lightcap, J. L., Kurland, J. A., and Burgess, R. L. (1982). Child abuse: A test of some predictions from evolutionary theory. Ethology and Sociobiology, 3, 61-67.

McCubbin, H. I., Jou, C. B., Cauble, A. E., Comeau, J. K., Patterson, J. M., &

Needle, R. H. (1980). Family stress and coping: a decade review. Journal of Marriage and the Family, 42(4), 125-141.

McCubbin, H. I., Wilson, L., & Patterson, J. M. (1979). Family Inventory of Life Events and Changes (FILE). St. Paul: Family Social Science, University of Minnesota.

McGoldrick, M., and Carter, E. A. (1980). Forming a remarried family. In E. A. Carter and M. McGoldrick (Eds.), The Family Life Cycle: A Framework for Family Therapy. New York: Gardner.

Malia, J. A., Norem, R. H., and Garrison, M. E. (1988, November). An examination of differences in the stress process in balanced, midrange, and extreme families using multi-sample LISREL analysis. Paper presented at annual meeting of National Council on Family Relations, Philadelphia, PA.

Martin, M. J., and Walters, J. (1982). Familial correlates of selected types of child abuse and neglect. Journal of Marriage and the Family, 44(2), 267-276.

Nelson, M., and Nelson, G. K. (1982). Problems of Equity in the reconstituted family: A social exchange analysis. Family Relations, 31, 223-231.

Norem, R. H., and Blundell, J. (1988). Farm families and marital disruption during a time of crisis. Pp. 21-31 in R. Marotz-Baden, C. Hennon, and T. Brubaker (Eds.), Families in Rural America. Stress: Adaptation and Revitalization. St. Paul, MN: National Council on Family Relations Press.

Norem, R. H., and Brown, W. C. (1983, November). Family health status indicators. Paper presented at annual meeting of National Council on Family Relations, St. Paul, MN.

Olson, D. H., Russell, C. S., and Sprenkle, D. H. (1983). Circumplex model of marital and family systems: VI. Theoretical update. Family Process, 22, 69-83.

Papernow, P. L. (1984). The stepfamily cycle: An experiential model of stepfamily development. Family Relations, 33, 355-363.

Pasley, K., and Ihinger-Tallman, M. (1982). Stress in second families. Family Perspectives, 16(4), 81-86.

Ransom, J. W., Schlesinger, S., and Derdeyn, A. (1979). A stepfamily in formation. American Journal of Orthopsychiatry, 49, 36-43.

Robinson, B. E. (1984). The contemporary American stepfather. Family Relations, 33, 381-388.

Santrock, J., Warshak, R., Lindbergh, R., and Meadows, L. (1982). Children's and parent's observed social behavior in stepfather families. Child Development, 53, 472-480.

Spanier, G. B., and Furstenberg, F. F. (1987). Remarriage and reconstituted families. Pp. 419-434 in M. B. Sussman and S. K. Steinmetz (Eds.), Handbook of Marriage and the Family. New York: Plenum Press.

SPSS, Inc. (1983). $SPSS^x$: A Complete Guide to $SPSS^x$ Language and Operations. New York: McGraw-Hill.

Strauss, M. A., Gelles, R. J., and Steinmetz, S. K. (1980). Behind closed doors: Violence in American families. New York: Doubleday.

Tabachnick, B. G., and Fidell, L. S. (1983). Using multivariate statistics. New York: Harper and Row.

Visher, E. B., and Visher, J. S. (1978). Common problems of stepparents and their spouses. American Journal of Orthopsychiatry, 48(2), 252-262.
Visher, E. B., and Visher, J. S. (1979). Stepfamilies: A guide to working with stepparents and stepchildren. New York: Brunner/Mazel.
Visher, E. B., and Visher, J. S. (1985). Stepfamilies are different. Journal of Family Therapy, 7, 9-18.
Walker, A. J. (1986). Reconceptualizing family stress. Journal of Marriage and the Family, 47(4), 827-837.
Whiteside, M. (1982). Remarriage: A family developmental process. Journal of Marital and Family Therapy, 8, 59-68.
Wilson, K. L., Zurcher, L., McAdams, D., and Curtis, R. L. (1975). Stepfathers and stepchildren: An exploratory analysis from two national surveys. Journal of Marriage and the Family, 37, 526-536.

The Transition to Stepgrandparenthood

Carolyn S. Henry
Cindi Penor Ceglian
Diane L. Ostrander

SUMMARY. Previous scholars have established developmental stages or tasks for remarriage, stepfamilies, and stepsibling relations. A parallel set of four developmental stages and corresponding tasks are presented for the transition to stepgrandparenthood. The stages include specific developmental tasks grandparents face as their adult-children marry spouses who have children from previous relationships. Implications of the developmental stages and tasks are presented.

In recent years family life practitioners and researchers have attended to a variety of transitions associated with stepfamilies, focusing upon the immediate stepfamily (Coleman & Ganong, 1990) while neglecting the transitions faced by extended family members (e.g., Chilman, 1983; Mills, 1984; Papernow, 1984). Yet, recent scholarship indicates stepfamily formation has important implications for extended family members such as stepgrandparents

---

Carolyn S. Henry, PhD, is Assistant Professor in the Department of Family Relations and Child Development, Oklahoma State University, Stillwater, OK 74078-0337. Cindi Penor Ceglian, MS, is Instructor and Diane L. Ostrander, PhD, is Assistant Professor in the Department of Human Development, Child and Family Studies, South Dakota State University, Brookings, SD 57007.

An earlier version of this article was presented at National Council on Family Relations Annual Conference, Philadelphia, PA (November, 1988).

[Haworth co-indexing entry note]: "The Transition to Stepgrandparenthood," Henry, Carolyn S., Cindi Penor Ceglian and Diane L. Ostrander. Co-published simultaneously in the *Journal of Divorce & Remarriage* (The Haworth Press, Inc.) Vol. 19, No. 3/4, 1993, pp. 25-44; and: *The Stepfamily Puzzle: Intergenerational Influences* (ed: Craig A. Everett), The Haworth Press, Inc., 1993, pp. 25-44. Multiple copies of this article/chapter may be purchased from The Haworth Document Delivery Center [1-800-3-HAWORTH; 9:00 a.m. - 5:00 p.m. (EST)].

(Brubaker, 1990). Although scholars have begun to examine step-grandparenthood as an integral part of the extended stepfamily system (Henry, Ceglian, & Matthews, in press; Sanders & Trygstad, 1989), minimal consideration has been given to the normative developmental stages and tasks associated with the transition to step-grandparenthood (Cicirelli, 1983).

Family developmental theory provides a means of describing the predictable stages and issues that families encounter over the family life cycle by focusing on role changes (Duvall & Miller, 1985) or emotional processes (McGoldrick & Carter, 1982). During the past decade, scholars have made advances in applying family developmental theory to identify normative transitions and processes associated with remarriage and stepfamilies. Specifically, developmental tasks or stages have been presented related to remarriage (Goetting, 1982; McGoldrick & Carter, 1982; Ransom, Schleisinger, & Derdeyn, 1979), stepfamilies (Mills, 1984; Papernow, 1984; Visher & Visher, 1982; Wald, 1981), stepsiblings (Rosenberg & Hajal, 1985), the adaptation of children to divorce (Wallerstein, 1983), and single-parent families (Hill, 1986).

Despite the applications of family developmental theory to stepfamilies, little is known about the transition to stepgrandparenthood. Based upon the work of Ransom et al. (1979), McGoldrick and Carter (1982) presented a set of developmental steps in the transition to remarried family life. These tasks focus around critical transition points such as ending the previous relationship; committing to the new relationship; announcing the decision to family and friends; and issues during remarriage, family formation, and as the realities of stepfamily life ensue (McGoldrick & Carter, 1982). The present article was designed to extend McGoldrick and Carter's (1982) model to present normative developmental issues associated with the transition into stepgrandparenthood, employing previous scholarship relating to grandparenting (Barranti, 1985; Hagestad & Lang, 1986) and stepfamilies (Coleman & Ganong, 1990; Einstein, 1982; Furstenberg & Spanier, 1984; Hobart, 1987; Wald, 1981). Thus, a model of the developmental stages and tasks in the transition to stepgrandparenthood are presented (see Table 1). These stages and tasks focus on the transition to stepgrandparenthood as stepgrandparent/stepgrandchild relations emerge from an adult-child's marriage to a spouse who has children from a previous marriage or relationship. In the following sections, these stages and tasks are discussed.

STAGE 1: ACCEPTING THE LOSSES

Consistent with Visher and Visher's (1979) observation that stepfamilies emerge through loss, the first stage in the transition to stepgrandparenthood involves developmental tasks associated with accepting the losses (see Table 1). Ransom et al. (1979) proposed the first developmental task for stepfamily formation is to mourn the loss of the previous family. Likewise, the transition to stepgrandparenthood often requires *grieving and mourning the loss* of previous relationships or hopes. For example, there may be a "loss" of a former son or daughter-in-law through death or divorce. Another possible loss is the loss of an idealized image of an intact family for the adult-child. As the loss is mourned, it is typical for both the adult-child and the grandparents to idealize the past by focusing on the positive and minimizing the negative qualities of the past relationship (Visher & Visher, 1979). For the older generation, the losses may be particularly difficult since the losses resulted from another's actions, allowing less of a sense of control (Hamon & Thiessen, 1990; Visher & Visher, 1982).

When an adult-child's marriage ends in divorce, grandparents may experience the loss of a desirable relationship for the adult-child with the former spouse, or relief that the adult-child is no longer in a difficult marriage (Milardo, 1987). In either case, grandparents face the task of *letting go of the fantasy of "a life-long happy marriage" between the adult-child and the adult-child's former spouse* (see Table 1). Further, feelings of loss may be intensified by the perception of pain in the adult-child or through the loss of a strong bond with the adult-child's former spouse (Cicirelli, 1983). Bengtson and Robertson (1985) reported it is especially common for grandmothers to experience the loss of a strong bond with their departing daughters-in-law.

Symptoms of grief over the losses include holding onto the past through continuing to display pictures of the adult-child's family that include the former spouse, or using statements such as, "I miss

Table 1

Developmental Stages and Tasks in the Transition to Stepgrandparenthood

---

STAGE 1: ACCEPTING THE LOSSES

Developmental Tasks:

Grieving and mourning the loss

Letting go of the fantasy of "a lifelong happy marriage" between the adult-child and the adult-child's former spouse

Accepting the loss of traditional grandparenthood

Accepting fears about changing relationships with grandchildren

Clarifying feelings about divorce and single parenting

Dealing with one's own feelings of anger, resentment, sadness, or failure

STAGE 2: ACCEPTING THE ADULT-CHILD'S SINGLE STATUS

Developmental Tasks:

Adjusting to increased permeability of family boundaries

Accepting reorganization of the adult-child's family

Acknowledging the ambiguity in family roles

Increasing contact with and support for adult-child without resuming parental roles

Accepting ambiguity in grandparenting roles and seeking acceptable ways to maintain relationships with grandchildren

Establishing a new relationship with the adult-child's former spouse

Supporting the contact of grandchildren with the adult-child's former spouse

Accepting the adult-child's new social network

STAGE 3: ACCEPTING THE ADULT-CHILD'S ENTRANCE INTO A NEW RELATIONSHIP

Developmental Tasks:

Adapting to redefinition of the adult-child's family boundaries

Acknowledge fears concerning the impact of a new relationship on all individuals involved

Establishing open communication in new relationships to avoid pseudomutuality

Placing the adult-child's former family into an historical perspective that allows grandchildren to have a sense of their roots and yet does not interfere with the acceptance of a new relationship

Preparing to accept the potential of new family members in the adult-child's family system

Acknowledging the existence of potential stepchildren and understanding their relationship with the adult-child's potential spouse

Considering how potential new family members can be integrated into the extended family

Providing a support system for grandchildren who fear their position in the new relationship or experience loyalty conflicts

STAGE 4: ESTABLISHING NEW RELATIONSHIPS WITHIN THE STEPFAMILY CONTEXT

Developmental Tasks:

Redefining family boundaries to include adult-child's new spouse and the stepgrandchildren

Developing realistic expectations for stepfamily living based upon an understanding of the uniqueness of stepfamily structures

Providing opportunities for developing bonds with the adult-child's new spouse and the stepgrandchildren

Clarifying expectations for grandparenting and stepgrandparenting roles

Restructuring family subsystems to accommodate expanded extended family systems

Understanding differences in the legal relationship with grandchildren and stepgrandchildren

Enhancing stepfamily integration through sharing information about family backgrounds and experiences with the adult-child's new spouse and the stepgrandchildren

Establishing terminology to use when referring to persons in the complex of stepfamily relationships

---

John. He was like my own son." Such symbols are signs of grief, which is a natural reaction to loss that needs to be experienced before grandparents are prepared to enact stepgrandparenting roles (Goldsmith, 1982).

A related developmental task is based upon entering "grandparent/grandchild" relationships in a manner different from traditional expectations (Ahrons & Bowman, 1982). That is, stepgrandparenthood does not emerge through biological or adopted grandchildren, rather with children who have a history that usually includes other grandparents. Thus, the task emerges of *accepting the loss of traditional grandparenthood* (see Table 1) and replacing the vision of entering into grandparental roles through a young adult-child marrying and having biological children with a stepfamily model (Kalish & Visher, 1982).

Further, research indicated that the contact of children with their grandparents is typically mediated through the middle generation (i.e., the child's parents; Barranti, 1985; Bengston & Robertson, 1985; Link, 1987; Robertson, 1975). Thus, grandparents may anticipate changes in the relationships with their grandchildren as part of the stage of accepting the losses. Grandparents, therefore, face the task of *accepting fears about changing relationships with grandchildren* (see Table 1; Gladstone, 1988). Possible changes in roles include greater parental roles or financial roles for grandparents whose adult-child is the custodial parent (Gerstel, 1988; Johnson, 1988; Johnson & Minton, 1982; Troll, 1983) or less consistency in contact when the adult-child is a non-custodial parent.

Since divorce and remarriage have increased dramatically over the past several decades (Glick & Lin, 1986; Troll, 1983), grandparents vary considerably in their views about the meaning of divorce and remarriage. For example, grandparents may fear or believe that the adult-child's divorce occurred as a result of their own failures as parents (Hyatt & Kaslow, 1985; Kalish & Visher, 1982). A developmental task for grandparents in this stage, then, is to *clarify their own values and feelings about divorce and single parenting* (see Table 1).

A related developmental challenge for grandparents is *dealing with one's own feelings of anger, resentment, sadness, or failure* that emerge from the losses (see Table 1). Scholarship relating to grieving indicates the process of grieving loss requires the recognition and expression of grief-related feelings (e.g., Brammer, 1988). It may be expected that the processes of accepting the losses will overlap with the next stage in the transition to stepgrandparenthood as grandparents continue to process their feelings.

STAGE 2: ACCEPTING THE ADULT-CHILD'S SINGLE STATUS

As grandparents clarify and begin to work through their feelings about the losses described in Stage 1, they may face an additional set of developmental tasks related to accepting the single status of the adult-child (Furstenberg & Spanier, 1984; see Table 1). In order for the adult-child to adapt to a changed family structure, the boundaries of the adult-child's family often open to allow for new friends, child care assistance, and others to become involved in the family system (McGoldrick & Carter, 1982). Thus, grandparents face the task of *adjusting to increased permeability of family boundaries* in the adult-child's family (see Table 1). Grandparents may have concerns about how these changing boundaries will influence their own relationships with their adult-children and grandchildren (Furstenberg & Spanier, 1984). These concerns reflect the lack of social norms related to the transition into single-parent families (Cherlin, 1978, 1981).

As the boundaries begin to change for the adult-child's family, ambiguity in roles is likely to result for a period of time (Pasley, 1987). The family continues to perform many of the same functions while adding new responsibilities. Yet, the family is composed of a different constellation of relationships to fulfill the tasks (Wald, 1981). For example, if the adult-child's former spouse previously enacted nurturing roles toward the children, they may wish to continue these roles (i.e., sharing co-parental roles; Ahrons & Rodgers, 1987). Since the social norms for single-parent families or binuclear families are ambiguous, the way that a particular family will attempt to enact former roles (e.g., nurturing roles) is subject to confusion. Accompanying the role changes for the adult-child's family are the developmental challenges for grandparents of *accepting reorganization of the adult-child's family* and *acknowledging the ambiguity in family roles* (see Table 1) as a normative part of the adult-child's single parent family structure (Furstenberg & Spanier, 1984).

Changes in the adult-child's family have implications for relationships between grandparents and the adult-child. In many cases, the grandparents seek to provide greater contact with and support for the adult-child (Duffy, 1982). Whereas divorced or widowed adult-children tend to seek emotional support from friends, most turn to parents for financial assistance (Gerstel, 1988; Johnson, 1988; Johnson & Minton, 1982). The developmental challenge that emerges for grandparents is *increasing contact with and support for the adult-child without resuming parental roles* (see Table 1). Johnson (1988) proposed the ideal situation is to provide support at a level of equal power, rather than as a parent resuming control over the adult-child's life.

Gerstel (1988) found that for the adult-child, the income level and degree of child care responsibilities influenced the degree of reliance upon grandparents during divorce and separation. Within the first year following a divorce, for example, women with custody of their children experience a 73% drop in their standard of living, while men experience a 42% increase in their standard of living (Gottlieb, Gottlieb, & Slavin, 1988). As a result, the female adult-child may more frequently be expected to seek financial support from her parents (Cherlin & Furstenberg, 1986). Hence, grandparents who may be on or anticipating a fixed retirement income are faced with decisions about the level of financial support they can realistically provide without risking their own future interests (Gottlieb et al., 1988).

Consistent with the task of accepting fears about changing roles with grandchildren indicated in Stage 1, changes in relationships with grandchildren may be expected. The nature of such changes may be closely related to whether the adult-child is a custodial or non-custodial parent (Kalish & Visher, 1982). The new role structure in the family of the adult-child poses the challenge of *accepting ambiguity in grandparenting roles and seeking acceptable ways to maintain relationships with grandchildren* (see Table 1). After divorce or death, grandparents whose adult-children are custodial parents often have increasing contact with and support for their grandchildren, often including the assumption of greater "parenting" and financial responsibilities for a time prior to remarriage (Kalish & Visher, 1982; Kornhaber & Woodward, 1981).

In contrast, grandparents whose adult-children are the non-custodial parents may experience decreased contact with their biological or adopted grandchildren due to a loss of contact with the custodial adult-child (Furstenberg & Spanier, 1984). This loss may be further exacerbated by the ambiguity of the legal rights for grandparents in most states (Wilson & DeShane, 1982). Furthermore, for non-custodial grandparents who retain contact with their grandchildren, visits may be limited to when the grandchildren see the non-custodial adult-child (i.e., parent; Kalish & Visher, 1982). Therefore, grandparents with adult-children who are non-custodial parents face the challenge of relinquishing old family patterns and establishing new ones that often incorporate infrequent contact with the grandchildren (Furstenberg & Spanier, 1984).

When the adult-child's former spouse has custody or joint custody of the grandchildren, the acceptance of a new "business-type" grandparenting role encompassing behaviors acceptable to the non-custodial adult-child and allowing for direct visitation with the grandchildren may be necessary in order to maintain contact with the grandchildren (Rodgers & Conrad, 1986). Grandparents vary considerably in how they feel toward the adult-child's former spouse. Some have strong bonds and find it difficult to let go of the former relationship. Others are faced with the challenge of balancing negative feelings they may have toward the parent's former spouse with a recognition of the importance of the parent-child bond between the grandchildren and the parent (i.e., the parent's former spouse). In any case, the developmental tasks emerge of *establishing a new relationship with the adult-child's former spouse* (see Table 1) and *supporting the contact of grandchildren with the adult-child's former spouse* (see Table 1).

As the adult-child becomes more adjusted to a single-parent lifestyle, grandparents face the developmental task of *accepting the parent's new social network* (see Table 1; Rodgers & Conrad, 1986). A divorced or widowed adult-child is likely to experience a transition from a couples social world to that of the formerly-married. For grandparents who are accustomed to the adult-child in the context of the former marital relationship, re-examination of their own perceptions and values about the social network of the adult-child may be necessary. Particularly challenging to grandparents is when the adult-child begins dating on a regular basis. The adult-child often introduces a potential mate to the grandparents only after the couple has developed a significant commitment to each other. The introduction, therefore, may be interpreted as an actual announcement of remarriage with the potential to impact grandparents' relationships with their grandchildren (Rodgers & Conrad, 1986).

STAGE 3: ACCEPTING THE ADULT-CHILD'S ENTRANCE INTO A NEW RELATIONSHIP

As grandparents begin to accept the single status of the adult-child, developmental tasks associated with the adult-child's entrance into a new relationship may develop (see Table 1). For example, grandparents face the task of *adjusting to a redefinition of the adult-child's family boundaries* as the adult-child enters a new dating relationship that has the potential for marriage (see Table 1). The role ambiguity experienced by grandparents as the adult-child's former marriage ended, as the single-parent family emerged, and as the adult-child enters a new relationship can result in accumulated stress for many grandparents (Rodgers & Conrad, 1986). The pile-up of stress resulting from the transitions in the adult-child's family may be particularly difficult for grandparents since their roles often change before they are ready for the change (McCubbin & Patterson, 1983). For example, the adult-child may be ready to enter a new marital relationship just as grandparents have come to accept their single status. Therefore, it is important for grandparents to *acknowledge their fears about the impact of the new relationship on all individuals involved* (see Table 1).

Establishing open communication between the grandparents and the person with whom the adult-child has developed a relationship is a necessary step in building a relationship with the potential new family member. Thus, grandparents face the developmental task of *establishing open communication in relationships to avoid pseudo-mutuality* (see Table 1). Pseudomutuality refers to outwardly appearing to accept the new relationship while internally experiencing anger, frustration, or resentment (Wynne, Ryckoff, Day, & Hirsch, 1958). If grandparents have resolved old issues and have established new relationships with the adult-child's former spouse and their grandchildren, they are more ready to establish open communication in the new relationship. Thus, a related developmental task is *placing the adult-child's former family into an historical perspective that allows grandchildren to have a sense of their roots and yet does not interfere with the acceptance of a new relationship* (see Table 1).

The next developmental challenge grandparents face relates to the potential of another change in the family structure of the adult-child as marriage becomes more likely. Grandparents face the challenge of *preparing to accept new family members (i.e., both a new spouse and stepgrandchildren) in the adult-child's family system* (see Table 1). Further, *acknowledgement of the existence of potential stepchildren and understanding their relationship with the adult-child's potential spouse* becomes an important issue (Kalish & Visher, 1982).

In addition, grandparents are likely to begin *considering how the potential new stepfamily members can be integrated into the extended family system* (see Table 1; Rodgers & Conrad, 1986). The initial meeting of the stepgrandparent and stepgrandchildren is initiated by the adult-child (i.e., parent) and is stressful for all involved (Lane, Van Zandt, & Davis, 1990). The stepgrandparents' acceptance of the stepgrandchildren may be mediated by this first meeting and how well they have accepted the adult-child's new spouse (Einstein 1982).

The extended family becomes increasingly complex as a new son-in-law or daughter-in-law, stepgrandchildren, and their extended family members enter the kin network (Visher & Visher, 1982). Potential stepgrandparents often experience confusion as these concerns become more eminent when the adult-child makes the decision to marry and establish a stepfamily system. Stepgrandparents, however, may be a vital link in the extended family system that provides the security needed for the remarried family to establish itself (Einstein, 1982).

In addition, the developmental task of *providing a support system for grandchildren who fear their position in the new relationship or experience loyalty conflicts* is an important issue for grandparents (Barranti, 1985; see Table 1). Although the transition to stepgrandparenthood focuses upon establishing new relationships with additional children, grandparents also face the continued changes in their relationships with their biological or adopted grandchildren. Thus, continued emphasis upon supportive quality relationships for grandchildren can facilitate the adaptation to potential stepgrandparental roles.

STAGE 4: ESTABLISHING NEW RELATIONSHIPS WITHIN THE STEPFAMILY CONTEXT

As the adult-child enters a stepfamily system, grandparents encounter a set of developmental tasks related to establishing new relationships within the stepfamily system (see Table 1). Grandparents do not make the choice to enter stepgrandparenthood, instead the choice is made when the adult-child chooses to marry a spouse with children (Kalish & Visher, 1982). Although grandparents enter the extended stepfamily system by default, they face the challenges of *redefining family boundaries to include the adult-child's new spouse and the stepgrandchildren* and *developing realistic expectations for stepfamily living based upon an understanding of the uniqueness of stepfamily structures* (Coleman & Ganong, 1985; see Table 1).

Visher and Visher (1979) suggest that stepfamilies differ from traditional nuclear families in several ways: (a) children have a biological parent (and usually grandparents) elsewhere, (b) family members have usually sustained a primary relationship loss, (c) the relationship between one parent and the children predates the marital relationship, (d) children often participate in more than one household, and (e) one adult (the stepparent) is not legally related to the children (the stepchildren). These characteristics distinguish stepfamilies from traditional nuclear families and have distinct implications for the transition to stepgrandparenthood. For example, grandchildren are likely to have previously established and usually continuing relationships with other sets of grandparents (Cherlin & Furstenberg, 1986). Stepgrandparents, however, who offer themselves as persons for the stepgrandchild to relate to may be especially well rewarded when the stepgrandchild lost a biological grandparent as a result of the adult-child's (i.e., the parent's) divorce (Kornhaber & Woodward, 1981; Lane et al., 1989; Visher & Visher, 1988). This stepgrandparent/stepgrandchild bond is likely to resemble that between a biological grandparent and a grandchild (Lane et al., 1989). Stepgrandparents who fail to develop such a bond appear to be responsible for this lack of a relationship, as stepgrandchildren easily adapt to the presence of step-kin since it provides a wider range of potential family from which to draw support (Furstenberg & Spanier, 1984). Stepgrandparents, therefore, face the task of *providing opportunities for developing bonds with the adult-child's new spouse and the stepgrandchildren* (see Table 1).

The entrance into stepgrandparenthood is inherently ambiguous due to the lack of social norms (Cherlin, 1978; 1981) and the predominance of misconceptions about stepfamily relations (Coleman & Ganong, 1985; Visher & Visher, 1979). Due to the lack of social norms, grandparents face the challenge of *clarifying expectations for grandparenting and stepgrandparenting roles*. When the adult-child with children marries a new spouse who has children (i.e., stepgrandchildren), grandparents are faced with the challenges of balancing and defining both grandparenting and stepgrandparenting roles. Grandparents may feel "competition" for the attention of their grandchildren from the adult-child's new in-laws (Cherlin & Furstenberg, 1986). This may be particularly threatening when grandparents have assumed semi-parental roles. Having adapted to the role changes of a single-parent adult-child, the grandparents now experience another set of changing role expectations (Kalish & Visher, 1982).

At the same time grandparents face changes in their relationships with their grandchildren or have concerns about how the adult-child's new in-laws will impact their relationship with their grandchildren, they face unclear expectations for their own stepgrandparenthood (Einstein, 1982). Fears may emerge that strengthening the "new" family means a breaking of ties with the "old" family (Kleinman, Rosenberg, & Whiteside, 1979). Viewing the stepfamily as a potential increase in interactions, however, where the stepgrandparents can influence the world even more than before may help reduce such fears and aid in the stepgrandparents' adjustment (Duffy, 1982; Trygstad & Sanders, 1989). As the stepfamily and stepgrandparents begin to learn more about the differences between the traditional nuclear family and stepfamilies, progress can be made toward clarifying stepgrandparental role expectations.

It may be expected that the nature of stepgrandparenthood will be somewhat different depending on factors such as the gender of the adult-child, the meaning of stepgrandparenting to the grandparent, the age of the stepgrandchildren, and the age of the stepgrandparent at the time the adult-child remarries (Bengtson & Robertson, 1985; Sanders & Trygstad, 1989). For example, the results of one study of remarried women indicated that remarried women and their children tend to be isolated from the extended family of their former spouse and hence integrate into the kin network of the present husband and stepfather (Anspach, 1976; Lane et al., 1989). In addition, similar to the variations that occur in the enactment of grandparenting roles (Kivnick, 1982; Neugarten & Weinstein, 1964; Robertson, 1975, 1977), variations in perceptions of the enactment of stepgrandparenting roles may be expected to occur (Henry, Ceglian & Matthews, in press; Sanders & Trygstad, 1989). Thus, grandparents face the challenge of *restructuring family subsystems to accommodate extended family systems* (e.g., other parents and grandparents; see Table 1).

Further, grandparents face the task of *understanding differences in the legal relationship with grandchildren and stepgrandchildren* (see Table 1). Typically, a lack of clarity in laws regarding stepgrandchildren occur (Wilson & DeShane, 1982). In general, stepgrandparents cannot safely assume that the degree of psychological bonding will serve as a basis for legal decisions. In cases where the adult child's new spouse adopts the adult-child's children, the legal relationship becomes more clearly established. To more fully understand their legal relationship to stepgrandchildren, stepgrandparents may wish to seek the advice of an attorney in their state of residence.

A related developmental task emerges as grandparents face the challenge of *enhancing stepfamily integration through sharing information about family background and experiences with the adult-*

child's new spouse and the stepgrandchildren (see Table 1). This task is related to Visher and Visher's (1979) concept of "myth of instant love" that may be evident as grandparents experience feelings of guilt for not experiencing bonding with the stepgrandchildren (e.g., not wanting to include new stepgrandchildren in activities with other grandchildren). Bonding with the adult-child's new spouse and the stepgrandchildren is likely to take time to establish (Einstein, 1982). By creating opportunities for bonds to develop, this process can be facilitated. For example, providing specific opportunities for the sharing of background may promote bonding in stepgrandparent/stepgrandchild relations (e.g., looking through family pictures, sharing memorabilia) by allowing for a knowledge and understanding of each other. Another way to enhance bonding between grandparents and stepgrandchildren is to gradually spend time together in enjoyable activities (Kornhaber & Woodward, 1981). In general, an increase in such self-disclosure, developing rituals, and spending time together is expected to yield a greater mutual understanding that opens the possibilities for bonding to occur (Galvin & Brommel, 1986; Whiteside, 1989).

A related developmental task in the transition to stepgrandparenthood is *establishing terminology to use when referring to persons in the complex of family relations* (see Table 1). Since the broader society has difficulty establishing a consistent set of terminology for stepfamily relations, it may be expected that specific grandparents may face the same difficulty. At this point, the family itself is faced with negotiating an acceptable set of terminology.

IMPLICATIONS FOR PRACTICE

There are several implications of the developmental tasks and stages of transition to stepgrandparenthood. First, the transition into stepgrandparenthood is a process rather than an event (Johnson, 1988). Although the developmental stages and tasks of transition to stepgrandparenthood have been divided into specific time frames, many of the tasks in more than one stage can occur simultaneously. Others may be earlier or later than presented in the model. The stages of transition to stepgrandparenthood were developed as a general model and variations are expected in specific families. The primary value in the model is the description and understanding of the *processes* and *issues* during the transition to stepgrandparenthood.

A second implication is that the process of the transition into stepgrandparenthood begins with a loss (Visher & Visher, 1979). The loss may be of the adult-child's former spouse through death or divorce. It may be a loss of the fantasy of a lifelong happy marriage for the adult-child. Thus, grieving the loss of the past or dreams that will not be fulfilled is the first step in the transition to stepgrandparenthood. The next part of the process is usually adaptation to the adult-child's single-parent family. Next, the grandparent adjusts to the entrance of the adult-child into a new relationship. These changes all impact grandparents and their family roles. After adapting to these changes, grandparents find themselves faced with a new set of challenges that accompany the transition to stepgrandparenthood.

A third implication is based on the idea that the transition to stepgrandparenthood results from a choice by the adult-child rather than by the grandparents (Kalish & Visher, 1982). The successful adaptation to stepgrandparenting roles requires an acceptance of the choices made by the adult-child. Issues in the grandparent/adult-child relationship may need to be dealt with before the transition to stepgrandparenting may be accomplished.

Fourth, although grandparents do not make the initial choice about entering stepgrandparenting roles they can be involved in enhancing stepfamily adaptation (Kalish & Visher, 1982). As a stepfamily negotiates and establishes new rules, roles, and responsibilities, these decisions impact, or can be impacted by, the grandparents. For example, a stepfamily decision to initiate a new holiday ritual may conflict with previously established family rituals. Since grandchildren may be part of three or more extended family systems (i.e., including maternal grandparents, paternal grandparents, and stepgrandparents), decisions regarding activities that normally include the extended family influence grandparents. Grandparents may vary in their adaptability to desires of the stepfamily related to such activities.

Fifth, perhaps the most important implication is that the unique developmental stages and qualities of stepfamilies need to be understood by extended family members as well as the stepfamily and the family life professional (Wald, 1981). Educating stepgrandparents about normative stepfamily development and the relinquishment of commonly held myths about stepfamilies can play a powerful role in the adaptation of grandparents to stepgrandparenting roles. Further, educating adult children about the transition into stepgrandparenting roles holds some potential for easing the transition.

CONCLUSION

This model of developmental stages and tasks in the transition to stepgrandparenthood has been developed to provide stepfamily members, grandparents, and professionals with a guide for understanding the process and issues involved in the transition to stepgrandparenthood. The model was developed through an integration and refinement of literature on grandparenting and stepfamily adjustment. Empirical data is necessary to further refine the model and more fully understand the issues and developmental concerns in the transition to stepgrandparenthood.

REFERENCES

Ahrons, C. R., & Bowman, M. E. (1982). Changes in family relationships following divorce of an adult child: Grandmother's perceptions. *Journal of Divorce, 5*, 49-68.

Ahrons, C. R. & Rodgers, R. H. (1987). *Divorced families: Meeting the challenge of divorce and remarriage.* New York: W. W. Norton & Co.

Anspach, D. (1976). Kinship and divorce. *Journal of Marriage and the Family, 38*, 323-330.

Barranti, C. C. R. (1985). The grandparent/grandchild relationship: Family resource in an era of voluntary bonds. *Family Relations, 34*, 343-352.

Bengtson, V. L. & Robertson, J. F. (1985) *Grandparenthood.* Beverly Hills: Sage.

Brammer, L. M. (1988). *The helping relationship: Process and skills* (4th ed.). Englewood Cliffs, NJ: Prentice-Hall.

Brubaker, T. H. (1990). Families in later life: A burgeoning research area. *Journal of Marriage and the Family, 52*, 959-981.

Cherlin, A. (1978). Remarriage as an incomplete institution. *American Journal of Sociology, 84*, 634-650.

Cherlin, A. (1981). *Marriage, divorce, remarriage.* Cambridge, MA: McGraw-Hill.

Cherlin, A. & Furstenberg, F. Jr. (1986). *The new American grandparent: A place in the family, a life apart.* New York: Basic Books, Inc.

Chilman, C. S. (1983). Remarriage and stepfamilies: Research results and implications. In E. D. Macklin & R. H. Rubin (Eds.), *Contemporary families and alternative lifestyles* (pp. 147-163). Beverly Hills, CA: Sage.

Cicirelli, V. G. (1983). Adult children and their elderly parents. In T. H. Brubaker (Ed.), *Family relationships in later life* (pp. 31-46). Beverly Hills, CA: Sage.

Coleman, M., & Ganong, L. (1985). Remarriage myths: Implications for helping profession. *Journal of Counseling and Development, 64*, 64-120.

Coleman M., & Ganong, L. (1990). Remarriage and stepfamily research in the 1980s: Increased interest in an old family form. *Journal of Marriage and the Family, 52*, 925-940.

Duffy, M. (1982). Divorce and the dynamics of the family kinship system. *Journal of Divorce, 5*, 3-18.

Duvall, E. M. & Miller, B. C. (1985). *Marriage and family development* (6th ed.). New York: Harper and Row.

Einstein, E. (1982). *The stepfamily: Living, loving and learning*. New York: MacMillan Publishing.

Furstenberg, F. F. Jr. & Spanier, G. B. (1984). *Recycling the family: Remarriage after divorce*. Beverly Hills, CA: Sage.

Galvin, K. M., & Brommel, B. J. (1986). *Family communication: Cohesion and change* (2nd ed.). Grandview, IL: Scott, Foresman.

Gerstel, N. (1988). Divorce and kin ties: The importance of gender. *Journal of Marriage and the Family, 50*, 209-219.

Glick, P. C., & Lin, S. L. (1986). Recent changes in divorce and remarriage. *Journal of Marriage and the Family, 48*(4), 737-747.

Goetting, A. (1982). The six stations of remarriage: Developmental tasks of remarriage after divorce. *Family Relations, 31*, 213-222.

Goldsmith, J. (1982). The postdivorce family system. McGoldrick, M., & Carter, E. A. (1982). The family life cycle. In F. Walsh (Ed.), *Normal family processes* (pp. 297-330). New York: Guilford Press.

Gladstone, J. W. (1988). Perceived changes in grandmother-grandchild relations following a child's separation or divorce. *The Gerontologist, 28*, 66-72.

Gottlieb, D. W., Gottlieb, I. B., & Slavin, M. (1988). *What to do when your son or daughter divorces*. New York: Bantam Books.

Hagestad, G. O. & Lang, M. E. (1986). The transition to grandparenthood. *Journal of Family Issues, 7*, 115-130.

Hamon, R. R. & Thiessen, J. D. (1990, November). *Coping with the dissolution of an adult child's marriage*. Paper presented at the National Council on Family Relations Annual Meeting, Seattle, WA.

Henry, C. S., Ceglian, C. P., & Matthews, D. W. (in press). The role behaviors, role meanings, and grandmothering styles of grandmothers and stepgrandmothers: Perceptions of the middle generation. *Journal of Divorce* Vol. 17, No.3/4, pp. 1-22, 1992.

Hill, R. (1986). Life cycle stages for types of single parent families: Of family developmental theory. *Family Relations, 35*, 19-29.

Hobart, C. (1987). Parent-child relation in remarried families. *Journal of Family Issues, 8*, 259-277.

Hyatt, R., & Kaslow, F. (1985). The impact of children's divorce on parents: And some contributing factors. *Journal of Divorce, 9*, 79-92.

Johnson, C. L. (1988). Postdivorce reorganization of relationships between divorcing children and their parents. *Journal of Marriage and the Family, 50*, 221-231.

Johnson, W. D., & Minton, M. H. (1982). The economic choice in divorce: Extended or blended family? *Journal of Divorce, 5*, 101-113.

Kalish, R. A., & Visher, E. (1982). Grandparents of divorce and remarriage. *Journal of Divorce, 5*, 127-140.

Kivnick, H. Q. (1982). Grandparenthood: An overview of meaning and mental health. *The Gerontologist, 22*, 59-66.

Kleinman, J., Rosenberg, E., & Whiteside, M. (1979). Common developmental tasks in forming reconstituted families. *Journal of Marital and Family Therapy, 5*, 79-86.

Kornhaber, A. & Woodward, K. L. (1981). *Grandparents/grandchildren: The vital connection*. New York: Anchor Press.

Lane, J., Van Zandt, S., Davis, B. (1990, June). *Intergenerational equity: Stepgrandparents and stepgrandchildren*. Presented at the American Home Economics Association Preconference Workshop, San Antonio, TX.

Link, M. (1987). The grandparenting role. *Lifestyles: A Journal of Changing Patterns, 8*, 157-164.

McCubbin, H. I., & Patterson, J. M. (1983). Family transitions: Adaptation to stress. In H. I. McCubbin and C. R. Figley (Eds.), *Stress and the family: Coping with normative transitions* (Vol 1., pp. 5-25). New York: Brunner/Mazel.

McGoldrick, M., & Carter, E. A. (1982). The family life cycle. In F. Walsh (Ed.), *Normal family processes* (pp. 167-195). New York: Guilford Press.

Milardo, R. M. (1987). Changes in network structure and interaction following divorce. *Journal of Family Issues, 8*, 81-93.

Mills, D. M. (1984). A model for stepfamily development. *Family Relations, 33*(3), 365-380.

Neugarten, B. L., & Weinstein, K. K. (1964). The changing American grandparent. *Journal of Marriage and the Family, 26*, 199-204.

Papernow, P. L. (1984). The stepfamily cycle: An experiential model of stepfamily development. *Family Relations, 33*(3), 355-363.

Pasley, K. (1987). Family boundary ambiguity: Perceptions of adult stepfamily family members. In K. Pasley and M. Ihinger-Tallman (Eds.), *Remarriage and stepparenting: Current research and theory* (pp. 206-224). New York: Guilford.

Ransom, W., Schlesinger, S., & Derdeyn, A. P. (1979). A stepfamily in formation. *Journal of Orthopsychiatry, 49*, 36-43.

Robertson, J. F. (1975). Interaction in three generation families, parents as mediators: Toward a theoretical perspective. *International Journal of Aging and Human Development*, *6*, 103-110.

Robertson, J. F. (1977). Grandmotherhood: A study of role conceptions. *Journal of Marriage and the Family*, *39*, 165-174.

Rodgers, R. H., & Conrad, L. M. (1986). Courtship for remarriage: Influences on family reorganization after divorce. *Journal of Marriage and the Family*, *48*, 767-775.

Rosenberg, E. B., & Hajal, F. (1985). Stepsibling relationships in remarried families. *Social Work*, *66*, 287-292.

Sanders, G. F., & Trygstad, D. W. (1989). Stepgrandparents and grandparents: The view from young adults. *Family Relations*, *38*, 71-75.

Troll, L. E. (1983). Grandparents: The family watchdogs. In T. H. Brubaker (Ed.), *Family relationships in later life* (pp. 63-74) Beverly Hills, CA: Sage.

Trygstad, D. W. & Sanders, G. F. (1989). The significance of stepgrandparents. *International Journal of Aging and Human Development*, *29*, 117-132.

Visher, E. B., & Visher, J. S. (1979). *Stepfamilies: Myths and realities*. Secaucus, NJ: Citadel Press.

Visher, J. S. & Visher, E. B. (1982). Stepfamilies and stepparenting. In F. Walsh (Ed.), *Normal family processes* (pp. 331-353). New York: Guilford Press.

Visher, J. S. & Visher, E. B. (1988). *Old loyalties, new ties: Therapeutic strategies with stepfamilies*. New York: Brunner/Mazel.

Wald, E. (1981). *The remarried family: Challenge and promise*. New York: Family Service Association of America.

Wallerstein, J. (1983). Children of divorce: The psychological tasks of the child. *American Journal of Orthopsychiatry*, *53*, 230-243.

Whiteside, M.F. (1989). Family rituals as a key to kinship connections in remarried families. *Family Relations*, *38*, 34-39.

Wilson, K. B., & DeShane, M. R. (1982). The legal rights of grandparents: A preliminary discussion. *The Gerontologist*, *22*(1), 67-71.

Wynne, L. C., Ryckoff, I. M., Day, J., & Hirsch, S. I. (1958). Pseudomutuality in the family relationships of schizophrenics. *Psychiatry*, *21*, 205-220.

Grandparents: A Special Resource for Children in Stepfamilies

Gregory E. Kennedy
C. E. Kennedy

SUMMARY. Responses to measures of relationship quality and range of activity with their grandparents by young adult grandchildren from stepfamilies (n = 55) were different from responses of young adult grandchildren from single-parent (n = 70) and intact families (n = 266). Analysis of variance comparisons revealed significant differences with grandchildren from intact families having the lowest scores, grandchildren from single-parent families in the middle, and those from stepfamilies highest. While cross-sectional data cannot demonstrate cause and effect, a possible implication from the data is that with divorce the child's relationship becomes closer with at least one grandparent as manifest by higher scores for those from single-parent families. In turn, the even higher scores by grandchildren from stepfamilies suggest that following the child's move from single-parent family life to stepfamily life, the relationship with the grandparent takes on increasing importance. Descriptive insight concerning the distinctive characteristics of grandparent/grandchild relationships in different family forms is provided by the grandchildren's rating of 29 reasons for closeness and 29 shared activities.

Gregory E. Kennedy, PhD, is Professor in the Department of Human Environmental Sciences, Central Missouri State University, Warrensburg, MO 64093. C. E. Kennedy, EdD, is Professor Emeritus, Department of Human Development and Family Studies, Kansas State University, Manhattan, KS 66506.

[Haworth co-indexing entry note]: "Grandparents: A Special Resource for Children in Stepfamilies," Kennedy, Gregory E., and C. E. Kennedy. Co-published simultaneously in the *Journal of Divorce & Remarriage* (The Haworth Press, Inc.) Vol. 19, No. 3/4, 1993, pp. 45-68; and: *The Stepfamily Puzzle: Intergenerational Influences* (ed: Craig A. Everett), The Haworth Press, Inc., 1993, pp. 45-68. Multiple copies of this article/chapter may be purchased from The Haworth Document Delivery Center [1-800-3-HAWORTH; 9:00 a.m. - 5:00 p.m. (EST)].

Literature on children of divorce, describing the developmental experiences of children during the years of living in a single-parent family, indicates that the child and resident parent become increasingly close during that time (Glenwick and Mowrey, 1986; Heatherington et al., 1985; Weiss, 1979). Grandparents, especially maternal grandparents, often become much more actively and intimately involved in the family life and in help and guidance in the care of the children during the years of single-parent family life (Cherlin and Furstenberg, 1986; Price-Bonham and Balswick, 1980).

However, as the family career changes and the resident parent and child move into a stepfamily career, the resident parent's interests move to include the new spouse. Many children at that time feel not only competition with the stepparent but also a sense of loss of closeness with resident parent (Brand and Clingempeel, 1987).

From a family systems perspective, close relationships between spouses, romantic bonding and other ingredients for high marital quality in stepmarriages may work against a stepchild's feeling of inclusion and security (Brand and Clingempeel, 1987; Minuchin, 1985). New family roles that remove from the child many of the adult-like collegial relationships and powers shared with the resident parent after divorce may often threaten and dishearten the child moving into the stepfamily.

Adjustments necessary in restructuring family roles in forming the stepfamily may conflict with developmental family and individual life cycle transitions. Heatherington and Anderson (1988) and McGoldrick and Carter (1980) describe the vulnerability to conflict for stepfamilies with adolescents. Adolescents are attempting to clarify their relationships with their biological parents and work on relationships with stepparents, while also attending to the developmental tasks of gaining autonomy and independence.

During the transition into stepfamily life, some children and adolescents may seek support and comfort through relationships with other caring adults outside the immediate family (Chapman, 1991). Some may turn back to attachment figures of the past (Brazzell and Acock, 1988; Weiss, 1982). A child's relationship with her or his biological grandparent can be one of the more stable relationships in a stepchild's changing world of adult relationships (Ihinger-Tallman and Pasley, 1987, Wilks and Melville, 1990). The grandparent's family "watchdog" role in defending and supporting the family during times of stress, such as divorce and single-parent family life has been noted (Troll, 1983; Hagestad, 1985).

Some consideration has been focused on the stepchild's relationship with stepgrandparents (Ahrons and Rodgers, 1987; Sanders and Trygstad, 1989). Our understanding of stepfamilies is severely limited by a scarcity of empirical information concerning the normative stages and transitions of the remarried family and wider kinship systems (Giles-Sims and Crosbie-Burnett, 1989; Spanier and Furstenberg, 1987). Little is known of children's relationship with their biological grandparents in stepfamilies (Bray and Berger, 1990).

The purpose of the present study was to investigate the quality of grandparent/grandchild relationships and the activities shared by grandchildren with their most-close grandparent. It was hypothesized that grandchildren from single-parent families would report a closer and more active relationship with their most-close grandparent than would grandchildren from intact families. A second hypothesis was that grandchildren from stepfamilies would report the closest and most active involvement with their grandparent.

METHOD

Sample

The 391 college students in the sample were enrolled in all sections of a family living course during the spring semester, 1990, at a midwestern university. This course is taken by approximately 60% of the students at the university and is generally representative of the student body by curriculum. Distribution of the students according to the family form in which they currently reside was as follows: 67% from intact families, 18% from single-parent families and 15% from stepfamilies. (Of the students from stepfamilies, 73% were from mother/stepfather families and 27% were from father/stepmother families.)

Forty-six percent were male and 54% were female. (Of the students from stepfamilies, 44% were male and 56% were female.) Eighteen percent of the respondents were from farms and rural areas; 36% were from towns of less than 40,000 people, 21% were from cities 40,000 to 150,000 people; 25% were from urban areas over 150,000 people. Three percent of the respondents identified their social class as "lower"; 56% said "working middle class–blue collar"; 37% chose the term "professional middle class–white collar"; the remaining 4% indicated "upper class." Eighty-five percent of the respondents identified themselves as White, 13% Black, 1% Asian, 1% Hispanic, 1% other. (Of the students from stepfamilies 90% were White and 10% were Black.) Sixty-five percent were freshmen, 19% sophomores, 9% juniors, 7% seniors. Participation was voluntary and anonymous.

Instrument

In the fall of 1989, 273 students who were enrolled in four randomly selected sections of the family living course completed a preliminary version of the instrument. Demographic characteristics of that sample were virtually identical with the present sample. Students were asked to choose the grandparent about whom they had the warmest memories. By means of a 25-item questionnaire those students described characteristics of the grandparent and of their relationship and activities with that grandparent, along with demographic information about themselves. The following two additional open-ended questions asked students to provide individualized descriptions of activities and relationships with that grandparent:

1. List five activities that are most characteristic of things you and this grandparent have done together.

2. Why do you think you have felt close to this grandparent?

The instrument developed for the present study used the same 25 questions as the preliminary questionnaire with 58 additional questions created on the basis of information the students provided in the open-ended questions of the preliminary version. From the lists provided by the 237 students in the preliminary study, twenty-nine statements of grandparent/grandchild activity and twenty-nine statements concerning reasons why grandchildren feel close to a grandparent were formed. Those statements encompassed the prevailing concepts expressed by students in the open-ended questions. Each statement was formed into a question using a Likert-type scale with a five-point range from "not characteristic" to "very characteristic." Students were asked to respond to each question as it related to their relationship with their most-close grandparent. A coefficient alpha (an internal consistency measure of reliability that is based on all the interitem correlations) was computed for each of the two sets of 29 statements, with Cronbach's alphas of .93 and .95. The standard deviations for all of the questions were in the range of 1.0 to 1.5.

RESULTS

Descriptive

More than half of the total sample (54%) described their relationship with their most-close grandparent as intimate or very close; 29% described it as close and 18% as somewhat or not very close. For the 55 grandchildren from stepfamilies, 73% said intimate or very close; 18% said close; 9% said somewhat close. Among the total sample identified as most-close grandparent, 67% were grandmothers and 33% grandfathers. For the grandchildren from stepfamilies, 62% identified grandmothers and 38% identified grandfathers as their most close grandparent. For the total sample 64% of the most-close grandparents were from the mother's side of the family; 36% were from the father's side of the family. For the grandchildren from stepfamilies, most selected a grandparent from the side of the family of the resident parent: 78% of grandchildren from mother/stepfather families selected a grandparent from the mother's side while 80% of those from father/stepmother families picked a grandparent from the father's side of the family. The focus of this study was on the relationship with the most-close grandparent. While many of the students from stepfamilies must have had stepgrandparents, only 5 chose a stepgrandparent as their most-close grandparent. Therefore, that number was too small to analyze.

Comparison of Family Forms

Both research hypotheses were supported. When compared with grandchildren from intact families, grandchildren from single-parent families consistently reported closer and more active relationships with their most-close grandparent. In turn, the responses of grandchildren from stepfamilies indicated a more close and active relationship with their grandparent than did either of the other two groups.

Tables 1-3 show that grandchildren from stepfamilies gave consistently stronger responses for most of the items describing: the quality of the grandparent/grandchild relationship (Table 1), the reasons for closeness with their grandparent (Table 2), and the kinds of activities shared (Table 3). This suggested that their relationship with their grandparent had a more predominant place in their lives than it had in the lives of the two other groups of grandchildren.

On four out of five items measuring QUALITY of the relationship (Table 1) grandchildren from stepfamilies gave significantly more positive responses. Differences among the three groups were significant at the .01 level in one-way analyses of variance. Among the 29 REASONS FOR CLOSENESS (Table 2), the responses of the grandchildren from stepfamilies were distinctive in that they expressed a stronger identity with most of the statements than did grandchildren from other family forms. On 25 out of the 29 items, analyses of variance showed differences among the three groups significant at the .05 level or better; on 11 of the items the differences were significant at .001. A similar pattern was present for the 29 shared ACTIVITY items (Table 3). For most of the items, grandchildren from stepfamilies indicated a greater involvement in shared activities with grandparents than did grandchildren from other family forms. On 15 items, analyses of variance showed differences among the groups significant at least at .05 level. On one of those, the pattern was reversed with grandchildren from stepfamilies having distinctively less involvement.

DISCUSSION

The expectation that responses of grandchildren from single-parent homes would be somewhat different from responses of grandchildren of intact families because of a greater presence of grandparents in the lives of single-parent families (Johnson, 1985) was confirmed. While supporting hypothesis two, the picture of a markedly greater involvement with grandparents by grandchildren from stepfamilies is provocative and suggests areas for further investigation.

The need that has been expressed for further study of parent/child relationships in stepfamilies might well include the need for study of the complementary function of the grandparent/grandchild relationship (Bray and Berger, 1990; Coleman and Ganong, 1990). The information from the present study suggests a pattern of progressive development in the grandparent/grandchild relationship as the grandchild moves into stepfamily life. At this point much of the discussion of the data in the study can only be speculative. The necessary information on the histories and dynamics of the families is not available to fully explain the differences reported. However, consideration of several dimensions in the pattern presented by these data can be helpful in reviewing possible perspectives for understanding life-stage changes in the career development of stepfamilies.

While the literature has established some expectation for a more active role for a grandparent in the life of a single-parent family (Cherlin and Furstenberg, 1986; Hagestad, 1985; Troll, 1983), the importance of the grandparent in the life of the grandchild in a stepfamily has not been a prominent feature in stepfamily literature. However, to assume that the styles of grandparental relationships do not change as the family moves from single-parent to stepfamily life would be to fail to appreciate the distinctness of the two family forms. It would also be a failure to appreciate the influence of family dynamics on the characteristics of the grandparent/grandchild relationship. The clear differences between the responses of grandchildren from single-parent families and stepfamilies suggests a definite change, a progression, in the grandparent/grandchild relationship.

Because these are not longitudinal data and because many variables (such as child's age at dissolution of parents' marriage, years residing in single-parent household, age at parental remarriage, years residing in stepfamily household, age of stepparent, presence

TABLE 1. MEAN SCORES OF ITEMS MEASURING GRANDPARENT RELATIONSHIP QUALITY

	Family Form			
Relationship Quality Elements	Intact (n=266)	Single-Parent (n=70)	Stepfamily (n=55)	F
Closeness with grandparent:				
5=intimately close...1=not close	3.3	3.5	3.9	7.12*
How well grandparent knew grandchild:				
3=very well...1=not very well	2.3	2.3	2.7	4.85*

How well grandchild knew grandparent:				
3=very well...1=not very well	2.2	2.3	2.4	1.45
Grandparent's influence on grandchild:				
3=very much...1=not very much	2.2	2.4	2.6	5.41*
"Grandparent/Grandchild communication				
mostly through parent" - statement:				
3=mostly not true...1=mostly true	1.9	2.0	2.3	4.91*

* p < .01.

TABLE 2. MEAN SCORES FOR ITEMS MEASURING REASON-FOR-CLOSENESS WITH GRANDPARENT

	Family Form of Grandchild			
	Intact	Single-Parent	Stepfamily	
Reason-for-Closeness	(n=266)	(n=70)	(n=55)	F
My grandparent is an enjoyable person to be with.	4.3	4.1	4.8	7.29***
Grandparent expresses love and appreciation for me.	4.1	4.0	4.7	5.77**
I have great admiration for my grandparent.	4.0	3.9	4.4	3.12
I can relax and feel comfortable around grandparent.	4.0	3.8	4.5	5.13**
My grandparent helps me feel proud of myself.	3.8	3.8	4.4	6.74**
Grandparent always available for help, support.	3.9	3.6	4.4	4.67**
Grandparent listens and treats me as an individual.	3.8	3.7	4.5	6.17**

Grandparent admiration makes me want to be a credit.	3.8	3.6	4.3	4.84**
Grandparent expresses affection with words, hugs.	3.7	3.5	4.4	8.37***
My grandparent has taught me many things.	3.5	3.7	4.1	4.04*
Grandparent gives advise, encourage, correction.	3.5	3.5	4.2	5.31**
Grandparent and I have spent much time together.	3.4	3.6	4.2	7.64***
Parents have wanted grandparent and me to be close.	3.5	3.5	3.7	1.84
Grandparent has many interests and ideas to share.	3.4	3.5	3.9	3.94*
My grandparent and I have shared many things together.	3.3	3.5	4.0	6.59**
We can talk easily.	3.3	3.3	4.1	8.00***
I have spent weekends or summer visiting grandparents.	3.2	3.2	4.3	10.57****
Special relationship because of my position in family.	3.1	3.6	4.0	7.81***
My grandparent and I do fun things together.	3.3	3.3	3.9	4.00*

TABLE 2. (CONTINUED)

Reason-for-Closeness	Family Form of Grandchild			
	Intact (n=266)	Single-Parent (n=70)	Stepfamily (n=55)	F
My grandparent puts me first over herself/himself.	3.5	3.2	3.6	2.33
Grandparent lonely, appreciates time spent together.	3.3	3.3	3.3	0.15
Grandparent and I similar in personality, appearance.	3.1	3.1	3.8	4.89**
Grandparent expresses strong religious faith.	3.2	3.2	2.3	9.95****

I see grandparent often; we live in same town.	2.8	3.5	2.8	4.35*
Grandparent took care of me when I was a child.	2.6	3.1	3.7	11.26****
Grandparent has singled me out for special attention.	2.6	2.8	3.6	8.51***
Grandparent's spouse is not living.	2.5	2.5	1.6	5.20**
For extended period time I lived with my grandparent.	1.7	2.4	3.0	15.74****
Grandparent took parent's place after divorce.	1.0	2.0	3.0	36.32****

5 = very characteristic, 1 = not characteristic

* $p < .05$ ** $p < .01$ *** $p < .001$ **** $p < .0001$

TABLE 3. MEAN SCORES FOR ITEMS MEASURING SHARED ACTIVITIES WITH GRANDPARENT

	Family Form of Grandchild			
	Intact	Single-Parent	Stepfamily	
Shared Activity	(n=266)	(n=70)	(n=55)	F
Being with family in family events, holidays, etc.	4.4	4.2	4.5	1.76
Eating, spending night at grandparent's house.	3.8	3.8	4.3	4.79*
Watching TV together.	3.5	3.5	3.8	1.22
Talking together about events in each others lives.	3.3	3.6	4.1	5.78**
Just being together, "messing around", "puttering".	3.3	3.5	3.9	4.51*
Eating out with grandparent.	3.1	3.1	3.7	4.27*

Playing games together - cards, charades, puzzles.	3.2	2.9	3.4	1.75
Shopping with grandparent for grandparent needs.	2.7	3.2	3.5	7.68***
Sharing recreational activities - fishing, camping.	2.9	2.7	3.1	0.97
Helping grandparent with gardening and yardwork.	2.8	2.9	2.9	0.13
Taking drives in the country.	2.8	3.0	3.5	4.33*
Talking together about personal concerns.	2.6	3.2	3.6	11.14****
Talking on the phone together.	2.7	3.0	3.3	4.54*
Attending events in which grandchild participates.	2.8	2.7	2.8	0.10
Sharing with grandparent in cooking.	2.6	2.6	3.0	1.85
Grandparent providing childcare.	2.4	2.9	3.4	11.21****
Learning skills from grandparent (crafts, sports).	2.5	2.8	3.0	3.83*
Helping grandparent with housework.	2.5	2.8	2.9	2.20
Attending church together.	2.7	2.6	2.0	3.86*

TABLE 3. (CONTINUED)

Shared Activity	Family Form of Grandchild: Intact (n=266)	Single-Parent (n=70)	Stepfamily (n=55)	F
Grandchild helping to care for grandparent when ill.	2.4	2.7	2.8	1.45
Shopping with grandparent for gifts for grandchild.	2.3	2.7	3.3	10.73****
Sharing with grandparent in crafts and hobbies.	2.3	2.4	2.6	1.09
Taking walks together.	2.2	2.3	2.5	0.57
Reading books and telling stories together.	2.2	2.3	2.5	0.98

Taking vacations or going on trips together.	2.1	2.4	2.9	5.86**
Attending sports and community events together.	2.2	2.4	2.7	2.88
Planning/preparing for parties, other celebrations.	1.8	2.2	2.4	4.94*
Helping grandparent with business, farm activity.	1.9	2.1	2.2	1.24
Writing letters to each other.	1.9	1.8	2.5	5.89**

5 = very characteristic, 1 = not characteristic

* $p < .05$ ** $p < .01$ *** $p < .001$ **** $p < .0001$

of stepsiblings and halfsiblings) that constitute the complexity of the stepfamily have not been investigated, the discussion of the results of this study might best proceed as a speculative scenario.

Such a scenario might be that as the child and resident parent moved into the stepfamily career, the resident parent devoted considerable attention to the stepparent. The child, in turn, remembered and reached out to the supportive identity of the grandparent/grandchild relationship. In the midst of changing family practices and new personalities in the family constellation, the familiar security of the grandparent/grandchild relationship may have taken on increased valence. This might be especially true if the remarriage occurred during the child's late school-age or adolescent years.

The more permeable intergenerational boundaries (Glenwick and Mowrey, 1986) that encouraged a greater collegial parent-child relationship during single-parent days may have become less permeable as the new family form of stepfamily was established. The beginning days of remarriage involve a period of restructuring and renegotiation of family rules and roles. This may come at a time when developmental family processes involve a parental move toward more flexibility and responsiveness to the maturational changes in children and adolescents (Chapman, 1991; Newman, 1989).

The emerging struggle for independence and identity, characteristic of late-school age and adolescence, may have heightened the child's emotional response–feelings of loss, perhaps of betrayal and need for survival. In the midst of the confusion and changes in the parent-child family situation, the sense of identity and security present in the grandparent/grandchild relationship remained steadfast. Therefore, the continuing and sustaining ties with the grandparent could be appropriated and enlarged by the child. Thus, we may perhaps understand the prominent place of grandparents in the lives of grandchildren from stepfamilies as reflected in the data of this study. Several themes in the responses of grandchildren from stepfamilies will be considered in the following paragraphs.

A Special Relationship

In our speculative scenario, if children felt a loss of position and intimacy with their move into the stepfamily, this was countered by the feelings of being singled out by their grandparent as a special person (Table 2). Grandchildren from stepfamilies seem to have a strong sense of closeness and pleasure in the presence of their grandparents (Tables 1 & 2). They were almost unanimous (mean of 4.8 on a 5-point scale, Table 2) in agreeing with the statement: "My grandparent is an enjoyable person to be with." More than other grandchildren, they found their grandparents easy to talk with and cited their grandparent's words of affection and hugs as reasons for their closeness.

Is it possible that after the resident parent remarries something happens in the relationship the child has with the grandparent? Children from stepfamilies gave higher ratings on the measures of relationship quality than did children from single-parent families. They more strongly indicated that their grandparent understood their feelings, knew their hopes and the activities with which they were involved. They more strongly affirmed that their grandparents were an influence in their lives by their values, behavior patterns and advice (Table 1).

The import from the data of this study shows grandchildren from stepfamilies in more frequent and closer contact with their grandparents. More of their time was individual, one-on-one, encounters. They ate together, shopped together, "puttered and messed around" together, talked together about what was going on in each others' lives. Table 3 presents a picture of comradeship that is stronger for grandchildren from stepfamilies than for grandchildren from other family forms. While letter writing was not a highly prevailing activity, the higher rating given it suggests that perhaps grandchildren from stepfamilies maintain contact with their grandparents even when direct contact is not possible.

Grandchildren in stepfamilies may reach out to affirm and develop a closer relationship with the grandparent as the larger and more varied family replaces the intimacy they remember. Perhaps the grandparent may be associated with nostalgia for previous days, which may have been difficult, but which are remembered for intimacy with the resident parent and the support of the grandparent. Often the most-close grandparent in the present study was the parent of the resident parent. Four out of five grandchildren who were in mother/stepfather families chose one of their mother's parents.

Likewise, in the father/stepmother families 80% of the grandchildren chose one of their father's parents. The point seems to be that the grandchild needs an adult with whom she/he feels a sense of continuity and identity. The grandparent may often be perceived by the child as the person offering (symbolizing) a trustworthy and stable relationship in a changing and unpredictable climate. Further understanding is needed concerning the complementary role of grandparents in the support system for children in stepfamilies. Kornhaber and Woodward (1981) have argued that all children need the presence of other caring adults, specifically grandparents, in addition to their parents.

Time Spent with Grandparent

Responses of grandchildren from stepfamilies present the picture of their having spent a lot of time with their grandparent, such as weekends and summer visits. Even more than those from single-parent families, grandchildren from stepfamilies reported being taken care of by grandparents and living with grandparents. Apparently, grandchildren in stepfamilies continue, perhaps even more than during single-parent family days, to spend time in the care of their grandparents (Kennedy, 1990). Particularly striking was the item "My grandparent took my parents place after divorce," which was affirmed more strongly by grandchildren from stepfamilies than by those from single-parent families. Is it possible that there is a different sense of loss of parent experienced by the child after remarriage? Does the child seek out more time with grandparent as a substitute parent?

Closeness versus Independence

Family dynamics vary in different family forms and researchers need to guard against deficit comparisons (Coleman and Ganong, 1990). However, these differences may contribute to difficulties for family members in the process of transition from one family form to another. Visher and Visher (1988) and White and Booth (1985) report that children in stepfamilies leave home earlier than do children in other family forms. Kennedy (1985) found that members of stepfamilies scored lower on measures of family connectedness. Chapman (1991) suggests that even if children do not leave home physically they may try to escape a troubled family situation by disengaging from the family and seeking support and comfort through their school activities, peer group, or through a relationship with some other caring adult.

Grandchildren in stepfamilies seem to maintain their relationship with their grandparents rather independently from their parents. While parents' support of the grandparent/grandchild relationship was important in all three family forms, comparisons by family form (Table 1) showed that grandchildren from stepfamilies, more than others, indicated their parents were not the primary communication link with their grandparents.

Attachment to grandparent could also be the grandchild's way of dealing with the loss of status. Some child may feel a loss status associated with their new family form. The stepfamily may inadvertently communicate this by seeking to emphasize a continuity with "normal" family identity and rejecting the stepfamily identity (Coleman and Ganong, 1987).

Perhaps, in some instances, the alliance with the grandparent was seen as establishing a base of operation on a more parallel level with the parent-stepparent dyad–healing the pain the child may have felt from loss of power. This may have sustained the child in a positive fashion, or, it could have contributed to a move toward greater separation. The possibility exists that grandparent/grandchild closeness could either impede the creation of stepfamily solidarity, or it could be an important resource sustaining the emotional well-being of the grandchild in times of developmental and environmental change and thus contribute to the larger goals of family life.

Future Study

The data from this study have presented grandchildren in stepfamilies as having a very meaningful and active relationship with at least one, a most-close, grandparent. The important place that this relationship may have in the developmental experiences of children in stepfamilies merits further investigation. It is possible that the grandparent/grandchild relationship in stepfamilies may have a more unique character and importance than has been heretofore known.

Understanding the reasons associated with the strong affirmation by stepfamily grandchildren of their relationship with their most-close grandparent requires knowledge of the developmental stages of family members at the time of remarriage. Future research examining the grandparental relationship within the context of life-stage developmental information would also want to address many issues presented by a family systems perspective to understanding career processes in stepfamilies. Included among those would be the paradoxical aspects of the importance of the support that close grandparental alignment gives to the child in a time of familial reorganization versus the potential interference that such affiliation may present to the building of solidarity in the stepfamily (Wilks and Melville, 1990). Such interference might relate not only to the incorporation of the resident parent and stepparent and stepsiblings but also add confusion to the building of associations with extended kin of the stepfamily. Understanding the imperative for such a grandparental relationship would require further understanding of the extent and characteristics of the child's experience of vulnerability and loss in the process of moving from a single-parent family to a stepfamily. Understanding the developmental needs of the child should be put alongside the formative concerns of the parent/stepparent dyad and considered within the broader context of the yet ill-defined family developmental tasks in the early stages of stepfamily life.

REFERENCES

Ahrons, Constance R. & Rodgers, Roy R. (1987). *Divorced Families: A Multidisciplinary Developmental Approach.* New York: W. W. Norton and Co.

Brand, Eulalee & Clingempeel, G. (1987). Interdependencies of marital and stepparent-stepchild relationships and children's psychological adjustment: Research findings and clinical implications. *Family Relations*, 36, 140-145.

Bray, James H. & Berger, Sandra H. (1990). Noncustodial father and paternal grandparent relationships in stepfamilies. *Family Relations*, 39, 414-419.

Brazzell, J. F. & Acock, A. C. (1988). Influence of attitudes, significant others, and aspirations on how adolescents intend to resolve a premarital pregnancy. *Journal of Marriage and the Family*, 50, 413-425.

Chapman, Steven F. (1991). Attachment and adolescent adjustment to parental remarriage. *Family Relations*, 40, 232-237.

Cherlin, Andrew J. & Furstenberg, Frank F. Jr. (1986). *The New American Grandparent.* New York: Basic Books.

Coleman, Marilyn & Ganong, Lawrence H. (1990). Remarriage and stepfamily research in the 1980s: Increased interest in an old family form. *Journal of Marriage and the Family*, 52, 925-940.

Coleman, Marilyn & Ganong, Lawrence H. (1987). The cultural stereotyping of stepfamilies. In Kay Pasley & Marilyn Ihinger-Tallman (Eds.), *Remarriage and Stepparenting: Current Research and Theory* (pp. 19-41). New York: Guilford Press.

Giles-Sims, Jean & Crosbie-Burnett, Margaret. (1989). Stepfamily research: Implications for policy, clinical interventions and further research. *Family Relations*, 38, 19-23.

Glenwick, David S. & Mowrey, Joel D. (1986). When parent becomes peer: Loss of intergenerational boundaries in single parent families. *Family Relations*, 35, 57-62.

Hagestad, Gunhild O. (1985). Continuity and Connectedness. In Vern L. Bengtson and Joan F. Robertson (Eds.), *Grandparenthood* (pp 31-48). Beverly Hills, CA: Sage Publications.

Heatherington, Mavis, & Anderson, E. R. (1988). The effects of divorce. In M. D. Levine and E. R. McAnarney (Eds.), *Early Adolescent Transitions* (pp. 49-67). Lexington, MA: Lexington Books.

Heatherington, Mavis, Cox, M., & Cox, R. (1985). Long-term effects of divorce and remarriage on adjustment of children. *Journal of American Academy of Child Psychiatry*, 24, 518-530.

Ihinger-Tallman, M. & Pasley, K. (1987). *Remarriage*, Beverly Hills: Sage.

Johnson, Colleen L. (1985). Grandparenting options in divorcing families: An anthropological perspective. In Vern L. Bengtson and Joan F. Robertson (Eds.), *Grandparenthood* (pp.81-96). Beverly Hills, CA: Sage.

Kennedy, Gregory E. (1990). College students' expectations of grandparent and grandchild role behaviors. *The Gerontologist*, 30, 43-48.

Kennedy, Gregory E. (1985). Family relationships as perceived by college students from single-parent, blended and intact families. *Family Perspective*, 19, 117-126.

Kornhaber, Arthur & Woodward, Kenneth L. (1981). *Grandparents/Grandchildren: The Vital Connection.* Garden City, NY: Anchor Press/Doubleday.

McGoldrick, Monica & Carter, Elizabeth A. (1980). Forming a remarried family. In Elizabeth A. Carter and Monica McGoldrick (Eds.) *The Family Life Cycle: A Framework for Family Therapy* (pp. 265-294). New York: Gardner Press.

Minuchin, Patricia. (1985). Families and individual development: Provocations from the field of family therapy. *Child Development*, 56, 289-302.

Newman, B. M. (1989). The changing nature of the parent-child relationship from early to late adolescence. *Adolescence* 24: 915-924.

Price-Bonham, Sharon & Balswick, J. O. (1980). The noninstitution: Divorce, desertion, and remarriage. *Journal of Marriage and the Family*, 42, 959-972.

Sanders, Gregory F. & Trygstad, Debra W. (1989). Stepgrandparents and grandparents: The view from young adults. *Family Relations*, 38, 71-75.

Spanier, G. B. & Furstenberg, Frank F. (1987). Remarriage and reconstituted families. In Marvin B. Sussman and Suzanne K. Steinmetz (Eds.), *Handbook of Marriage and the Family* (pp. 419-434). New York: Plenum Press.

Troll, Lillian E. (1983). Grandparents: The family watchdogs. In Timothy H. Brubaker (Ed.), *Family Relationships in Later Life* (pp. 63-74). Beverly Hills, CA: Sage Publications.

Visher, Emily B. & Visher, John S. (1988). *Old Loyalties, New Ties: Therapeutic Strategies with Stepfamilies*. New York: Bruner/Mazel.

Weiss, R. S. (1982). Attachment in adult life. In C.M. Parkes and J. Stevenson-Hinde (Eds.), *The Place of Attachment in Human Behavior* (pp. 171-184) New York: Basic Books.

Weiss, R. S. (1979). *Going It Alone: The Family Life and Social Situation as a Single Parent*. New York: Basic Books.

White, Lynn K. & Booth, Alan. (1985). The quality and stability of remarriages: The role of stepchildren. *American Sociological Review*, 50, 689-698.

Wilks, C. & Melville, C. (1990). Grandparents in custody and access disputes. *Journal of Divorce*, 13, 1-14.

Relationships with Former In-Laws: Normative Guidelines and Actual Behavior

Candan Duran-Aydintug

SUMMARY. Very few studies examined how divorce affects individuals' relationships with their former in-laws. In this study the normative aspect of this relationship, the actual contact, and the nature of support obtained from former in-laws were explored. Data obtained through in-depth interviews indicated that the quantity and the quality of the interaction between former spouses and their former in-laws depended on the quality and quantity of this relationship before the separation/divorce. Respondents' actual behavior was in agreement with their own norms but not with the perceived societal ones. The quality of the relationship established with in-laws during the marriage also affected asking and receiving support from former in-laws.

INTRODUCTION

The process of divorce entails a restructuring of the kinship system. The questions: "What happens to a person's relationship

---

Candan Duran-Aydintug, PhD, is Assistant Professor in the Department of Sociology, University of Colorado, Denver.

This paper was presented to the American Sociological Association, Pittsburgh, 1992.

[Haworth co-indexing entry note]: "Relationships with Former In-Laws: Normative Guidelines and Actual Behavior," Duran-Aydintug, Candan. Co-published simultaneously in the *Journal of Divorce & Remarriage* (The Haworth Press, Inc.) Vol. 19, No. 3/4, 1993, pp. 69-81; and: *The Stepfamily Puzzle: Intergenerational Influences* (ed: Craig A. Everett), The Haworth Press, Inc., 1993, pp. 69-81. Multiple copies of this article/chapter may be purchased from The Haworth Document Delivery Center [1-800-3-HAWORTH; 9:00 a.m. - 5:00 p.m. (EST)].

with his or her in-laws after divorce, and what are the normative expectations regulating this interaction" are relevant not only in terms of informing us about familial processes in general, but also because we know so little about the nature of the former affinal relationship (Ambert, 1988).

According to David Schneider (1980, p. 289), there are "no formal, clear, categorical limits to the domain of kinship" in American society. Thus the system has no effective rules defining the limits or boundaries of any kinship system (Schneider, 1980; Schneider and Cottrell, 1975). This means that following marital dissolution, the normative flexibility of the kinship system allows individuals to make their own choices about whether or not to interact with former in-laws when they are no longer connected by an intact marriage (Furstenberg and Spanier, 1984; Johnson, 1988a). Although speculation abounds (Goode, 1956; Bohannan, 1971), the existence and nature of norms characterizing a separated/divorced person's relationship with his or her former in-laws has not been systematically studied.

Only a handful of studies describe the patterns of interaction with in-laws after divorce. Generally, divorced men and women report distinctly less contact with the relatives of their former spouse after the break-up of their marriages, while contact with their own kin increases slightly, especially among women (Ambert, 1988; Anspach, 1976; Furstenberg and Spanier, 1984; Rosenberg and Anspach, 1973; Serovich, Price, and Chapman, 1992; Spicer and Hampe, 1975; Weiss, 1975).

Except for one study, in which parents of former spouses were the unit of analysis (Ahrons and Bowman, 1982), these studies, based on data collected from former spouses, also suggest significant gender differences in frequency of contact with former affines. Even when proximity and the presence of children are controlled, women more often than men are found to maintain ties with former affines (Ambert, 1988). This gender difference is explained by the role that women play in the kinship network. Women have been described as the "kinkeepers," the crucial link in the kinship network, the primary catalysts for interaction regardless of geographical separation (Adams, 1968; Troll, Miller, and Atchley, 1979). After divorce, women often maintain relationships with in-laws, many of whom they have learned to think of as family or friends during the marriage. On the other hand, most men are reported to discontinue their relationships with in-laws after divorce probably because men infrequently establish bonds with in-laws strong enough to survive a marital break-up (Weiss, 1975).

Another general finding is that parents, compared to nonparents, interact more frequently with former in-laws, and custodial parents interact more than noncustodial ones (Ambert, 1988; Anspach, 1976; Johnson 1988b; Spicer and Hampe, 1975). Results from a recent study indicated that the gender difference loses its significance when attention is paid to custodial versus noncustodial status (Ambert, 1988). That is, custody seems to be a more significant variable than gender. As women are awarded custody more often than men (Price and McKenry, 1988), custody status also explains at least some of the reported gender difference. There are very few studies that focus on this relationship if the divorced couple does not have common children. This lack of investigation is based on the assumption that relationships with affinal relatives that have developed through one's marriage will dissolve with divorce if there are no grandchildren present.

Other variables that play a role in behavior to in-laws are the support received from in-laws during and after divorce, the quality of the former spousal relationship, whether former in-laws are considered as relatives and the quality of coparenting among former spouses (Cherlin and Furstenberg, 1986; Furstenberg and Spanier, 1984; Serovich, Price, and Chapman, 1992; Spanier and Thompson, 1984).

The purpose of this study is to explore (1) the personal and societal norms that separated and divorced persons hold or perceive that guide their relationship with their former in-laws; (2) individuals' interaction with their in-laws after divorce and the factors that affect this relationship; and (3) whether or not former in-laws are seen as a source of support.

METHODS

The data to be reported here were collected through personal in-depth interviews between May and November of 1990. A random sample of divorced and legally separated couples was drawn from two counties (Latah and Whitman) in the Pacific Northwest. One research criterion required that the former spouses live within 2 1/2 hours (by ground transportation) of each other. The second criterion was that at least one of the former spouses has to reside in either Latah or Whitman county.

The sampling frame was prepared from court records of divorce decrees filed between January 1988 and April 1990 in the superior courts of the two counties. Based on the conception of marital dissolution as a process rather than a static life event, the respondents were sampled in different stages of divorce. From the sampling frame a sample of 60 couples was drawn: 20 couples who filed for or who obtained a divorce between January and April of 1990; 20 couples who were granted a divorce in 1989; and 20 couples who were divorced in 1988.

Almost all information was obtained from both members of a couple. In 12 cases information was gathered from only single individuals because their former spouses could not be located. For the purposes of this research it was decided to interview former spouses with common children as well as those who had no children in common.

In this study the response rate was 78.3%. This percent was reduced because of location problems since 16 individuals had moved out of state. In fact, only 10 persons who were contacted refused to participate.

The respondents interviewed were predominantly white with only 5 Hispanic respondents and 2 African Americans. Approximately 90 percent of the sample had a mean gross income in the $25,000-35,000 range. The men and women interviewed ranged in age from 19 to 48, with a mean of 35.3 years for women and 38.2 years for men. Prior to separation or divorce the couples were married from 1 to 25 years, with an average length of marriage of 11.7 years. Six of the participants were remarried at the time of the interview, and 7 ex-couples did not have common children from their marriage. In the divorced-with children category there were 24 mother custody, 6 father custody, and 10 joint parenting cases. The ages of the children ranged from 3 to 17, with a mean of 10.5 years.

In only 4 divorce cases were the common children over 18 years old, and therefore, no custody decisions were made.

FINDINGS

Personal and Societal Norms

To explore the norms regarding the interaction of separated/divorced persons with their former in-laws the respondents were asked the following question: "How do you think that divorced persons with or without children from the dissolved marriage should interact with their former in-laws?" A very high consensus emerged among the respondents on three norms: (1) interaction based on friendship, (2) the importance of grandparents, and (3) the role of the custodial parents in providing the link between the children and grandparents.

The majority (90.4%) of the respondents agreed that one should continue to interact with one's former in-laws only if the quality of that relationship during the marriage was satisfactory. That is, if the bonds established with the in-laws are strong enough to survive the marital break-up, and if the person considers them either as family or friends, then interaction was expected and encouraged to continue. On the other hand, if the spouse was the only link between them, and if, for whatever reasons, a meaningful relationship was never established between them, then the respondents agreed that this interaction should not be forced even if the marriage produced children. These respondents also agreed that even if one chooses not to interact with the former in-laws, one still should treat them courteously in public and not talk about them in front of the children.

Only 9.6% of the sample stated that one should not interact with former in-laws after divorce no matter what the quality of this relationship was during the marriage. Their reasons were that a continuing relationship makes a person feel awkward, makes one uncomfortable, and because one can never trust them, as parents will always side with their own children "if push comes to shove."

Cherlin and Furstenberg (1986), in their study of American

grandparents, note that if a separated/divorced person and his/her former in-laws do not interact it does not necessarily follow that children's interaction with the grandparents are negatively affected. This finding makes sense in light of the second norm that emerged from the data. This norm is about children's interaction with grandparents. Almost all of the respondents mentioned the importance of paternal and maternal grandparents in children's lives and acknowledged the critical role of grandparents in preserving family ties, linking the child to other members of the kindred, and providing the child with a sense of family history. However, respondents held firmly to the belief that acknowledging the importance of grandparents should not pressure the parents to interact with their former in-laws as long as they make sure that their children's interaction with the grandparents does not deteriorate.

In this sample, both custodial and noncustodial parents agreed that it is the custodial parent's responsibility to ensure that maternal and paternal grandparents interact with the children the same amount of time, if not more, after separation or divorce. In joint custody cases both parents are expected to share this responsibility.

When asked about the societal expectations, again 90.4% agreed that this interaction only becomes an issue for others when children are involved. Both parents and nonparents agreed that society does not expect nonparents to continue their relations with former in-laws, and if they choose to do so they are not supported by relatives and friends. It was perceived that only parents, especially custodial parents, were expected to have relations with their former in-laws and only for the children's sake. A mother of two summarized the majority's opinion:

> I think people expect a difference here. Like if you have children then you have to stay in touch with your former in-laws, and if you don't then this relationship is expected to fade out. I know that they only have do's and don'ts for mothers who have the custody of the children as they have the responsibility to keep the link between grandparents and children. I don't agree with this, but this is the way others think. (012 = 488w)

More than 75% of the respondents stated that these "unrealistic" expectations from others who did not experience divorce places them under unnecessary tension. Nonparents especially felt that they had to justify to others why they continued to interact with former in-laws. Conversely parents who did not continue contact felt under pressure to justify their actions. There was a clear and definite disagreement between the respondents' expectations of themselves and the perceived expectations of others, usually the never-divorced people.

Frequency of Contact

In this study the respondents were asked two questions regarding the frequency of contact after separation/divorce with the former in-laws: (1) Now: How often do you interact with your former in-laws? (2) How do you interact with them: Visits, phone calls, cards, letters; and who initiates these interactions? Following Ambert (1988) reported frequency of contact was coded as follows:

alternatives	coded as
once a week or more; every other week; once a month	frequent
every other month, 3-4 times a year	irregular
once a year; less than that; never	rarely/never

The questions about actual interaction were relevant for 84 out of 94 respondents, as the former in-laws of 10 participants were not alive. The interaction of 23.8% of the respondents was reported as frequent, 38.1% reported irregular interaction, and another 38.1% of the respondents fell into the rarely/never interaction category. In coding these responses, only information about the parents' in-law was used even though some subjects mentioned interaction with other in-laws. These findings agree with previous studies that divorced individuals generally cease to interact with their in-laws after their marriage dissolves. In this study, however, the percentage of the frequently and irregularly interacting participants (61.9%) is higher than that reported in studies by Ambert (1988), Anspach (1976), Serovich, Price, and Chapman (1992), and Spicer and Hampe (1975). In these studies interaction with former in-laws averaged around 30%. The fact that these data were gathered from individuals who were separated for three years and longer may account for the differences in reported frequency of contact.

The most frequent mode of interaction for respondents was mutual phone calls, followed by mutual visits. It should be noted, however, that not all of the respondents who reported frequent interaction reported mutuality in interaction. Four out of twenty participants in this category stated that they themselves very infrequently initiate interaction, but their former in-laws call them frequently. All of these respondents were mothers who had sole custody of their children. In these cases, grandparents initiated all the effort to keep this interaction going because they feared that if they did not the relationship between them and their grandchildren would weaken. According to these mothers, the grandparents did not trust them to guarantee that this relationship would continue and so they themselves took action. In doing so, though, they not only kept the interaction going with the grandchildren, but with the mother as well. One of these mothers described this relationship as "close encounters of a different kind":

> It is strange and I don't know how to explain it to you. They are scared that one day I will take the kids and move far away. I think that's why they are on the phone all the time, to make sure. (014 = 390w)

Contrary to the results of most studies (Ambert, 1988; Anspach, 1976; Spicer and Hampe, 1975; Weiss, 1975), this study failed to find gender differences in interaction patterns. In fact, in the frequent and rarely/never interaction categories men and women were distributed equally (in the first category 10 men and 10 women; and in the second category 16 men and 16 women). In the infrequent interaction category out of 32 respondents twenty are male and twelve are female.

Analysis of the data also suggests, as previous studies reported

(Ambert, 1988; Anspach, 1976; Johnson, 1988b; Spicer and Hampe, 1975), that parents, regardless of their custody status, interact with in-laws more frequently than childless couples. A further examination of the data, however, did not distinguish custody status as an important variable, so these findings do not support the results of the previous studies.

The lack of gender or custody differences suggested a need for a closer look at the reasons to interact or not to interact that were reported by the respondents. Eighty percent of the respondents who frequently interact with their former in-laws said the reason for this interaction was the quality of the interaction established during marriage. For these individuals, gender or custody status was not relevant. These respondents treated their former in-laws still as a part of their family, or as their close friends. The remaining four women in this category are the mothers who are being sought out and contacted by their former in-laws.

In the rarely/never interaction category 78.1% of the respondents stated that the reason they did not interact with their in-laws was that they never felt close to them during the marriage, but interacted with them to please the spouse and kept these feelings from children. The remaining respondents said they thought they had fairly close relationships during marriage, and they were planning on interacting with their in-laws after divorce. However, during separation and divorce the in-laws either blamed them, made them feel uncomfortable, or showed no support, so these respondents reevaluated the previous decision and chose not to interact. Only one of these respondents attributed the nonexistent relationship partly to the fact that they were no longer living in the same locality. No other respondent in any of the categories mentioned distance as an important factor.

During the other parts of the interview it became clear that the reasons for divorce did not influence respondents' frequency of contact with their in-laws. Most of the respondents repeatedly said that divorce happened between the spouses and divorcing the spouse did not necessitate a divorce from in-laws. Length of marriage, however, seemed to have an effect on this relationship. Many frequently interacting respondents indicated that the quality of this relationship, feeling as a family member or perceiving them as good friends, was established over a number of years. On the average, respondents in this group were married longer than the ones in the rarely/never interaction category.

Parents who established effective coparental relationships indicated that their children spent as much time with both sets of grandparents as they did before marital dissolution. Other parents, custodial and noncustodial, stated that they were making an effort to preserve this link, but they admitted that the frequency of grandchild and, especially, noncustodial grandparent interaction declined slightly after their divorce.

These findings show that there exists a personal norm/actual behavior congruence for these respondents. No matter what they believe the society's expectations are for divorced individuals, in general, they let their own rules guide them.

Former In-Law as a Source of Support

Some respondents mentioned lack of support as one of the reasons not to interact with former in-laws. Therefore, how support affected this interaction or lack of it was also analyzed. Respondents were asked whether they sought support (in any form, specified by the respondent) from their in-laws after separation/divorce. All of the respondents who interacted with their in-laws frequently and 50% of the ones in the irregular mentioned that they received support from them during the divorcing process and afterwards. This support usually took the form of emotional/moral support and less frequently it was in the form of offering services. Contrary to the findings of Spanier and Hanson (1982) and Spanier and Thompson (1984), in this study gender and custody status were not the determinants of receiving support. Again it was the quality of the relationship established during marriage. In fact, this trusting and strong relationship enabled the majority of these respondents to ask for support (emotional, financial or service) in the first place. As one woman said:

> When we first got separated I stayed with her almost for two weeks. Lots of emotional support . . . And now I can ask her whenever I need something, I know I can trust her. We always

> had this kind of a relationship, she trusts me, too, you know. (007 = 290w)

Custodial and noncustodial parents mentioned that the former in-laws (especially the former mother-in-laws) supported them not only because they always had close relationships but also because the grandparents wanted to play an instrumental role in the grandchildren's adjustment to the divorce. All in all, it appears that former in-laws helped them out because they liked them and because of the grandchildren. Those respondents who interacted with their former in-laws on an infrequent basis mentioned that they did not ask for support at all. Seven of the thirty-two respondents in this category mentioned that they would have gotten support from their in-laws because of the children if they had asked for it. The majority of the respondents in the rarely/never interaction category stated that they did not ask their former in-laws for support, as their former relationships with them was not really close. A divorced man said:

> I asked help from my first in-laws because at the time I had my daughter all to myself and I didn't know what to do. They were very supportive, and they helped me out, but see we were really close to each other during the time I was married to their daughter. This time [after a second divorce] I didn't even ask for sympathy, I don't need it from them. I'd cut my ties with them and had my peace. (041 = 789h)

A small minority (9.4%) mentioned that they did ask for support (moral and service), but they were turned down because their former in-laws took sides with their own children and voiced criticism and blame. These individuals decided not to maintain interaction with their former in-laws.

CONCLUSIONS

This study is unique in the sense that it is the first one in the literature to explore the normative aspects of the former in-law relationship. Respondents' own norms about this interaction differed from what they perceived the societal norms were. Their actual behavior, though, was in agreement with their own norms, not with perceived societal ones. They chose to continue or discontinue interaction with their former in-laws based on their previous relationships with them. This emerged as the major determinant of this interaction. Respondents did not perceive length of marriage, reasons for divorce, or presence of children as affecting this relationship.

Receiving support from former in-laws was not determined by gender or type of custody either. Again the quality of the relationship established with in-laws during the marriage and in the early stages of the divorcing process seemed to be the major determinant. Former in-laws were more likely to support parents (both custodial and noncustodial) to ensure their relationship with their grandchildren. Respondents suggested that if the relationship prior to divorce had been a trusting one then they were as likely to interact with former in-laws as they did with their own blood relatives and seek support from them as they sought support from their own families.

Too often, only minimal attention has been given to former in-laws, as in-laws have usually been considered to be a lesser part of the family. Future studies need to determine more accurately what normative guidelines and what processes are involved in the formation of one's in-law network in order to explain the differential role behaviors between blood relatives and in-laws during marriage and after divorce.

REFERENCES

Adams, B.N. (1968). *Kinship in an Urban Setting*. Chicago: Markham Publishing Company.

Ahrons, C.R., & Bowman, M.E. (1982). "Changes in family relations following divorce of adult children: Grandmothers' perceptions." *Journal of Divorce*, 5, 49-68.

Ambert, A.M. (1988). "Relationships with former in-laws after divorce: A research note." *Journal of Marriage and the Family*, 50, 679-686.

Anspach, D.F. (1976). "Kinship and divorce." *Journal of Marriage and the Family*, 38, 343-350.

Bohannan, P. (1971). "The six stations of divorce." In P. Bohannan (ed.), *Divorce and After*. Garden City: Doubleday.

Cherlin, A., & Furstenberg, F.F., Jr. (1986). *American Grandparenthood*. New York: Basic Books.

Furstenberg, F.F., Jr., & Spanier, G.B. (1984). *Recycling the Family: Remarriage after Divorce*. Beverly Hills: Sage.

Goode, W.J. (1956). *After Divorce*. Glencoe, Ill: Free Press.

Johnson, C.L. (1988a). *Ex Familia*. New Brunswick: Rutgers University Press.

________ . 1988b. "Post-divorce reorganization of the relationships between the divorced and their parents." *Journal of Marriage and the Family*, 50, 221-231.

Price, S.J., & McKenry, P.C. (1988). *Divorce*. Newbury Park, CA: Sage.

Rosenberg, G.S., & Anspach, D.F. (1973). *Working Class Kinship*. Lexington: Lexington Books.

Schneider, D.M. (1980). *American Kinship: A Cultural Account*. Englewood Cliffs, NJ: Prentice-Hall.

Schneider, David M., and Cottrell, C.B. (1975). *The American Kin Universe: A Genealogical Study*. Chicago: Department of Anthropology, University of Chicago.

Serovich, J.M; Price, S.J., & Chapman, S.F. (1992). "Former in-laws as a source of support." *Journal of Divorce and Remarriage*, 17, 17-25.

Spanier, Graham B., and Hanson, Sarah. (1982). "The role of extended kin in the adjustment to marital separation." *Journal of Divorce*, 5, 533-548.

Spanier, Graham B., and Thompson, Linda. (1984). Parting: *The Aftermath of Separation and Divorce*. Beverly Hills CA: Sage.

Spicer, Jerry W., and Hampe, Gary D. (1975). "Kinship interaction after divorce." *Journal of Marriage and the Family* 37: 113-119.

Troll, Lillian E., Miller, Sheila J. and Atchley, Robert. (1979). *Families in Later Life*. Belmont: Wadsworth.

Weiss, Robert S. 1975. *Marital Separation*. New York: Basic Books.

Differentiation from Ex-Spouses and Stepfamily Marital Intimacy

Joshua M. Gold
Donald L. Bubenzer
John D. West

SUMMARY. Based on Masheter's (1991) results supporting the relationship between attachment to an ex-spouse and personal functioning, this study explored the relationship between attachment to an ex-spouse and spousal well-being, specifically marital intimacy in stepfamilies. The sample consisted of 127 volunteer spouses who completed the Masheter (1991) inventory as the measure of differentiation from ex-spouses and the PAIR as the measure of marital intimacy. The study found a significant positive relationship between the two variables. These findings suggest that the relationship between ex-spouses and between current spouses is an important component of counseling with stepfamily couples.

As a reflection of the growing incidence of divorce and remarriage (Bumpas, Sweet, & Martin, 1990; Coleman & Ganong, 1990; Dolan & Lown, 1985; Goetting, 1982; Hetherington & Clingempeel, 1988; Norton, 1987), stepfamilies have been designated as the fastest growing family configuration in American society. By the

---

Joshua M. Gold, PhD, is Assistant Professor of Marriage and Family Counseling, at Fairfield University, Fairfield, CT 06430-7524. Donald L. Bubenzer is Associate Professor and John D. West is Professor in Counseling & Human Development Services at Kent State University, Kent, OH.

[Haworth co-indexing entry note]: "Differentiation from Ex-Spouses and Stepfamily Marital Intimacy," Gold, Joshua M., Donald L. Bubenzer and John D. West. Co-published simultaneously in the *Journal of Divorce & Remarriage* (The Haworth Press, Inc.) Vol. 19, No. 3/4, 1993, pp. 83-95; and: *The Stepfamily Puzzle: Intergenerational Influences* (ed: Craig A. Everett), The Haworth Press, Inc., 1993, pp. 83-95. Multiple copies of this article/chapter may be purchased from The Haworth Document Delivery Center [1-800-3-HAWORTH; 9:00 a.m. - 5:00 p.m. (EST)].

year 2000, the number of stepfamilies has been forecast to exceed the number of nuclear families in American society (Bryan, Ganong, Coleman & Bryan, 1985). The stepfamily unit is theorized to consist of parents/spouses, the step, biological, and mutual child(ren), and the non-residential parent(s) (Poppen & White, 1984; Visher & Visher, 1985; 1988). Traditional models of family functioning are based on the first-marriage family and emphasize intra-familial dynamics. This emphasis on intra-familial dynamics may preclude consideration of the relationship between extra-familial members of stepfamilies. This study wanted to add to the understanding of stepfamily dynamics by focusing on the relationship between stepfamily spouses and their ex-spouses. As the marital dyad is designated as the leadership in the family system (Haley, 1976; Minuchin & Fishman, 1982), an understanding of the factors that contribute to marital functioning would be crucial to the functioning of the stepfamily unit.

Among the variables theorized as related to stepfamily functioning is the degree of differentiation between the stepfamily spouse and his/her ex-spouse. Differentiation can be defined as emotional independence from a subsystem (Bowen, 1976). Well-differentiated persons express feelings of individual separateness from, yet connectedness to, the larger system (Boszormenyi-Nagi & Sparks, 1973). Such persons are described as flexible, adaptable, and self-sufficient, based on their ability to use their intellectual capacity as fully as possible, unimpeded by conflicting pressures of family sanctioning mechanisms (Bowen, 1978).

Carter and McGoldrick (1988) suggested that spouses in stepfamilies carry three sets of emotional "baggage" from (a) family of origin, (b) the first marriage, and (c) the period of separation and divorce prior to the remarriage. Issues of guilt, loyalty conflicts, hurt, failure, anger and bitterness may interfere with the creation of appropriate boundaries and affective differentiation, and the new marital relationship in the stepfamily.

Stepfamily literature has repeatedly identified the relationship between ex-spouses as an area of concern of stepfamily spouses (Ahrons & Rogers, 1987; Crosbie-Burnett, 1989; Goetting, 1982; Hutchinson, 1989; Mills, 1984; Nolan, Coleman & Ganong, 1984; Osborne, 1983; Roberts & Price, 1985; Stanton, 1986; Visher &

Visher, 1985, 1988). In addition, the empirical literature supports a significant positive relationship between differentiation from ex-spouses and measures of personal emotional adjustment (Tschann, Johnston & Wallerstein, 1989) and measures of marital satisfaction/adjustment (Anderson & White, 1986; Bray, Berger, Mann, Silverblatt & Gershenhorn, 1987; Goodman-Lezin, 1985, Guisinger, Cowan & Schuldberg, 1989; Roberts & Price, 1989). However, further investigation of differentiation from ex-spouses and spousal functioning in the stepfamily is needed to more fully understand these dynamics (Vemer, Coleman, Ganong, & Cooper, 1989).

Marital intimacy has been described as one of the more descriptive dimensions of the marital relationship and can be viewed as a mediator of higher order relational qualities such as mutuality, interdependence, trust, commitment, and caring (Sabatelli, 1988). In addition, the cultivated intimacy of couples has been labeled as the best indicator of whether couples plan to continue or terminate their relationship (Kersten, 1990). However, the study of marital intimacy is one of the least addressed topics in family literature (Kantor & Okun, 1989). As stepfamily couples are more likely to divorce than are first-married couples (Furstenberg & Spanier, 1984), the study of marital intimacy can be theorized as crucial to the maintenance of the stepfamily unit.

Two studies (Waring, Patton, Neron & Linker, 1984; Waring, Redon, Corvinelli, Chalmers, & Vander Laan, 1983) supported the positive relationship between marital intimacy and individual functioning. Four studies (Harper & Elliott, 1988; Kersten, 1990; Speisman, Bartis, White & Costos, 1985; Tolstedt & Stokes, 1983) supported the positive relationship between marital intimacy and marital satisfaction/adjustment. In addition, several studies list marital intimacy as one of several factors predictive of stepfamily functioning (Bray, Berger, Mann, Silverblatt & Gershenhorn, 1987; Ganong & Coleman, 1989; Roberts & Price, 1989). However, stepfamily marital intimacy has yet to be directly studied.

This exploratory study asked "What is the relationship between differentiation from ex-spouses and stepfamily marital intimacy?" The study intended to examine sample responses by gender and by family configuration.

METHODOLOGY

Participants

The sample for this study consisted of 200 spouses recruited through their membership in chapters of the Stepfamily Association of America. Chapter contact persons were used to advertise the study, to inform the researcher of the number of interested couples from the chapter, and to disseminate the survey packages to the volunteer couples. Follow-up mailing to the chapter contacts resulted in a response rate of 127 spouses (60.4%).

The sample consisted of 69 men and 58 women. Of the 69 men, 30 were part of biological father/stepmother families and 39 were part of complex stepfamilies. Of the 58 women respondents, 19 were part of biological mother/stepfather families and 39 were part of complex stepfamilies. Men's ages ranged from 25-64 years (mean = 39.0, sd. = 8.2) and women's ages ranged from 22-62 years (mean = 34.6, sd. = 8.0). Sixty-four respondents (50%) reported residential children and 63 respondents (50%) reported visiting children. None of the respondents reported residential and nonresidential children. Sixty-one spouses (47.7%) reported the birth of a mutual child to the blended family couple and 66 respondents (52.3%) reported no mutual child. The majority of the participants in this study reported at least some college education, and none reported failing to complete high school. The majority of respondents reported out-of-home employment. None of the participants reported being unemployed or retired. The majority of the respondents in this study were Caucasian, with approximately 25% of the sample being African-American. The majority of participants reported Protestant as religious affiliation, with equal numbers reporting Catholic, Jewish, Other, or None. Household incomes of the sample ranged from \$20,000- \$100,000+, with 14.8% reporting income between \$20,001 and \$40,000, 29.5% reporting income between \$40,001 and \$60,000, 33.0% reporting income between \$60,001 and \$80,000, 11.4% reporting income between \$80,001 and \$100,000, and 11.4% reporting income of over \$100,000.

Instrumentation

Differentiation from ex-spouses. For the purposes of this study, the construct of differentiation was operationalized as the degree of emotional attachment and interpersonal conflict between ex-spouses. The What Happens Between Ex-Spouses After Divorce questionnaire was developed to assess these constructs (Masheter, 1991). Emotional attachment is measured through response to a 10-item, 5-point Likert scale. Interpersonal conflict is measured through response to a 6-item, 5-point Likert scale. Factor loading analysis demonstrated significant differences ($p < .001$) between the two scales. The Cronbach's alpha was established as .70 for the attachment scale and .85 for the conflict scale. Masheter (1991) found the scales to have significant negative predictive validity ($p < .01$) with a measure of personal well-being on a sample of 265 respondents.

Marital intimacy. The Personal Assessment of Intimacy in Relationships (PAIR) uses five indices to measure self-reported marital intimacy: (a) emotional intimacy (closeness of feeling); (b) social intimacy (experiences of common friends and similarities in social networks); (c) intellectual intimacy (experiences of sharing ideas); (d) sexual intimacy (experiences of sharing general affection and/or sexual activity); and, (e) recreational intimacy (experiences of sharing interest in hobbies and leisure time activities) (Schaefer & Olson, 1981). Split-half reliability figures ranging from .70 to .77 have been established. Scale-by-scale concurrent validity was established with the Locke-Wallace Marital Adjustment Scale ($p < .001$) and with the cohesion, expressiveness, and conflict subscales of the Family Environment Scales ($p < .01$) in predicted directions (Schaefer & Olson, 1981). The predictive validity of the PAIR has been established with measures of career and marital stress (Thomas, Albrecht & White, 1984), coalitions in the family-of-origin (West, Zarski & Harvill, 1986), measures of marital adjustment (Harper & Elliott, 1988; Quinn & Davidson, 1986), and with measures of marital disaffection (Kersten, 1990).

RESULTS

It was hypothesized that there would be no significant relationships between self-reported differentiation from ex-spouses and self-reported marital intimacy of stepfamily spouses by gender or by family configuration. As neither instrument provides a total score, only scale by scale correlations could be calculated. These relationships were assessed through the calculation of five Pearson Product Moment Correlation Coefficients between the two subscales of the differentiation instrument and the five scales of the marital intimacy instrument.

For men, a significant negative relationship ($p < .01$) was found between emotional attachment to ex-spouse and measures of emotional, social, sexual, and intellectual marital intimacy. A significant negative relationship also was found between conflict with ex-spouse and measures of emotional intimacy ($p < .01$), intellectual intimacy ($p < .05$) and recreational intimacy ($p < .01$). For women, a significant negative relationship ($p < .01$) was found between emotional attachment to ex-spouse and emotional, social, sexual, and intellectual marital intimacy. A significant negative relationship was also found between conflict with ex-spouse and measures of emotional intimacy ($p < .05$), sexual intimacy ($p < .05$), and recreational intimacy ($p < .01$).

For men in biological father/stepmother couples, a significant negative relationship ($p < .05$) was found between emotional attachment to the ex-spouse and measures of emotional and recreational marital intimacy. For women in biological mother/stepfather couples, no significant relationships were found. For couples in complex blended families, a significant negative relationship was found between emotional attachment to ex-spouse and emotional intimacy ($p < .01$), social intimacy ($p < .01$), sexual intimacy ($p < .05$), and intellectual intimacy ($p < .05$). A significant negative relationship was also found between conflict with ex-spouse and measures of emotional intimacy ($p < .01$), sexual intimacy ($p < .05$), and recreational intimacy ($p < .01$). Tables 1 and 2 summarize the correlational results. Based on these results, the null hypothesis was rejected.

DISCUSSION

Theoretically, the negative relationship between emotional attachment and conflict with ex-spouses and stepfamily marital inti-

Table 1

Summary of the Correlations between Differentiation and Intimacy Scores by Gender of Respondent

Correlations	Subjects	
Diff/Intimacy	Men (n=69)	Women (n=58)
Attach/Emot.	-.584**	-.391**
Attach/Soc.	-.433**	-.508**
Attach/Sex.	-.428**	-.338**
Attach/Int.	-.524**	-.341**
Attach/Rec.	-.137	-.123
Conf/Emot.	-.360**	-.314*
Conf/Soc.	-.141	-.180
Conf/Sex.	-.209	-.307*
Conf/Int.	-.282*	-.156
Conf/Rec.	-.326**	-.362**

*p<.05; **p<.01.

macy is consistent with Bowen's (1976) view that the ability to establish relationships based on objectivity and emotional distance with extra-familial subsystems would be predictive of higher levels of marital functioning. This finding also is consistent with the Structural Therapy emphasis on clear boundaries to denote the primacy of the current marital dyad and the independent functioning of that subsystem, free from the intrusion of other family subsystems (Minuchin & Fishman, 1982). The finding is consistent with the Strategic concept of clear generational alliances as indicative of positive family functioning (Madanes, 1981). In the case of stepfamily

Table 2

Summary of the Correlations between Differentiation and Intimacy by family Configuration

Correlations	Subjects		
Diff/Intimacy	Father Stepmother Family (n=30)	Mother Stepfather Family (n=19)	Complex Step Family (n=39)
Attach/Emot.	-.418*	-.121	-.451**
Attach/Soc.	-.347	-.226	-.580**
Attach/Sex.	.026	-.383	-.343*
Attach/Int.	-.236	-.052	-.406*
Attach/Rec.	-.383*	-.183	-.198
Conf/Emot.	-.322	-.105	-.417**
Conf/Soc.	-.031	.021	-.264*
Conf/Sex.	.030	-.307	-.340*
Conf/Int.	-.019	-.142	-.191
Conf/Rec.	-.030	-.262	-.424*

*p<.05; **p<.01.

couples, the generations would refer to the past and present marital dyads, with the subordination of the previous marital coalition to the current marital alliance for healthy family functioning.

In terms of the clinical implications of these results, the relationship between differentiation from the ex-spouse and current marital intimacy further emphasizes the tasks facing stepfamily spouses, specifically: (a) the facilitation of the primary attachment between current spouses; (b) the establishment of clear boundaries around the blended family unit of spouses, residential, and mutual children; and (c) the ongoing relationship with the ex-spouse(s) in terms of parental responsibilities and the resolution of emotional issues from the previous marriage(s) (Ahrons & Rogers, 1987; Carter & McGoldrick, 1988; Poppen & White, 1984; Sager, Brown, Crohn, Engel, Rodstein & Walker, 1983; Visher & Visher, 1988).

Previous studies have identified the relationship between ex-spouses as an area of concern for partners in stepfamilies (Adams & Taylor, 1983; Anderson & White, 1986; Bray, Berger, Mann, Silverblatt & Gershenhorn, 1987; Ganong & Coleman, 1989; Pasley & Inhinger-Tallman, 1989; Roberts & Price, 1987, 1989; Schultz & Schultz, 1987). However, those studies did not specify how the relationship between ex-spouses may effect marital functioning. The results of this study suggest the resolution of the emotional and conflictual relationships between ex-spouses has a significant impact on the marital dynamics of the stepfamily. An ongoing relationship between ex-spouses, either in terms of feelings of closeness or conflict, has been shown to interfere with feelings of marital intimacy in the current marriage. In addition, the family configuration with the most anticipated contact between ex-spouses (complex stepfamilies) presented the most significant relationships between attachment/conflict with ex-spouses and marital intimacy.

This investigation is the first study of marital intimacy of stepfamily spouses. Its findings may assist in describing the spouses' development of marital intimacy in the new stepfamily. Stepfamily couples cannot utilize the honeymoon period of a young marriage to create the spousal connection that later accommodates the arrival of children. The stepfamily marriage involves the immediate creation of the parental role, whether the children reside with the new couple or with the absent spouse. This simultaneous demand of parental and spousal roles has been theorized to result in one relationship, usually the spousal relationship, being neglected (Goetting, 1982). Counselors need to direct couples' attentions to both the parental and spousal functions in the stepfamily (Hutchinson, 1989; Roberts & Price, 1985; Stanton, 1986; Visher & Visher, 1988). Intervention in the spouses' relationship is intended to legitimize their rights as partners, as well as their duties as parents. Within this framework, the spouses can decide how best to develop and communicate their feelings of marital intimacy.

These results also imply that counselors working with stepfamilies need to be aware of the dynamics between the current and ex-family systems. The optimum relationship between the two systems would not be characterized by disengagement between the current spousal/parental and ex-spousal/parental systems nor by over-involvement of the systems. It would, however, permit resolution of the ongoing tasks of child care, visitation and financial matters between the two households. In addition, it would allow for the creation of marital intimacy by the spouses in the new stepfamily.

In acknowledging this study's limitations, the lack of adequate representation of respondents who report racial/ethnic origins other than Caucasian and of respondents in the lower income categories may raise concerns about how reflective the findings of this study may be of those populations. The methods of data collection employed in this study presented a lack of opportunity for follow-up with non-respondents. Such a follow-up would have helped determine if nonrespondents demonstrated significantly different profiles from those volunteers who initially completed the study's instruments.

This initial study began the process of examining the relationship between differentiation from ex-spouses and stepfamily marital intimacy. The results offer an admonition to stepfamily spouses and to the professionals who work with these spouses to ensure that the old marital relationship is truly "over" while working on the new relationship.

REFERENCES

Adams, P.K., & Taylor, M.K. (1983). Characteristics and attitudes of parents in stepfamilies (ERIC Document Reproduction Service No. 274 429).

Ahrons, C., & Rogers, R. (1987). *Divorced families: A multidisciplinary developmental view.* New York: W.W. Norton.

Anderson, J.Z., & White, G.D. (1986). An empirical investigation of interaction and relationship patterns in functional and dysfunctional nuclear families and stepfamilies. *Family Process, 25,* 407-422.

Boszormenyi-Nagi, I., & Sparks, G.U. (1973). *Invisible loyalties: Reciprocity in intergenerational family therapy.* New York: Harper & Row.

Bowen, M. (1976). Theory in the practice of psychotherapy. In P.J. Gruerin (Ed.). *Family therapy: Theory and practice*. (pp. 42-90). New York: Gardner Press.

Bowen, M. (1978). *Family therapy in clinical practice*. New York: Jason Aronson.

Bray, J.H., Berger, S.H., Mann, T., Silverblatt, A.H., & Gershenhorn, S. (1987, April). Parenting practices and family process during early remarriage. Paper presented at the Biennial Meeting of the Society for Research in Child Development, Baltimore.

Bryan, S.H., Ganong, L.H., Coleman, M., & Bryan, L.R. (1985). Counselors' perceptions of stepparents and stepchildren. *Journal of Counseling Psychology, 32*, 279-282.

Bumpas, L., Sweet, J., & Martin, T.C. (1990). Changing patterns of remarriage. *Journal of Marriage and the Family, 52*, 747-756.

Carter, B., & McGoldrick, M. (1988). *The changing family life cycle: A framework for family therapy*. (2nd ed.). New York: Gardner Press.

Coleman, M., & Ganong, L.H. (1990). Remarriage and stepfamily research in the 1980s: Increase interest in an old family form. *Journal of Marriage and the Family, 52*, 925-940.

Crosbie-Burnett, M. (1989). Application of family stress theory to remarriage: A model for assessing and helping stepfamilies. *Family Relations, 38*, 323-332.

Dolan, E.M., & Lown, J.M. (1985). The remarried family: Challenges and opportunities. *Journal of Home Economics, Fall*, 36-40.

Furstenberg, F.F. Jr., & Spanier, G.B. (1984). The risk of dissolution in remarriage: An examination of Cherlin's hypothesis of incomplete institutionalization. *Family Relations, 33*, 433-441.

Ganong, L.H., & Coleman, M. (1989). Preparing for remarriage: Anticipating the issues, seeking solutions. *Family Relations, 38*, 28-33.

Goetting, A. (1982). The six stations of remarriage: Developmental tasks of remarriage after divorce. *Family Relations, 31*, 213-222.

Goodman-Lezin, S. (1985, August). The remarried family: Variables affecting adjustment to stepmothering. Paper presented at 93rd Annual Convention of the American Psychological Association, Los Angeles.

Guisinger, S., Cowan, P.A., & Schuldberg, D. (1989). Changing parent and spouse relations in the first years of remarriage of divorced fathers. *Journal of Marriage and the Family, 51*, 445-456.

Haley, J. (1976). *Problem solving therapy*. New York: Colophan Books.

Harper, J.M., & Elliott, M.L. (1988). Can there be too much of a good thing? The relationship between desired level of intimacy and marital adjustment. *The American Journal of Family Therapy, 16*(4), 351-360.

Hetherington, E.M., & Clingempeel, G. (1988, March). Coping with remarriage: The first two years. Paper presented at the 34th Annual Meeting of the Southeastern Psychological Association, New Orleans.

Hutchinson, L.C. (1989, March). How many parents? Support for stepfamilies. Paper presented at the Annual Meeting of the American Association for Counseling and Development, Boston.

Kantor, D., & Okun, B.F. (1989). *Intimate environments: Sex, intimacy and gender in families*. New York: The Guilford Press.

Kersten, K.K. (1990). The process of marital disaffection: Interventions at various stages. *Family Relations*, *39*, 257-265.

Madanes, C. (1981). Strategic family therapy. San Francisco: Jossey-Bass.

Masheter, C. (1991). Postdivorce relationship between ex-spouses: The roles of attachment and interpersonal conflict. *Journal of Marriage and the Family*, *53*, 103-110.

Mills, D.M. (1984). A model for stepfamily development. *Family Relations*, *33*, 365-372.

Minuchin, S. (1982). Reflections on boundaries. *American Journal of Orthopsychiatry*, *52*, 655-663.

Nolan, J., Coleman, M., & Ganong, L. (1984). The presentation of stepfamilies in marriage and family textbooks. *Family Relations*, *33*, 559-566.

Norton, A.J. (1987). Families and children in the year 2000. *Children Today*, *16*(4), 6-9.

Osborne, J. (1983). Stepfamilies: The restructuring process (ERIC Document Reproduction Service No. 264 040).

Pasley, K., & Inhinger-Tallman, M. (1989). Boundary ambiguity in remarriage: Does ambiguity differentiate degree of marital adjustment and integration? *Family Relations*, *38*, 46-52.

Poppen, W.A., & White, P.N. (1984). Transition to the blended family. *Elementary School Guidance and Counseling*, *19*(1), 50-61.

Quinn, W.H., & Davidson, B. (1986). Marital type and the marital relationship. *Journal of Divorce*, *9*, 117-134.

Roberts, T.W., & Price, S.J. (1985). A systems analysis of the remarriage process: Implications for the clinician. *Journal of Divorce*, *9*(2), 1-21.

Roberts, T.W., & Price, S.J. (1987). Instant families: Divorced mothers marry never-married men. *Journal of Divorce*, *11*(1), 71-91.

Roberts, T.W., & Price, S.J (1989). Adjustment in remarriage: Communication, cohesion, marital and parental roles. *Journal of Divorce*, *13*(1), 17-43.

Sabatelli, R.M. (1988). Measurement issues in marital research: A review and critique of contemporary survey instruments. *Journal of Marriage and the Family*, *50*, 891-915.

Sager, C.J., Brown, H.S., Crohn, H., Engel, T., Rodstein, E., & Walker, L. (1983). *Treating the remarried family*. New York: Brunner/Mazel.

Schaefer, M.T., & Olson, D.H. (1981). Assessing intimacy: The PAIR inventory. *Journal of Marital and Family Therapy, January*, 47 -60.

Schultz, N.C., & Schultz, C.L. (1987). Affection and intimacy as a special strength of couples in blended families. *Australian Journal of Sex, Marriage and the Family*, *8*(2), 66-72.

Speisman, J.C., Bartis, S., White, K.M., & Costos, D. (1985). Marital adjustment and congruence in intimacy maturation (ERIC Document Reproduction Service No. 261 278).

Stanton, G.W. (1986). Preventive intervention with stepfamilies. *Social Work, May-June*, 201-206.

Thomas, S.P., Albrecht, K., & White, P. (1984). Determinants of marital quality in dual-career couples. *Family Relations, 33*, 513-521.

Tolstedt, B.E., & Stokes, J.P. (1983). Relation of verbal, affective, and physical intimacy to marital satisfaction. *Journal of Counseling Psychology, 30*, 573-580.

Tschann, J.M., Johnston, J.R., & Wallerstein, J.S. (1989). Resources, stressors and attachment as predictors of adult adjustment after divorce: A longitudinal study. *Journal of Marriage and the Family, 51*, 1033-1046.

Vemer, E., Coleman, M., Ganong, L.H., & Cooper, H. (1989). Marital satisfaction in remarriage: A Meta-analysis. *Journal of Marriage and the Family, 51*, 713-725.

Visher, E.B., & Visher, J.S. (1985). Stepfamilies are different. *Journal of Family Therapy, 7*, 9-18.

Visher, E.B., & Visher, J.S. (1988). *New loyalties, old ties*. New York: Brunner/ Mazel.

Waring, E.M., Patton, D., Neron, C.A., & Linker, W. (1986). Types of marital intimacy and prevalence of emotional illness. *Canadian Journal of Psychiatry, 31*, 720-726.

Waring, E.M., Reddon, J.R., Corvinelli, M., Chalmers, W.S., & Vander Laan, R. (1983). Marital intimacy and mood states in a nonclinical sample. *The Journal of Psychology, 115*, 263-273.

West, J.D., Zarski, J.J., & Horvill, R. (1986). The influence of the family triangle on intimacy. *American Mental Health Counselors Association Journal, 8*, 166-174.

The Presence of Children and Blended Family Marital Intimacy

Joshua M. Gold
Donald L. Bubenzer
John D. West

SUMMARY. This study is an effort to add to the understanding of spousal dynamics in blended families. The survey of 88 couples investigated the effects of family configuration, residence of children, and birth of a mutual child on husbands' and wives' self-reported marital intimacy. Significant interaction effects were found for residence of children on spouses' marital intimacy and for birth of a mutual child on wives' marital intimacy.

Family therapists working with blended family systems may become overwhelmed by the complexity of blended family dynamics. Blended family systems are composed of the current spouses, absent biological parents, residential children whose birth predates the marriage, nonresidential children, present grandparents, mutual children whose birth postdates the current marriage and ex-in-laws (Miller & Moorman, 1989). Based on this constellation of boundary

Joshua M. Gold, PhD, is Assistant Professor of Marriage and Family Counseling, Graduate School of Education & Allied Professions, 223 Canisius Hall, Fairfield University, Fairfield, CT 06430-7524. Donald L. Bubenzer, PhD, is Associate Professor and John D. West, EdD, is Professor, Counseling and Human Development Services, 310 White Hall, Kent State University, Kent, OH 44242-0001.

[Haworth co-indexing entry note]: "The Presence of Children and Blended Family Marital Intimacy," Gold, Joshua M., Donald L. Bubenzer, and John D. West. Co-published simultaneously in the *Journal of Divorce & Remarriage* (The Haworth Press, Inc.) Vol. 19, No. 3/4, 1993, pp. 97-108; and: *The Stepfamily Puzzle: Intergenerational Influences* (ed: Craig A. Everett), The Haworth Press, Inc., 1993, pp. 97-108. Multiple copies of this article/chapter may be purchased from The Haworth Document Delivery Center [1-800-3-HAWORTH; 9:00 a.m. - 5:00 p.m. (EST)].

issues and interaction patterns, family therapists are presented with a myriad of areas of attention. In the study of blended family dynamics, parenting concerns of blended family spouses have been well researched. However, less attention has been directed towards the blended family spousal dynamics.

Marital intimacy has been labeled as one of the least addressed topics in the family literature (Kantor & Okun, 1989). However, the "cultivated intimacy" (Wynne & Wynne, 1986, p. 384) of couples has been specified as the best indicator of whether couples plan to continue or to terminate their relationship (Kersten, 1990). In light of weakening financial, social, and legal impairments to divorce, this emotional bond between spouses has become more heavily emphasized as the motive for couples to remain together (Kersten, 1990).

Marital intimacy has been identified as a crucial task of the process of marital adjustment and as a component of spouses' evaluation of marital satisfaction (Sabatelli, 1988). The literature offers several conceptualizations of the construct of marital intimacy (Birtchnell, 1986; Combrinck-Graham, 1989; L'Abate & Sloan, 1984; Schaefer & Olson, 1981). These definitions agree that marital intimacy can be seen as one of the more descriptive dimensions of marital relationships and can be viewed as a mediator of higher order relational qualities such as mutuality, interdependence, trust, commitment, and caring (Sabatelli, 1988).

The initial development of marital intimacy is seen to be a spousal task within the "newly married" stage of the couple's life. The goal of this stage is the formation of a spousal identity, encompassing the partners' expression of marital intimacy, free from the intrusion of family-of-origin and, as of yet, unencumbered by parenting responsibilities. However, blended family couples cannot utilize the honeymoon period of a young marriage to create the spousal connection that later accommodates the arrival of children (Papernow, 1984). The blended family marriage involves the immediate creation of the parental role, whether the children reside with the new couple or with the absent spouse. This simultaneous demand of parental and spousal roles has been found to result in one relationship, usually the spousal relationship, being neglected (Goetting, 1982).

A review of the empirical literature over the past decade revealed no specific studies of marital intimacy in the blended family. However, previous studies did support the positive relationship between marital intimacy and individual functioning in the marital dyad (Waring, Patton, Neron, & Linker, 1986; Waring, Redon, Corvinelli, Chalmers, & Vander Laan, 1983) and the positive relationship between marital intimacy and marital satisfaction/adjustment (Harper & Elliott, 1988; Kersten, 1990; Speisman, Bartis, White, & Costos, 1985; Tolstedt & Stokes, 1983). The blended family literature cited marital intimacy among several factors predictive of blended family functioning (Bray, Berger, Mann, Silverblatt, & Gershenhorn, 1987; Crosbie-Burnett, 1984; Ganong & Coleman, 1989; Roberts & Price, 1989). However, blended family marital intimacy has yet to be directly studied.

The blended family literature has repeatedly reported family configuration (Clingempeel & Brand, 1985; Coleman and Ganong, 1987; Crosbie-Burnett, 1984; Gross, 1986; Guisinger, Cowan, & Schuldberg, 1989; Roberts & Price, 1987; Schultz & Schultz, 1987), residence of children (Ambert, 1986; Crosbie-Burnett, 1989; Goetting, 1982; Kosinski, 1983; Pasley, Inhinger-Tallman, & Coleman, 1984; Stanton, 1986; Turnbull & Turnbull, 1983) and birth of a mutual child (Amato, 1987; Goetting, 1982; Nolan, Coleman, & Ganong, 1984; Papernow, 1984; Visher & Visher, 1985) as salient blended family demographic variables. This study will report these demographic variables but also seeks to investigate their effects on blended family marital intimacy.

To date, blended family research seems to have concentrated on stepparent/stepchild dynamics, perhaps at the expense of the study of blended family spousal dynamics (Skeen, Covi & Robinson, 1985). As satisfaction with parental and spousal roles would seem to be crucial to blended family success, this study sought to integrate the presence of children and marital intimacy as a dynamic of spousal functioning in the blended family.

METHOD

Subjects

A total of 145 volunteer couples were recruited through their membership in local chapters of the Stepfamily Association of

America. Of the 145 survey packages distributed to the couples, 88 survey packages (60.7%) were completed and returned.

A review of the demographic information revealed 30 (34.1% of the total sample) simple blended families of biological father/stepmother; 19 (21.6% of the total sample) simple blended families of biological mother/stepfather; and 39 (44.3% of the total sample) complex blended families. The ages of the husbands in this sample ranged from 25-64 (mean = 39.0). The ages for wives in this sample ranged from 22-62 (mean = 34.6).

The presence of children in these families is evenly divided between those families with (44 families, 50%) and without (44 families, 50%) residential children, and with (42 families, 47.7%) and without (46 families, 52.3%) a mutual child. The majority of the participants (79.5% of wives, 71.6% of husbands) report at least a college degree. None of the participants reported lack of completion of high school. The majority of the participants (86% of wives, 100% of husbands) report part-time or full-time, out-of-home employment. None of the participants reported being unemployed or retired. The majority of participants (74% of wives and husbands) were Caucasian, with approximately 25% of the sample being African-American. None of the participants reported Hispanic, Native American, or Asian as racial/ethnic background. The majority of participants reported Protestant as religious affiliation, with equal numbers reporting Catholic, Jewish, Other or None as religious affiliation. Household incomes ranged from $20,001 to $100,000+ with an average of $55,000. No households in this sample reported incomes under $20,000.

Procedures

Chapter contact persons were used in the advertisement of the study and the dissemination of materials to volunteer couples. The volunteer respondents were directed to return the completed instruments directly to the researcher via the stamped, self-addressed, enclosed envelope.

Instrument

For the purposes of this study, marital intimacy was measured through use of the Personal Assessment of Intimacy in Relationships (PAIR). The PAIR uses five indices of self-reported marital intimacy. These five components are: (a) emotional intimacy (closeness of feeling); (b) social intimacy (experiences of common friends and similarities in social networks); (c) intellectual intimacy (experiences of sharing ideas); (d) sexual intimacy (experiences of sharing general affection and/or sexual activity); and (e) recreational intimacy (experiences of sharing interest in hobbies and leisure time activities) (Schaefer & Olson, 1981).

In terms of the instrument's psychometric properties, the PAIR's split-half reliability established acceptable alpha coefficients of .70-.75. Test-retest reliability figures have not been established. Scale-by-scale concurrent validity was established with the Locke-Wallace Marital Adjustment Scale ($p < .001$), with the cohesion, expressiveness, and conflict subscales of the Family Environment Scales ($p < .01$) in the predicted direction, and with the Waring Intimacy Questionnaire ($p < .01$) (Schaefer & Olson, 1981). Previous studies (Harper & Elliott, 1988; Quinn & Davidson, 1986; Thomas, Albrecht, & White, 1984; West, Zarski, & Harvill, 1986; Worthington, Buston, & Hammonds, 1989) support the predictive validity of the PAIR with measures of marital satisfaction/adjustment.

Statistical Analysis

The data for this study was analyzed by use of a repeated measures MANOVA with family configuration, residence of children, and birth of a mutual child serving as the between-group factors, with gender of respondent serving as the repeated measures factor, and the five subscales of marital intimacy serving as the dependent variables.

RESULTS

This study explored the effects of family configuration, residence of children and birth of a mutual child on marital intimacy scores of husbands and wives. The MANOVA involving these three variables produced no significant 3-way interaction effects (see Table 1).

The analysis yielded two significant interaction effects. The results

Table 1

MANOVA with Overall Subscales by Family Configuration x Residence of Children x Birth of a Mutual Child

Univariate F Tests with (2, 76)DF

Variable	SS	MS	F	Sig. of F
Emotional	21.4245	10.7122	.8785	.420
Social	43.2966	21.6478	2.4188	.096
Sexual	43.3411	8.3793	2.4669	.092
Intellectual	15.4712	7.6246	1.0146	.367
Recreational	29.1797	12.0388	1.2119	.303

Multivariate Tests of Significance

Test Name	Value	Approx. F	Sig. of F
Pillais	.1295	1.0105	.437
Hotellings	.1395	.9905	.455
Wilks	.8743	1.0005	.466

show significant interaction effects for residence of children × family configuration on spouses' emotional ($p < .01$), social ($p < .05$), sexual ($p < .01$), and recreational ($p < .01$) intimacy scores. Further analyses of this interaction effect suggested that biological parents in blended families with residential children reported significantly greater intimacy than did biological parents in blended families without residential children. Conversely, stepparents in blended families with residential children reported significantly less marital intimacy than did stepparents in blended families with non-residential children (see Table 2).

A significant interaction effect for family configuration × birth of a mutual child on social intimacy was noted. Further analysis of this result found that wives in blended families with a mutual child

Table 2

MANOVA with Overall Subscales by Family Configuration x Residence of Children

Effect... Family Configuration x Residence of Children

Univariate F-Tests with (2,76)DF

Variable	SS	MS	F	Sig of F
Emotional	148.9477	74.4738	6.1074	.003
Social	77.9108	38.9554	4.3527	.016
Sexual	111.7947	55.8973	6.6709	.002
Intellectual	42.1433	21.0717	2.7637	.069
Recreational	122.6127	61.3063	5.0923	.008

Multivariate Tests of Significance

Test Name	Value	Approx. F	Sig. of F
Pillais	.2640	2.2205	.020
Hotellings	.3458	2.4548	.010
Wilks	.7401	2.3391	.014

reported significantly greater social intimacy than did wives in families without a mutual child (see Table 3).

DISCUSSION

This study's research question focused on the effects of family configuration, residence of children, and birth of a mutual child on the marital intimacy scores of husbands and of wives. Analyses of these results show that spouses in simple blended families reported contrasting responses to the presence of children. This finding expands Ambert's (1986) conclusion that spouses in blended families with residential children report greater marital intimacy than do spouses in blended families with nonresidential children. The re-

Table 3

MANOVA with Overall Subscales by Family Configuration x Birth of a Mutual Child

Effect... Family Configuration x Birth of a Mutual Child

Univariate F-Tests with (2,76)DF

Variable	SS	MS	F	Sig of F
Emotional	54.2319	27.1159	2.2237	.115
Social	72.3964	36.1982	4.0446	.021
Sexual	19.2554	9.6277	1.1490	.322
Intellectual	26.6564	13.3282	1.7481	.181
Recreational	2.3210	1.1605	.0964	.908

Multivariate Tests of Significance

Test Name	Value	Approx. F	Sig. of F
Pillais	.1440	1.1329	.342
Hotellings	.1592	1.1304	.344
Wilks	.8596	1.1318	.343

sults of this study suggest that, for the biological parent, the presence of children seems linked to greater marital intimacy. However, for the stepparent, the presence of children seems linked to less marital intimacy. Conversely, stepparents in blended families with nonresidential children reported greater marital intimacy, while biological parents in those families reported less marital intimacy. Spouses in complex blended families with residential children reported greater marital intimacy than did spouses in complex blended families with nonresidential children.

The significant interaction of family configuration × birth of a mutual child may be a random effect, as evidenced by the lack of significance of the multivariate tests of significance. Conversely, this result may support the contention of Amato (1987) that birth of a mutual child facilitates blended family cohesion.

Implications

This investigation is the first study of marital intimacy of blended family spouses. Its findings may assist in describing the effects of the presence of children on spouses' perceptions of intimacy in the new marriage.

Therapeutic intervention in the spouses' relationship is intended to legitimize their rights as partners, as well as their duties as parents. The interaction of family configuration and residence of children on the marital intimacy scores of spouses implies spouses need to recognize their differing feelings about children in the home. While biological parents may feel residential children facilitate marital intimacy, stepparents may feel that residential children hamper marital intimacy. This finding may reflect the difficulty of the creation of a positive relationship between stepparent and stepchild, resulting in the triangulation of the biological parent, stepparent, and child. This difficulty may also reflect the diffuse boundaries between the spousal and child subsystems, possibly fostering competition between stepparent and stepchild for the affections and attention of the spouse/biological parent. Professionals also need to introduce this issue in premarital counseling, to share with the couple the differing views each may hold of the new household and assist in the resolution of this potentially divisive issue. This result implies that no one solution (residential or nonresidential children) will satisfy both partners. Rather, exploration of the family and marital dynamics surrounding this issue may help the partners become more aware of the feelings of the other and facilitate a sense of family cohesion around the solution of this issue.

In addition, accommodation to the residence of children with the blended family needs to be arranged in a manner not to interfere with the fledgling spousal relationship. Negotiation around the common spousal identity and the differing parental functions unique to blended families need to be explored. Care must be taken to ensure the parental function does not take precedence over the spousal function. Spouses need to recognize the legitimacy of their relationship and be encouraged to develop the special vehicles through which to communicate their senses of marital intimacy.

The uncertain findings regarding the effects of a mutual child on marital intimacy require further study. This study does not resolve the role of the mutual child in the blended family system. Its finding suggests that the social life of blended family wives may revolve around the new child. As with new parents in first-marriage families, the birth of a child may serve to affirm family identity and to include the new family in child-focused, as well as adult-focused, activities.

CONCLUSION

This study sought to emphasize spousal, rather than parental, dynamics in blended families. The study wanted to add to the understanding of the presence of children on marital functioning of the blended family by exploring the effects of family configuration, residence of children, and birth of a mutual child on blended family marital intimacy.

REFERENCES

Amato, P.R. (1987). Family process in one-parent, stepparent and intact families: The child's point of view. *Journal of Marriage and the Family*, *49*, 327-337.

Ambert, A.M. (1986). Being a stepparent: Live-in and visiting stepchildren. *Journal of Marriage and the Family*, *48*, 795-804.

Birtchnell, J. (1986). The imperfect attainment of intimacy. *Journal of Family Therapy*, *8*, 153-172.

Bray, J.H., Berger, S.H., Mann, T., Silverblatt, A.H., & Gershenhorn, S. (1987, April). Parenting practices and family process during early remarriage. Paper presented at the Biennial Meeting of the Society for Research in Child Development, Baltimore.

Clingempeel, W.G., & Brand, E. (1985). Quasi-kin relationships, structural complexity, and marital quality in stepfamilies: A replication, extension and clinical implications. *Family Relations*, *34*, 401-409.

Coleman, M.T., & Ganong, L. (1987). Marital conflicts in stepfamilies: Effects on children. *Youth and Society*, *19*(2), 151-172.

Combrinck-Graham, L., & Kerns, L. (1989). Intimacy in families with young children. In D. Kantor & B.F. Okun (Eds.). *Intimate environments: Sex, intimacy and gender in families* (pp. 74-92). New York: The Guilford Press.

Crosbie-Burnett, M. (1984). The centrality of the step relationship: A challenge to family theory and practice. *Family Relations, 33*, 459-463.

Crosbie-Burnett, M. (1989). Application of family stress theory to remarriage: A model for assessing and helping stepfamilies. *Family Relations, 38*, 323-332.

Furstenberg, F.F. Jr., & Spanier, G.B. (1984). The risk of dissolution in remarriage: An examination of Cherlin's hypothesis of incomplete institutionalization. *Family Relations, 33*, 433-441.

Ganong, L.H., & Coleman, M. (1989). Preparing for remarriage: Anticipating the issues, seeking solutions. *Family Relations, 38*, 28-33.

Goetting, A. (1982). The six stations of remarriage: Developmental tasks of remarriage after divorce. *Family Relations, 31*, 213-222.

Gross, P. (1986). Defining post-divorce remarriage families: A typology based on the subjective perceptions of children. *Journal of Divorce, 10*, 205-217.

Guisinger, S., Cowan, P.A., & Schuldberg, D. (1989). Changing parent and spouse relations in the first years of remarriage of divorced fathers. *Journal of Marriage and the Family, 51*, 445-456.

Harper, J.M., & Elliott, M.L. (1988). Can there be too much of a good thing? The relationship between desired level of intimacy and marital adjustment. *The American Journal of Family Therapy, 16*(4), 351-360.

Hutchinson, L.C. (1989, March). How many parents? Support for stepfamilies. Paper presented at the Annual Meeting of the American Association for Counseling and Development, Boston.

Kantor, D., & Okun, B.F. (1989). *Intimate environments: Sex, intimacy and gender in families.* New York: The Guilford Press.

Kersten, K.K. (1990). The process of marital disaffection: Interventions at various stages. *Family Relations, 39*, 257-265.

Kosinski, F.A., Jr. (1983). Improving relationships in stepfamilies. *Elementary School Guidance and Counseling, 17*(3), 200-207.

L'Abate, L., & Sloan, S. (1984). A workshop format to facilitate intimacy in married couples. *Family Relations, 33*, 245-250.

Miller, L.F., & Moorman, J.E. (1989). Married couple families with children. In Bureau of the Census (Ed.) *Studies in marriage and the family* (pp. 27-31). Washington: US Government Printing Office.

Nolan, J., Coleman, M., & Ganong, L. (1984). The presentation of stepfamilies in marriage and family textbooks. *Family Relations, 33*, 559-566.

Papernow, P.L. (1984). Thickening the "middle ground": Dilemmas and vulnerabilities of remarried couples. *Psychotherapy, 24*, 630-639.

Pasley, K., Inhinger-Tallman, M., & Coleman, C. (1984). Consensus styles among happy and unhappy remarried couples. *Family Relations, 33*, 451-457.

Poppen, W.A., & White, P.N. (1984). Transition to the blended family. *Elementary School Guidance and Counseling, 19*(1), 50-61.

Quinn, W.H., & Davidson, B. (1986). Marital type and the marital relationship. *Journal of Divorce, 9*, 117-134.

Roberts, T.W., & Price, S.J. (1985). A systems analysis of the remarriage process: Implications for the clinician. *Journal of Divorce, 9*(2), 1-21.

Roberts, T.W., & Price, S.J. (1987). Instant families: Divorced mothers marry never-married men. *Journal of Divorce, 11*(1), 71-91.

Roberts, T.W., & Price, S.J. (1989). Adjustment in remarriage: Communication, cohesion, marital and parental roles. *Journal of Divorce, 13*(1), 17-43.

Sabatelli, R.M. (1988). Measurement issues in marital research: A review and critique of contemporary survey instruments. *Journal of Marriage and the Family, 50*, 891-915.

Schaefer, M.T., & Olson, D.H. (1981, January). Assessing intimacy: The PAIR inventory. *Journal of Marital and Family Therapy*, 47-60.

Schultz, N.C., & Schultz, C.L. (1987). Affection and intimacy as a special strength of couples in blended families. *Australian Journal of Sex, Marriage and the Family, 8*(2), 66-72.

Skeen, P., Covi, R.B., & Robinson, B.E. (1985). Stepfamilies: A review of the literature with suggestions for practitioners. *Journal of Counseling and Development, 64*, 121-125.

Speisman, J.C., Bartis, S., White, K.M., & Costos, D. (1985). Marital adjustment and congruence in intimacy maturation (ERIC Document Reproduction Service No. 261 278).

Stanton, G.W. (1986, May-June). Preventive intervention with stepfamilies. *Social Work*, 201-206.

Thomas, S.P., Albrecht, K., & White, P. (1984). Determinants of marital quality in dual-career couples. *Family Relations, 33*, 513-521.

Tolstedt, B.E., & Stokes, J.P. (1983). Relation of verbal, affective, and physical intimacy to marital satisfaction. *Journal of Counseling Psychology, 30*, 573-580.

Turnbull, S.K., & Turnbull, J.M. (1983). To dream the impossible dream: An agenda for discussion with stepparents. *Family Relations, 32*, 227-230.

Visher, E.B., & Visher, J.S. (1985). Stepfamilies are different. *Journal of Family Therapy, 7*, 9-18.

Visher, E.B., & Visher, J.S. (1988). *New loyalties, old ties*. New York: Brunner/Mazel.

Waring, E.M., Patton, D., Neron, C.A., & Linker, W. (1986). Types of marital intimacy and prevalence of emotional illness. *Canadian Journal of Psychiatry, 31*, 720-726.

Waring, E.M., Redden, J.R., Corvinelli, M., Chalmers, W.S., & Vander Laan, R. (1983). Marital intimacy and mood states in a nonclinical sample. *The Journal of Psychology, 115*, 263-273.

West, J.D., Zarski, J.J., & Horvill, R. (1986). The influence of the family triangle on intimacy. *American Mental Health Counselors Association Journal, 8*, 166-174.

Worthington, E.L., Jr., Buston, B.G., & Hammonds, T.M. (1989). A component analysis of marriage enrichment: Information and treatment modality. *Journal of Counseling and Development, 67*, 555-564.

Wynne, L.C., & Wynne, A.R. (1986). The quest for intimacy. *Journal of Marital and Family Therapy, 12*, 383-394.

The Effects of Postdivorce Attachment on Coparenting Relationships

Brenda S. Dozier
Donna L. Sollie
Steven J. Stack
Thomas A. Smith

SUMMARY. Whether ongoing attachment to the former spouse affects postdivorce relationships has been a source of debate and controversy for several years. The purpose of this study was to further explore post-divorce attachment by examining the influence of both friendly and dependent types of attachment on the coparenting relationship. The sample consisted of 95 respondents (54 women and 41 men) who were divorced and not remarried. Results indicated that friendlier attachment is not only conducive to a more supportive and shared coparenting relationship, but also decreases conflict around childrearing. The predicted inverse relationship between dependent attachment and shared and supportive coparenting was not found. Instead, dependent attachment was positively related to supportive and shared coparenting, but only for women. There were no gender differences on the attachment and coparenting variables. Custodial status did not differentiate the respondents on the dependent variables. Discussion centered on the implications of types of

---

Brenda S. Dozier, MS, is a doctoral student. Donna L. Sollie, PhD, and Thomas A. Smith, PhD, are Associate Professors in the Department of Family and Child Development, School of Human Sciences, Auburn University, 203 Spidle Hall, Auburn University, AL 36849. Steven J. Stack, PhD, is Professor in the Department of Sociology, College of Liberal Arts, Auburn University, 6090 Haley Center, Auburn University, AL 36849.

[Haworth co-indexing entry note]: "The Effects of Postdivorce Attachment on Coparenting Relationships," Dozier, Brenda S., Donna L. Sollie, Steven J. Stack and Thomas A. Smith. Co-published simultaneously in the *Journal of Divorce & Remarriage* (The Haworth Press, Inc.) Vol. 19, No. 3/4, 1993, pp. 109-123; and: ***The Stepfamily Puzzle: Intergenerational Influences*** (ed: Craig A. Everett), The Haworth Press, Inc., 1993, pp. 109-123. Multiple copies of this article/chapter may be purchased from The Haworth Document Delivery Center [1-800-3-HAWORTH; 9:00 a.m. - 5:00 p.m. (EST)].

attachment for continuing coparenting relationships between divorced parents.

In recent years, questions about whether or not divorced spouses can relate effectively with one another have been a topic of controversy. Divorce researchers in the 1970's and early 1980's viewed both postdivorce attachment and any continued relationship between divorced spouses as being indicative of poor individual adjustment. Divorce researchers have equated attachment to dependency (Weiss, 1975), preoccupation with the divorced spouse (Berman, 1985; Brown, Felton, Whiteman, & Manela, 1980), and to the bereavement process (Kitson, 1982). The focus of previous research has been upon negative aspects of attachment, but this prevailing wisdom has recently been challenged as positive aspects of postdivorce attachment have been further examined (Masheter, 1988). The present study explores the influence of both healthy and unhealthy forms of attachment on postdivorce coparenting relationships.

John Bowlby (1969) formulated the original attachment theory maintaining that attachment is a normal outgrowth of strong, close relationships, and includes both positive and negative feelings toward the attachment figure. He also likened attachment in adulthood to attachment behaviors experienced in infancy. Recently, Bowlby (1983) noted that the concept of dependency, used by some clinicians to refer to attachment behaviors experienced by divorced persons, excludes the beneficial attachment that may be experienced toward a significant other. Other research lends support to viewing attachment as having both beneficial and detrimental aspects for adults. Hazan and Shaver (1987), basing their work on Bowlby (1969), explained that attachment in adulthood is similar to attachment in infancy, and that, as in early childhood, both healthy and unhealthy forms of attachment can develop in adults. Similarly, Kitson, Babri, Roach, and Placidi (1989) reviewed the literature on adjustment to divorce and suggested that if attachment is defined according to Bowlby (1969) as strong affectional bonds to significant others, then distress at the end of close relationships, "is neither surprising nor a sign of weakness or dependency" (p.17).

Recent divorce research suggests that more than one type of attachment exists and that attachment influences not only personal well-being, but is also important for the tenor of the postdivorce relationship. Masheter (1988), also basing her conceptualization of attachment upon Bowlby (1969), brought new insight to the area of postdivorce relationships which accommodates "healthy" as well as "unhealthy" types of postdivorce attachment. Masheter included both parents and nonparents in her sample, and she identified two aspects of attachment, the extent of friendliness with the ex-spouse and the extent of dependence on the ex-spouse. Masheter concluded that most divorced individuals do maintain some contact with their divorced spouses and that most are satisfied with that amount of contact. In line with other studies (Brown et al., 1980; Kitson, 1982), Masheter reported that men have higher levels of dependence and lower levels of well-being than women. In addition to having a greater dependent attachment, Masheter found that males also have friendlier attachment than females, suggesting that overall, males are likely to be more emotionally involved with their divorced spouse. In general, for both males and females, Masheter found that increased postdivorce contact decreases hostility and increases friendliness.

Masheter's (1988) work on postdivorce relationships reflects the view of attachment as having a positive as well as a negative component. Her research indicates that divorced spouses continue to relate with one another after divorce by exhibiting both positive and negative types of attachment behaviors. Masheter's work further indicated that parents experience more hostility and conflict in their postdivorce interactions than do nonparents. Thus, the type of attachment between divorced spouses, which reflects the emotional tone of their changed relationship, is likely to impact their interactions concerning childrearing.

It is these two aspects of divorce–the emotional aspect and the childrearing aspect–that have been repeatedly identified as the most distressful aspects of the divorce experience (Bohannan, 1970; Hetherington, Cox & Cox, 1976; Weiss, 1975). However, Masheter's (1988) work, like that of others in the attachment area, has tended to focus on the feelings and interactions associated with the divorced spouse relationship. Although Masheter included parents in her study, she asked only two questions about parenting issues, and these questions focused on conflict. The focus of the postdivorce attachment literature has been on the divorced couple and has neglected to take into account how attachment impacts on the coparental relationship.

Children are obviously affected by divorce, and how the divorced spouses relate has clear implications for the children's well-being. Results from numerous studies have found associations between disrupted parenting, interpersonal conflict between spouses, and children's psychological distress (Hetherington, Cox, & Cox, 1976; Wallerstein, 1986, 1987; Wallerstein & Kelly, 1980). Wallerstein (1987) also reported that divorced families can buffer the psychological distress faced by children when both parents are available, stable, and responsive to the children's needs. Ahrons (1981), a forerunner in postdivorce research, examined several aspects of coparenting relationships. These included quality of coparental communication (conflict or support) and shared parenting responsibilities. Overall, Ahrons found that those divorced individuals who have some degree of harmony, those who interact frequently, and those who do not dissolve their relationship are better able to cooperate as parents. Additionally, Hess and Camara (1979) suggested that amicable coparenting relationships can serve to reduce some of the role-overload that custodial parents face, as well as lessen the sense of loss for many non-custodial parents.

While these studies indicate beneficial effects of coparenting for both the children and the divorced spouses, the literature on coparenting has neglected to take into account the divorced individual's feelings about the former spouse. Since coparenting involves some type of continued relationship and interaction between divorced spouses, further examination of the level of friendliness and the level of dependence warrants attention.

The literature suggests that a friendlier attachment between divorced spouses will be related to more supportive coparenting interactions. On the other hand, more dependent attachment will be related to conflictual coparenting interactions. Although the literature on gender differences is less clear-cut, it appears likely that males will be more likely than females to have both higher dependent and friendly attachment scores, more conflict, less support, and less shared parenting.

METHOD

Sample

A sample of 132 divorced individuals was recruited from Parents Without Partners (PWP) organizations in six cities of the Southeastern United States. Of the 132 respondents who completed the questionnaires, 95 met the criteria for this study: (l) legally divorced once with at least one minor child (18 years old or younger) from that marriage, or legally divorced more than one time, but with a minor child or children from only one marriage, and (2) a minor child or children who lived in the household with either the mother or father.

The 95 respondents, 41 males and 54 females, ranged in age from 28 to 54 years, with a mean age of 42 years (SD = 5.32). Eighty-one percent of the subjects had been married one time, with a mean length of marriage of 13 years and three months (SD = 6.87). Time since divorce ranged from one month to 17 years, with a mean of five years and three months (SD = 4.69). The majority of the males did not initiate the divorce (80%), whereas 43% of the females did not initiate divorce. Most of the respondents had some post-high-school education (79%), and annual incomes averaged $25,500 a year for men, and $17,500 annually for women.

Subjects had an average of two children; almost one-half of the fathers (46%) and over three-fourths of the mothers (81%) served as custodial parents. Over one-half of the non-custodial fathers (51%) and over one-third of the non-custodial mothers (37%) reported that they visit their children at least twice a month.

Procedure

Questionnaires were administered at PWP functions and after the data were collected, respondents and nonrespondents were invited to participate in a discussion about postdivorce relationships, led by the first author.

Measures

Postdivorce attachment was measured by a 14-item Likert scale that included the ten items from Masheter's (1988) attachment scale, and four additional dependent attachment items from scales developed by Berman (1985) and Weiss (1975). This revision of Masheter's scale is comprised of two dimensions. The first dimension assesses *friendliness*, or the extent to which the respondent considers the divorced spouse a friend all or most of the time and the extent to which the respondent dislikes or gets upset with the divorced spouse. Higher scores reflect friendlier attachment. The items from this dimension are the same items in Masheter's affect dimension. The second dimension is *dependence*, or the extent to which the respondent has ambivalent feelings toward the divorced spouse or is preoccupied with thoughts about the divorced spouse. A higher score indicates greater dependence on the ex-spouse.

Factor analyses using varimax rotation were computed using the 14-item attachment scale (see Table 1). Two factors with eigenvalues greater than 1.0 were obtained. Six items loaded strongly on the first factor, friendliness, and are identical to the six items included in Masheter's affect dimension. These items generally reflect the degree of friendly feelings toward the divorced spouse. Examples are: "Though our marriage is over, I like my divorced spouse as a person." "I can't spend more than a few minutes with my divorced spouse without getting upset." "Though we are divorced, we get along now." "I really dislike my divorced spouse." These friendliness items showed weak loadings on the second factor. The second factor also showed strong loadings for six items which reflected dependence. Examples of these six dependence items are: "I can't stop thinking about my divorced spouse." "I miss my divorced spouse very much." "Since my divorce, I feel like a part of me is missing." These six dependence items loaded weakly on the first factor. Two of the items were not retained in the final scales. The first of these two items, which had moderate loadings on both factors, was an item indicating neutral feelings for the divorced spouse. The second item, which reflected ambivalent feelings, had very low loadings on both factors.

The oblique factor rotation shows a correlation of .30 between the two factors, indicating that the factors of friendliness and dependence are related, but do not reflect the same construct. Cronbach's

TABLE 1. Factor Item Loadings and Alpha Coefficients for the Attachment Scale

Item		Factor 1	Factor 2
Friendliness (Coefficient Alpha = .90)			
1.	Like as a person	.88	.15
2.	Get upset when around	.65	.02
4.	Get along now	.84	.02
5.	Really dislike	.82	.15
6.	Know ex is my friend	.83	.10
7.	Want to forget	.80	.11
Dependence (Coefficient Alpha = .86)			
9.	Can't stop thinking about	.05	.75
10.	Miss very much	.19	.85
11.	Think about our marriage	.10	.74
12.	Interested/curious in ex	.50	.60
13.	Part of me is missing	.12	.77
14.	Reminded of exspouse	.13	.79
Items not retained			
3.	Don't feel much for	.42	.45
8.	Have mixed feelings about	.01	.26

coefficient alphas for the two subscales of friendliness and dependence were .90 and .86, respectively.

Coparenting was measured by two scales that assessed quality and amount of sharing (Ahrons, 1981). *Quality of coparental communication* is reflected in *conflict* (four items) and *support* (six items). Examples of the items are: "When you and your former spouse discuss parenting issues how often does an argument result?," and "Do you feel that your former spouse understands and is supportive of your special needs as a custodial (or non-custodial) parent?" Cronbach's reliability coefficients for the present sample were .88 on the conflict scale and .81 on the support scale.

Shared parenting was measured by a 10 item scale that assessed the content of interactions shared around childrearing responsibilities. Examples include: "Do you and your former spouse share making major decisions regarding your children's lives?" "Discussing school and/or medical problems?" "Making day to day decisions regarding your children's lives?" Cronbach's coefficient alpha for the present sample was .96.

RESULTS

In order to assess the relationships between attachment and coparenting, Pearson correlation coefficients were computed for the sample as a whole, and also separately for males and females. Mean scores for males and females on the postdivorce variables are summarized in Table 2. The expectation that friendlier attachment would be positively related to a more supportive coparenting relationship and shared parenting, and inversely related to a more conflictual coparenting relationship, was supported for the sample as a whole (see Table 3).

Pearson correlations also yielded similar results when computed separately for males and females (see Table 4). For males, strong relationships were found between friendlier attachment and a more supportive coparenting relationship and between friendlier attachment and shared parenting, while a strong inverse relationship was detected between friendlier attachment and a conflictual coparenting relationship. For females, moderate relationships were found between friendlier attachment and a more supportive coparenting relationship, and between friendlier attachment and shared parenting, and a strong inverse relationship was indicated between friendlier attachment and a conflictual coparenting relationship.

The expectation that dependent attachment would be inversely related to a more supportive coparenting relationship and shared parenting, and positively related to a more conflictual coparenting relationship was not supported. Instead, for the sample as a whole, statistically significant relationships in the opposite direction be-

TABLE 2. Means and Standard Deviations of Attachment and Coparenting for Males and Females

Variables	Males		Females	
	Mean	SD	Mean	SD
Attachment				
Friendliness	19.83	6.02	17.93	7.30
Dependence	11.41	3.96	11.09	4.76
Coparenting				
Conflict	11.15	4.67	10.68	4.96
Support	17.94	5.83	16.16	6.57
Shared	24.12	12.23	20.83	10.83

tween dependent attachment and supportive coparenting and shared parenting were indicated, but there was no statistically significant relationship between dependence and conflict (see Table 3).

Gender differences on attachment and coparenting were expected, but results of the present study indicated that males and females are similar on both types of attachment and on coparenting behaviors. Analyses of variance yielded no significant differences between males and females on type of attachment (friendliness: $F = 1.84$, $df = 1/93$, $p > .05$; dependence: $F = 0.12$, $df = 1/93$, $p > .05$) or on conflictual ($F = 0.22$, $df = 1/93$, $p > .05$), supportive ($F = 1.88$, $df = 1/93$, $p > .05$), and shared parenting ($F = 1.92$, $df = 1/93$, $p > .05$) aspects of coparenting. Overall, then, the results indicated that males and females are similar on both types of attachment and on coparenting behaviors.

Thus, the hypotheses received mixed support. Friendlier attachment was related to more supportive coparenting interactions, as

TABLE 3. Correlations Between Attachment and Coparenting Variables

	Friendliness	Dependence	Conflict	Support	Shared
Friendliness	___				
Dependence	.32*	___			
Conflict	-.77**	-.09	___		
Support	.56**	.41**	-.31*	___	
Shared	.57**	.31*	-.30*	.76**	___

* $p < .01$. ** $p < .001$.

predicted. However, dependent attachment was not related to coparenting for males, and showed a positive rather than the predicted negative relationship for females. No gender differences on attachment and coparenting behaviors were found.

In order to further enhance our understanding of the postdivorce experience, the influence of two other variables on the relationship between type of attachment and coparenting were also examined. The two additional variables were custodial status and presence of children 14 years and older versus under 14 years. Analysis of variance yielded non-significant results for the impact of custodial/non-custodial status on friendliness (F = 0.02, df = 1/93, p > .05) and dependence (F = 0.37, df = 1/93, p > .05), and on aspects of coparenting: conflict (F = 0.38, df = 1/93, p > .05), support (F = 0.19, df = 1/93, p > .05), and shared parenting (F = 0.89, df = 1/93, p > .05). Analysis of variance resulted in a statistically significant relationship between dependent attachment and parents with children under the age of 14 (F = 4.84, df = 1/93, p < .05). Nonsignificant results were obtained for the effects of children's age on friendliness (F = 0.00, df = 1/93, p > .05) and all coparenting variables: conflict (F = 1.28, df = 1/93, p > .05), support (F = 2.12, df = 1/93, p > .05), and shared parenting (F = 3.71, df = 1/93, p > .05).

TABLE 4. Correlations Between Attachment and Coparenting Variables for Males and Females

	Friendliness	Dependence	Conflict	Support	Shared
			Males		
Friendliness	—				
Dependence	.03	—			
Conflict	-.82**	-.01	—		
Support	.70**	.17	-.60**	—	
Shared	.66**	-.10	-.51*	.76**	—
			Females		
Friendliness	—				
Dependence	.47*	—			
Conflict	-.76**	-.14	—		
Support	.47*	.54**	-.13	—	
Sharing	.51**	.60**	-.14	.77**	—

* $p < .01$. ** $p < .001$.

DISCUSSION

Once the marital relation ends, does the relationship between divorced spouses dissolve? What about parenting after divorce? The more traditional view of attachment emphasizes dependency and proposes that a "clean break" is the best way to deal with divorce. More recent work, which considers both beneficial and disruptive types of postdivorce attachment, suggests that it is not necessarily harmful for divorced spouses to be friendly, and in fact a friendly relationship may reap positive results for the individual (Masheter, 1988). However, less is known about how attachment between divorced spouses may affect their interactions around childrearing issues and the children. We would expect to see similar positive results for the coparenting relationship if spouses are friendly.

The results of this study upheld that expectation. The effect of attachment, as reflected on a friendliness dimension (hostile to friendly), was positively related to coparenting. These findings indicate that friendlier attachment is conducive to a more supportive and shared coparenting relationship. Furthermore, the present study found that the friendlier the attachment, the less likelihood of conflict around childrearing. Additionally, these patterns were quite similar for males and females.

These results provide support for an expanded view of attachment behavior between divorced spouses that allows for a continued relationship with friendly overtones that has positive implications both for the parents and for their children. These beneficial aspects of attachment provide a picture that is directly opposite that indicated by the more usual depiction of postdivorce attachment, which has focused on negative aspects of attachment and has equated attachment with dependency.

Findings from this study also suggest that the greater the dependence on the divorced spouse, the more supportive and the more shared interactions are received around childrearing. However, this pattern held only for women. Interestingly, dependent attachment was not related to any of the coparenting variables for men. Perhaps those women with greater dependence make extra efforts to involve the divorced spouse in joint parenting interactions as a way to increase contact with the divorced spouse and thus help to meet their dependence needs. Since dependence is reflected in missing and wanting to be with the divorced spouse, it would seem that the dependent person would have high expectations about continued interactions and be likely to experience disappointment when those expectations are not met.

One way to express this disappointment could be through resentment and conflict concerning the children. However, these more dependent individuals did not experience greater conflict with their divorced spouses. Possibly these more dependent women feel pressured to avoid hostile contact with their divorced spouses and they may also feel a greater reliance on the divorced spouse. Or, it might be that those women are more dependent on their former spouse because their children are younger. Dependent attachment scores were higher for parents with younger children. Another interpretation of the results on dependence and coparenting is that mothers are able to separate their own feelings for the divorced spouse from their perceptions of the child's need for a positive relationship with both parents, and thus work to insure that a continued positive coparental relationship exists, even when their own feelings of attachment have not been resolved.

Research on attachment has consistently found males to experience more dependent attachment than females (Brown et al., 1980; Kitson, 1982; Masheter, 1988). In the present study, it was hypothesized that males also would have more negative coparenting experiences and report greater conflict, since previous studies (e.g., Berman, 1985; Brown et al., 1980; Masheter, 1988) found that dependent attachment was related to greater interpersonal conflict. However, results from the present analyses found that males and females have very similar scores on both type of attachment and coparenting, including conflict. Thus, the predicted gender differences were not evident.

A major difference in this study's sample, compared to other studies, concerns custodial status. Ahrons' (1981) sample included only mothers with child custody, whereas this study included both custodial fathers (46%) and custodial mothers (81%). At first glance, it may appear that male and female respondents in this sample were more alike because nearly half of the fathers had custody. In other words, because other studies looked only at females with custody, this sample may have reduced some of the expected gender differences. Males for this sample may be more similar to females and less emotionally involved (friendlier or dependent) with their divorced spouses than males in other studies because they have custody and are more involved with their children. However, when custodial/non-custodial status was compared for both types of attachment and coparenting, no gender differences were found. Further clarification of the influence of gender on attachment and coparenting is definitely needed.

There are limitations in this study that should be noted. The sample is not a random sample and thus caution should be taken when generalizing these findings. Parents Without Partners groups are representative of only a portion of all divorced individuals. Additionally, the high percentage of custodial fathers in this study does not reflect typical custody patterns. However, the use of a PWP sample does have the advantage of providing access to respondents who are parents and have not remarried (Weiss, 1975). This type of sample is more likely to be representative of the general population than a clinic sample, which is of particular importance when trying to more fully understand dimensions of attachment. Further studies are needed to assess both postdivorce attachment and coparenting with other populations (e.g., other divorced populations and remarrieds).

Despite these limitations, the present study does provide insight into postdivorce relationships and evidence that aspects of attachment are definitely related to coparenting, thus refining our view about continued relationships between divorced spouses. Clinicians, family members, and friends may offer more support to individuals who experience divorce if they are open to the possibility of amicable ongoing postdivorce relationships.

Further conceptual and empirical work on the concept of attachment is needed to clarify the nature of postdivorce spousal relationships and aid in the understanding of how people redefine these relationships. Indicative of this need is the recent discussion by Kelly (1988) and Berman (1988) on the various merits and problems of applying the concept of attachment to postdivorce relationships. Kelly (1988) suggested that, ". . . there may be gradations and variants of attachment behaviors following divorce that are adaptive in terms of long-term adjustment" (p. 331). Berman (1988) stated that, ". . . attention to the adaptive role of attachment is crucial" (p. 335). Both emphasized the need to further investigate positive or adaptive aspects of attachment. The present study provides support for their shared conclusion, expanding our understanding of the positive aspects of attachment affecting postdivorce relationships, especially the coparental one.

REFERENCES

Ahrons, C. R. (1981). The continuous coparental relationship between divorced spouses. *American Journal of Orthopsychiatry, 51*, 413-429.

Berman, W. H. (1985). Continued attachment after legal divorce. *Journal of Family Issues, 6*, 375-392.

Berman, W. H. (1988). The attachment bond as a unique aspect of divorce. *Journal of Family Psychology, 1*, 333-336.

Bohannan, P. (1970). *Divorce and after.* New York: Anchor Books.

Bowlby, J. (1969). *Attachment and loss.* New York: Basic Books.

Bowlby, J. (1983). Attachment and loss. *Annual Progress in Child Psychiatry and Child Development, 16*, 29-47.

Brown, P., Felton, B. J., Whiteman, V. & Manela, R. (1980). Attachment and distress following marital separation. *Journal of Divorce, 3*, 303-317.

Hazan, C. & Shaver, P. (1987). Romantic love conceptualized as attachment. *Journal of Personality and Social Psychology, 52*, 511-524.

Hess, R. D. & Camara, K. A. (1979). Postdivorce family relationships as mediating factors in consequences of divorce for children. *Journal of Social Issues, 35*, 79-97.

Hetherington, E., Cox, M., & Cox, R. (1976). Divorced fathers. *Family Coordinator, 25*, 417-428.

Kelly, J. B. (1988). Refining the concept of attachment in divorce. *Journal of Family Psychology, 1*, 329-332.

Kitson, G. C. (1982). Attachment to the spouse after divorce: A scale and its application. *Journal of Marriage and the Family, 44*, 379-393.

Kitson, G. C., Babri, K. B., Roach, M. J., & Placidi, K. S. (1989). Adjustment to widowhood and divorce. *Journal of Family Issues, 10*, 5-32.

Masheter, C. (1988). *Postdivorce relationships between ex-spouses.* Unpublished dissertation. University of Connecticut, Storrs.

Wallerstein, J. S. & Kelly, J. B. (1980). *Surviving the breakup: How children and parents cope with divorce.* New York: Basic Books.

Wallerstein, J. (1986). Child of divorce: An overview. *Behavioral Sciences and the Law, 4*, 105-118.

Wallerstein, J. (1987). Children of divorce: Report of a ten-year follow-up of early latency-age children. *American Journal of Orthopsychiatry, 57*, 199-211.

Weiss, R. S. (1975). *Marital separation.* New York: Basic Books.

An Exploratory Study of Stepsibling Subsystems

Lawrence Ganong
Marilyn Coleman

SUMMARY. Measures of stepsibling relations, step/parent-child relations, and stepfamily relations were taken from both adults and children in 105 stepfamilies. Children's interactions with half-siblings and siblings were slightly more positive than with stepsiblings (especially cross-sex stepsibling pairs) although all relationships were relatively positive. Parents in families with stepsibling subsystems felt closer to their biological children than parents who did not have stepchildren. They also felt stepchildren negatively affected their relationship with their biological children. When stepsibling subsystems are present, parents more often discipline only their biological children. When stepsibling subsystems are not present the stepparent is more likely to be perceived as playing a parental role, including disciplining the stepchildren. In general, adults in stepfamilies have more difficulty than do children coping with stepsibling subsystems. In the absence of stepsibling subsystems, the tendency is to incorporate the nuclear family model.

Most studies of the effects of living in a stepfamily on children have focused on how the remarital relationship influences children

---

Lawrence Ganong, PhD, is Associate Professor in the Department of Human Development and Family Studies, School of Nursing, University of Missouri. Marilyn Coleman, EdD, is Professor and Chairperson in the Department of Human Development and Family Studies, University of Missouri-Columbia, 31 Stanley Hall, Columbia, MO 65211.

[Haworth co-indexing entry note]: "An Exploratory Study of Stepsibling Subsystems," Ganong, Lawrence and Marilyn Coleman. Co-published simultaneously in the *Journal of Divorce & Remarriage* (The Haworth Press, Inc.) Vol. 19, No. 3/4, 1993, pp. 125-141; and: *The Stepfamily Puzzle: Intergenerational Influences* (ed: Craig A. Everett), The Haworth Press, Inc., 1993, pp. 125-141. Multiple copies of this article/chapter may be purchased from The Haworth Document Delivery Center [1-800-3-HAWORTH; 9:00 a.m. - 5:00 p.m. (EST)].

(Ganong & Coleman, 1984, 1986). An assumption underlying much of this work is that childrens' emotional and behavioral adjustment to stepfamily living is a function of marital conflict or other marital problems (Coleman & Ganong, 1987). Another assumption is that stepchildrens' adjustment is a direct effect of the stepparent-stepchild relationship. Rosenberg and Hajfal (1985) have argued that these assumptions imply a "dripolator effect," in which influences from the "top" of the stepfamily system filter down to the "bottom." They suggest, however, that there also might be "percolator effects" in stepfamilies, where influences from relationships at the bottom "bubble to the top," resulting in either negative or positive effects on the family. One major source of these "percolator effects" may be the relationships between stepsiblings.

Although research on siblings is limited compared to other areas of family study, it is known that siblings have a profound influence on each other (Bank & Kahn, 1985). Siblings are believed to perform several important functions, among them: identification, protection from parents and others, mutual regulation of behavior, socialization, support, and the exchange of direct services. Sibling relationships can be extremely important in a child's psychological development.

In stepfamilies, children may have quite varied sibling relationships. They may acquire stepsiblings and, eventually, half-siblings in addition to siblings they had prior to the remarriage. Stepchildren may also reside either full-time or part-time with a combination of siblings, stepsiblings, and half-siblings. What is the nature of these various stepsibling and half-sibling bonds? Do stepsiblings provide stress-buffering effects similar to siblings or do stepsiblings increase the stressors related to parental remarriage? Only a handful of researchers have examined the relationship between stepsiblings (Duberman, 1975; Ganong & Coleman, 1987), despite the estimation that nearly 50% of the children in stepfamilies have at least one stepsibling (Bumpass, 1984).

This study was an exploratory examination of stepsibling relationships. The purpose of the study was to assess the impact of the stepsibling subsystem on the stepfamily system. Specifically, we asked these questions: What is the nature of stepsibling relationships? How do stepsibling relationships differ from half-sibling or sibling relationships? What effect do stepsibling subsystems have on children's relations with parents and stepparents? What effect do stepsiblings have on the stepfamily unit?

METHOD

Subject Recruitment

The first wave of families was obtained through the marriage license records of one central Missouri county for the year 1983. All marriage license records were reviewed for this year; those that were remarriages for one or both partners were selected for follow-up. A snowball technique was used as well; additional families were suggested by participating families at the conclusion of the interviews. Additional families volunteered to participate in response to media notices about the study.

Initial contact with families was made via a letter informing them of the general purposes of the study. A few days later a phone call was made to determine: (a) if the family met the criteria for inclusion in the study and, if so, (b) if they were interested in participating. Criteria for inclusion were: (a) at least one partner must have been married previously, (b) the wife must have been younger than 45 at time of remarriage, and (c) one or both partners have at least one child from a previous marriage between the ages of 6 and 18 that resided in the household more than half-time.

Data were collected from all household members via a lengthy semi-structured interview format. Interviews were conducted with the entire family together, with the remarried couple only, and with each household member individually. Standardized questionnaires were administered to all family members at the conclusion of the interviews.

Sample

The sample consisted of 105 adult females, 100 adult males, 99 male children, and 75 female children from 105 stepfamilies. Fifty-three families had stepsibling subsystems; in 20 families the stepsiblings lived together and in 33 of these families they did not live together most of the time. Of these 53, 31 were stepfather households, 2 were stepmother households, and 20 had both a stepfather and a stepmother in the household.

Of the 52 stepfamilies with no stepsibling subsystems, 35 were stepfather households and 17 were stepmother households. Nine of these families had only one child, the rest had sibling and half-sibling subsystems.

These stepfamilies had been together a mean of 4 years (the range was 1 to 16 years). The families were generally middle class and the adults were well-educated (45% of the husbands and 39% of the wives had college degrees). Further descriptions of the families in this sample may be found in Ganong and Coleman (1988).

The children who participated in the interviews ranged in age from 7 to 20; their mean age was 13. The mean age of their 207 stepsiblings was 15, the mean age of their 80 half-siblings was 8.3, and the mean age of their siblings was 14.4 years.

The stepfamilies in which there were stepsibling subsystems differed from those without stepsiblings in several ways. Those families with stepsiblings had more children, the wives were older (mean age 38 compared to 33 for women in stepfamilies not having a stepsibling subsystem), the husbands also were older (mean age 42.3 compared to 34.7 for those without stepsibling subsystems), wives had slightly less education (15 years compared to 14 years), they were less likely to have cohabited prior to remarriage, they were less likely to have had a child born to the remarriage, and adults were more likely to have been married prior to this marriage. Stepfamilies with stepsibling subsystems did not differ from those without stepsiblings in husband's education, SES, years together, children's age at divorce and remarriage, and children's age at the time of the study.

Measures

Data were gathered from both adults and children on measures of stepsibling relations, step/parent-child relations, and stepfamily relations.

Stepsibling Relationships

Parent's Views. Parent's views of the nature of stepsibling relations were obtained with a series of open-ended questions: How often are both sets of children staying with you? Have your children benefitted from their relationship with their stepsiblings? Have there been problems in the relationships between your children and your spouses' children? How would you rate the relationship between your children and your spouse's children? The responses to these questions were coded and summarized to provide some descriptive information from the parent's perspectives.

Children's Views. A series of 9 items were used to assess how frequently children interacted with the other children in the stepfamily system. Each of the 9 items was asked for every other child under the age of 20, regardless of whether they resided in the same household or not. All stepsiblings, half-siblings, and siblings were included. Respondents indicated on a 5 point scale (1 = never, 5 = always) how frequently the statement was true. Items included: S/he fights with me, S/he teaches me things, S/he helps me do things, S/he plays with me, S/he ignores me, S/he is a friend to me, I ignore him/her, I teach him/her things, I help him/her do things. Items were coded so that higher scores indicate more negative interactions. A Stepsibling Interaction Scale total score was calculated by summing responses to these 9 items. The higher the score, the less positive the interactions.

Stepparent-Child Relationships

Stepparent's Views. Stepparents were asked to indicate how close their relationship with each of their stepchildren was on a scale ranging from 1 to 5 (1 = not at all close, 5 = extremely close). Biological parent-child relations were assessed by having parents indicate their perceptions of how close they were to each of their children using the same 5 point scale. Those who live in stepfamilies that had stepsibling subsystems were asked, "Has the relationship with your stepchildren affected the way you have gotten along with your children?"

Children's Views. A number of measures were used to assess how children viewed their parents and stepparents. They were asked a series of questions about discipline: who made the rules for them, who was the primary decision-maker regarding children, and who punished them. They were asked also to choose from among several labels the one that best described how their stepparent related to them (e.g., parent, friend, teacher). Finally, several statements drawn from the clinical literature on stepfamilies (Ganong & Coleman, 1986), were included to measure perceptions of the residential parent and stepparent. Children were asked to indicate on a five point scale how frequently the statements were true about their stepfamily situation (1 = never, 5 = always). The items included: I feel like I have to choose between my mother and father, I feel like I am being unfaithful to my dad (or mom) when I'm having fun with my stepdad (or stepmom), I get along fine with all my parents and stepparents, I wish I could spend more time with my nonresidential parent, I wish my residential parent would show more affection to me, I wish my stepparent would show more affection to me.

Stepfamily Relationships

Parent's Views. Adults were asked the extent to which 11 stepfamily issues derived from the clinical literature were problems experienced in their family (Pasley & Ihinger-Tallman, 1984). They were first asked if they had ever experienced the problems and, if so, to what degree (1 = slight problem, 3 = serious problem). They were then asked to indicate to what degree they were still experiencing the problem.

Children's Views. Statements drawn from the clinical literature were used to assess children's views of their families (Ganong & Coleman, 1986). Children were asked to indicate how often the statements were true for them (1 = never, 5 = always). Statements included: I wish my family was more like other families, I am a member of two households, My family is just like any other family, I talk about my stepfamily with my friends.

RESULTS

Stepsibling Relationships

Parent's Views. Parents were asked to report on the frequency of contact between their children and their spouse's children. There was quite a range in the frequency of contact between stepsiblings; 10% had no contact, 50% were together a "few days each year," 15% were together "a few days each month," and 25% were together "most of the time." Parents estimated the number of days the stepsiblings shared the same household. The median was 65 days per year; 32% spent more than 3 weeks in the same residence, 30% spent more than 180 days in the same household, 22% lived together all of the time. Of those who did not reside in the same household, 21% spent holidays, 26% spent weekends, 11% spent summers only, 15% spent summers and holidays, and 27% had other arrangements.

We asked the parents to identify any problems they perceived between the stepsiblings. Slightly over half (57%) were able to identify some problems: 39% perceived "normal" sibling rivalry, 33% saw jealousy between the stepsiblings, 12% reported that sharing space was a problem, 12% felt that the children had nothing in common with their stepsiblings, and 4% identified competition as a source of trouble in stepsibling relations. Most rated the stepsibling relationship as a positive one; 77% felt that having stepsiblings benefitted their children. Thirteen percent rated the quality of their children's relationship with their stepsiblings as "excellent," 65% rated them as "good," 18% as "fair," and only 4% as "poor."

Children's Views. Children's relations with their stepsiblings were analyzed in a 3 (type of sibling; stepsibling, half-sibling, or biological sibling) X 2 (residence; whether the target child lived with the respondent or not) X 4 (type of gender combination; male-male, male-female, female-male, or female-female, depending on the gender of the respondent and the gender of the target child) multivariate analysis of covariance, with age differences between the children as the covariate. Age difference was used as a covariate since this variable has been found to influence the frequency of sibling interaction (Vandell, Minnett, & Santrock, 1987). The dependent variables were the 9 items on the Stepsibling Interaction Scale and the total scale score. Only children under the age of 20 were used as targets, and only children under the age of 18 were respondents for this analysis.

The multivariate analysis revealed main effects for type of sibling (F (18, 744) = 3.31, $p < .0001$), residence (F (9, 372) = 2.98,

p = .0019), and gender combination (F (27, 1087) = 1.94, p = .0029). There was also an effect for the type of sibling X gender combination interaction (F (54, 1901) = 1.44, p = .02). Examination of the univariate analysis indicated that type of sibling differences were found for 6 of the 10 comparisons, with 3 more comparisons approaching statistical significance (see Table 1). Differences were found on how frequently the target fought, helped, and played with the respondent and how frequently the respondent taught and helped the target. There was also a difference on the total scale score. At the .10 level, how frequently the target taught, ignored, and was a friend to the respondent was different. The interaction effect was statistically significant for two items, "S/he teaches me" and "I teach him/her."

Compared to siblings, stepsiblings were fought with less, taught less, and helped less frequently. Compared to half-siblings, stepsiblings were played with less, taught less, and helped less often. On the total scale score, half-siblings were responded to more positively than stepsiblings.

Cross-sex pairs of stepsiblings taught each other less often than cross-sex siblings, cross-sex half-siblings, and same-sex pairs of all types of siblings. There were no differences between pairs of brothers, stepbrothers, and half-brothers or between pairs of sisters, stepsisters, and half-sisters.

Effects of Stepsibling Subsystems on Stepparent-Child Relationships

Parent's Views. The closeness of adult's relationships with their children or stepchildren was analyzed with two 2 (gender of adult) by 2 (gender of child) by 2 (presence of stepsiblings) analysis of variance tests, one test for parents' ratings of their closeness to children and one for stepparents' ratings of their closeness to their stepchildren. To control for the fact that different numbers of children and stepchildren were being rated by these adults (some had one child in the stepfamily and some had several), the oldest child in each household was selected as the target child to which adults' responses were analyzed.

For stepparents perceived closeness to stepchildren, there were no significant main effects or interaction effects. For parents per-

Table 1. Means and Standard Deviations on Step/sibling Interaction Items

Item	Stepsiblings n=207	Half-siblings n=91	Siblings n=164	F
S/he fights	2.32^a (1.30)	2.38^a (1.21)	3.07^c (1.25)	3.67*
S/he teaches	3.62 (1.09)	3.62 (1.38)	3.34 (1.23)	2.74
S/he helps	3.14^a (1.03)	3.24^a (1.30)	2.97^b (1.70)	5.29**
S/he plays	3.16^a (1.27)	2.70^b (1.24)	3.09^a (1.28)	3.63*
S/he ignores	2.02 (1.04)	1.73 (.95)	2.37 (1.21)	2.92
S/he is a friend	2.11 (1.23)	1.93 (1.17)	2.13 (1.30)	2.32
I ignore them	2.10 (1.08)	1.89 (1.03)	2.33 (1.99)	1.24
I teach them	3.67^a (1.11)	2.67^b (1.33)	3.18^c (1.23)	10.61***
I help them	3.14^a (1.05)	2.53^b (1.19)	2.77^c (1.03)	10.55***
Relationship Score	25.38^a (5.90)	22.69^b (5.49)	25.25^a (6.54)	5.92**

Note. Scores with different subscripts are significantly different from each other. Low scores represent more positive interactions.

* $p < .05$
** $p < .01$
*** $p < .001$

ceived closeness to their children, the only significant main effect was for presence of stepsiblings (F = 4.22, df = 1,94, p < .05). Those who were in families with stepsibling subsystems reported feeling closer to their biological children than those without stepsibling subsystems. There were no significant interaction effects (see Table 2).

In addition, nearly half (44%) of the parents felt that the presence of stepsiblings had affected their relationships with their children, and most (71%) thought the influence had been negative (e.g., having less time with their children, added tension, discipline problems).

Table 2. Univariate Effects for Gender of Parent, Child Gender, and Presence of Stepsiblings on Parent's and Stepparent's Closeness to Children

Effects	Parents' Closeness	Stepparents' Closeness
Gender of Parent	1.67	1.19
Gender of Child	.01	2.40
Presence of Stepsiblings	4.22*	.09
Gender of parent X gender of child	.01	.07
Gender of parent X stepsibling	1.67	.37
Gender of child X stepsiblings	.09	.55

* $p < .05$

Children's Views. Three questions about discipline were analyzed with chi square tests. These results indicate that discipline may be handled differently in stepfamilies that have stepsibling subsystems and those that do not. Children who did not have stepsibling subsystems were more likely to say that stepparents made the rules in their households, while those with stepsiblings more often indicated that rules were made by both their parent and stepparent (x = 7.268, *df* = 2, *p* = .05). However, regarding decisions made about discipline, children with stepsiblings more often perceived only their parent to be the decision-maker, while stepparents were more likely to be identified as the decision-maker about discipline in families without stepsibling subsystems (x = 8.125, *df* = 2 , *p* = .05). Although the difference was not significant, a larger number of those children without stepsiblings indicated that their stepparents, rather than their parents, "got after them" when they did something wrong (X = 5.028, *df* = 2, *p* = .08). Taken together, these results indicate that parents are more likely to take the lead in disciplining their biological children when there are also stepchildren in the family.

We also asked children to tell us what kind of role their stepparent took in relationship to them. Those without stepsiblings were more likely to report that their stepparent took the role of "parent," whereas those with stepsiblings were more likely to report that the stepparent took the role of a "friend" or "teacher" (X = 6.1. *df* = 2, *p* = .05).

Responses to the clinical statements (e.g., I wish my family was more like other families) were analyzed with 2 (presence of stepsiblings) by 2 (gender of parent) by 2 (gender of child) multivariate analyses of variance tests. No main effects were found for presence of stepsiblings, F (7, 89) = .15, p = .99. The other main effects were also not significant (parent gender F (7, 89) = >87, p = .53, and child gender F (7,89) = .41, p = .90). None of the interaction effects were significant.

Effects on the Family

Parent's Views. Adult respondents were asked about the extent to which 11 stepfamily issues derived from the clinical literature were problems experienced in their family (see Table 3 for results). No differences in the frequency of occurrence were reported between families with stepsibling subsystems and those without for six of the issues: disagreements over raising the children, what children should call their stepparent, inheritance issues, sexual attraction between stepfamily members, stepchildren feeling torn loyalty between the parent and stepparent of the same gender, and children feeling responsible for their parents' divorce. Differences were found on five issues, however. Those adults whose families had stepsiblings reported having more problems with: stepparent-stepchild conflict, the stepparent feeling like an outsider, visiting children feeling like outsiders, and children hoping that their parents would reunite. The only problem that was greater for those with no stepsibling subsystems was the issue of stepparents adopting stepchildren.

In addition to these 11 issues, two other questions were relevant only to those with stepsiblings. Thirty-nine percent of the parents said they had experienced some problems with feeling they were neglecting their own children and nearly two-thirds (62%) reported some stepsibling conflicts.

Children's Views. Data were analyzed with 2 (presence of stepsiblings) by 2 (gender of parent) by 2 (gender of child) multivariate analysis of variance tests. The main effect of presence of stepsiblings (F (4, 103) = .34, p = .85) was not significant. The main effect for parent gender was also not significant (F (4, 103) = 1.68, p = .16), but the child gender effect was, (F (4, 103) = 3.63, p < .01).

Table 3. Means and Standard Deviations for Adults' Responses to Frequency of Stepfamily Problems

Problems	Adults From Stepfamilies Without Stepsibling Subsystems n=103	Adults From Stepfamilies With Stepsibling Subsystems n=95
Stepparent - child conflict	2.77 (.89)	3.28* (1.10)
Disagreements over childrearing	2.63 (.78)	2.86 (.91)
Name for Stepparent	2.35 (.61)	2.36 (.65)
Adoption of Stepchildren	2.14 (.52)	2.01* (.10)
Inheritance issues	2.18 (.47)	2.24 (.63)
Sexual attraction	2.04 (.26)	2.15 (.55)
Stepparent feels like an outsider	2.53 (.62)	2.72 (.93)
Noncustodial children feel like outsiders	2.27 (.69)	2.68* (.89)
Loyalty conflicts	2.61 (.86)	2.81 (.98)
Children hoping parents reunite	2.52 (.85)	2.85* (.98)
Children feelings responsible for divorce	2.39 (.73)	2.75** (1.05)

Note. Higher scores indicate problems more severe.

* $p < .05$
** $p < .01$

Males more frequently talked about their stepfamilies than females did. There were no interaction effects.

DISCUSSION

Stepsibling Relationships

The results of this study appear to indicate that the presence of stepsiblings in a household is a greater problem for the parents than it is for the children. For our sample of children it is likely that stepsiblings were important figures in their development even though time and opportunities for mutual influence and socialization was more limited for stepsiblings (i.e., 52% spent more than half the year in the same residence; 48% weekends, holidays, and summers only).

Responses of some children seemed idiosyncratic. For example, one 10-year-old boy seemed genuine in expressing the extreme closeness he felt to his older stepsister in spite of the fact he had only seen her two or three times in his life. Raised as an only child, the concept of having a sibling seemed very important to him. Hero worship of an older stepsibling may be a fairly common phenomena causing the child to perceive the relationship positively even when there is little interaction. In other cases, a child was viewed negatively by stepsiblings and biological siblings as well.

Other responses appeared to be age-related. For example, because half-siblings were always younger than the respondent it is not surprising that the half-sibling was perceived as fighting with and helping the respondent less. Nor is it surprising that the respondent perceived the younger half-sibling playing with them more and that they taught and helped them more than either siblings or stepsiblings. The study is limited, however, in what can be concluded regarding the effects of age differences between stepsiblings or about the effects related to the child's age when they acquire stepsiblings.

There were many indications that children do not distinguish between siblings and half-siblings. In fact, several children spontaneously objected to our use of the term half-brother or half-sister during the interview. This was not true for the terms stepsister and stepbrother.

The problems between stepsiblings most often identified in this study were consistent with what is reported in the clinical literature. For example, children reported problems derived from having to share resources such as parental attention, and space (e.g., one adolescent boy was irate at having to share his bedroom with his preschool-aged stepbrother).

The fact that cross-sexed stepsiblings taught each other less than cross-sexed siblings and half-siblings and same-sexed siblings of all types may be related to the age of the sample. The mean age of the children participating in the interviews was 13, and the mean age of their stepsiblings was 15. Sexual tension may have been a factor among these pubescent stepsiblings causing them to maintain emotional distance or it may be that adolescents of the opposite sex assume there is little to be learned from each other.

In spite of the fact that 57% of the children identified problems with their stepsiblings, the majority rated the stepsibling relationship as better than average. This could be due to a number of things. The children may have had very low expectations for their stepsiblings and, therefore, weren't disappointed with their relationships. It's also possible they felt guilty about jealous feelings they had towards stepsiblings and denied those feelings. Others may have worked hard to get along with stepsiblings in order to please their parent. A combination of these and other factors may have been operating.

Spontaneously offered comments about stepsiblings elicited in the interviews were basically benign–seldom were extremely positive or negative comments made about stepsiblings. The benign attitude towards stepsiblings shows up in the comparisons between stepsiblings and siblings as well. Significant differences between stepsiblings and siblings (i.e., they fought with and helped siblings, and were helped and taught more by siblings than stepsiblings) indicates, in general, that relations with stepsiblings are more passive.

Parent/Child Relations

Parents who have both biological children and stepchildren felt closer to their biological children than parents who had biological children and no stepchildren. Two possible explanations seem manifest. The first is that parents with both biological and stepchildren have a comparison group not available to those without stepchildren. Biological children may look better when compared to stepchildren than they do when compared to some hypothetical standard. Comments made by the biological parents insinuate that a second reason for more positive evaluations of biological children occurs because of defensiveness.

"He compares Sue (her child) to Kate and John (his children) which I think is unfair. He doesn't see them often, and they're on their best behavior."

"When there is an argument between Sam (her child) and Mark (his child), he jumps in and blames it on Sam."

"Joe expects my children to be a certain way that they're not . . . they're my children and I love them just the way they are, and they're not like his children."

"I protect Tim (her child) when Alan is critical. Alan protects his kids when I'm critical."

Some parents also commented that they felt they were neglecting their own children and that the presence of stepchildren had a negative effect on their relationship with their biological children. They may have rated their own children more positively because they felt guilty about this.

Having both children and stepchildren definitely appeared to create tension. When asked about differences in the way the couple dealt with the children, among those citing differences, the common response was that the biological parent was overprotective or too easy on the child, and the stepparent expected too much of the children. Many variations of this theme were shared.

"She thinks I'm too strict and I think she's too lenient. When I tell him 'no' she sticks up for him, and she and I fight."

"He's more lenient with his kids and less with mine than I am. I think he sees his kids through rose-colored glasses. He is not tuned in with my child's needs."

This defensive posture may have caused parents to actually feel closer, or to exaggerate their perceived closeness, to their biological child.

Interestingly, in those families without stepsibling subgroups, the stepparent was perceived more as a parent than in families where both adults had children. The stepparent did more disciplining and was more often seen in the role of parent. It may be that because these families are less complex (i.e., have fewer step relationships) they attempt to use the nuclear model for their family. Considering the dearth of information regarding healthy stepfamily models, it is not surprising that this is the case. It should be noted that length of time spent as a stepfamily was similar for those with stepsibling subsystems and those without. Therefore, the differences in stepfamily dynamics were not time related.

It could be concluded from this study that stepsibling subsystems are not inherently positive or negative for the children. However, parents appear to struggle with discomfort (eg., feeling like an outsider) and with loyalty issues in the presence of a stepsibling subsystem. There is some evidence that stepfamilies tend to replicate a nuclear family model when stepsibling subsystems are not present. Clearly, more research is needed on this potentially important stepfamily relationship.

REFERENCES

Ambert, A.M. (1986). Being a stepparent: Live-in and visiting stepchildren. *Journal of Marriage and the Family, 48*, 795-804.

Achenbach, T. (1978). The Child Behavior Profile: Boys aged 6-11. *Journal of Consulting and Clinical Psychology, 46*, 478-488.

Bank, S.P., & Kahn, M. D. (1982). *The sibling bond.* New York: Basic Books.

Beer, W. (1989). *Strangers in the house.* News Brunswick: Transaction Publishers.

Bernstein, A. C. (1989). *Yours, mine, and ours: How families change when remarried parents have a child together.* New York: Charles Scribner's Sons.

Bumpass, L. (1984). Some characteristics of children's second families. *American Journal of Sociology, 90*, 608-623.

Coleman, M., & Ganong, L. (1987). Marital conflict in stepfamilies: Effects on children. *Youth and Society, 19*, 151-172.

Ganong, L., & Coleman, M. (1984). Effects of remarriage on children: A review of the empirical literature. *Family Relations, 33*, 389-406.

Ganong, L., & Coleman, M. (1986). A comparison of clinical and empirical literature on children in stepfamilies. *Journal of Marriage and the Family, 48*, 309-318.

Ganong, L. & Coleman, M. (1987). Stepchildren's perceptions of their parents. *Journal of Genetic Psychology, 148*, 5-17.

Lang, M. & Tisher, M. (1983). *Children's Depression Scale Manual.* Victoria, Australia: Australian Council for Education Research.

Rosenberg, E., & Hajfal, F. (1985). Stepsibling relationships in remarried families. *Social Casework: The Journal of Contemporary Social Work, 66,* 287-292.

Pasley, K., & Ihinger-Tallman, M. (1984). *Remarried family life.* Pullman, WA: Unpublished instrument.

Stittman, A., Orme, J., Evans, D., Feldman, R., & Keeney, P. (1984). A brief measure of children's behavior problems: The Behavior Rating Index for Children. *Measurement and evaluation in counseling and development, 17,* 83-90.

Vandell, D., Minnett, A., & Santrock, J. (1987). Age differences in sibling relationships during middle childhood. *Journal of Applied Developmental Psychology, 8,* 247-257.

A Meta-Analytic Comparison of the Self-Esteem and Behavior Problems of Stepchildren to Children in Other Family Structures

Lawrence H. Ganong
Marilyn Coleman

SUMMARY. A meta-analysis was based on published studies that compared the self-esteem or behavior problems of stepchildren to children in nuclear and single-parent households. Twenty-four studies produced 57 effect sizes. Results showed generalizable differences in self-esteem between children in stepfamilies and nuclear families but not between stepchildren and children in single-parent households. Stepchildren's internalizing and externalizing behaviors were slightly greater than nuclear family children, but not single-parent family children. Discussion focused on the interpretation of these results within the limitations of the designs employed in the studies.

In spite of the fact that parental remarriage and the formation of stepfamilies is not a new phenomenon (Sweetzer, 1985), it is only

---

Lawrence H. Ganong, PhD, is Associate Professor in School of Nursing/Department of Human Development and Family Studies, University of Missouri. Marilyn Coleman, EdD, is Professor and Chairperson in the Department of Human Development and Family Studies, University of Missouri, 31 Stanley Hall, Columbia, MO 65211.

[Haworth co-indexing entry note]: "A Meta-Analytic Comparison of the Self-Esteem and Behavior Problems of Stepchildren to Children in Other Family Structures," Ganong, Lawrence H., and Marilyn Coleman. Co-published simultaneously in the *Journal of Divorce & Remarriage* (The Haworth Press, Inc.) Vol. 19, No. 3/4, 1993, pp. 143-163; and: *The Stepfamily Puzzle: Intergenerational Influences* (ed: Craig A. Everett), The Haworth Press, Inc., 1993, pp. 143-163. Multiple copies of this article/chapter may be purchased from The Haworth Document Delivery Center [1-800-3-HAWORTH; 9:00 a.m. - 5:00 p.m. (EST)].

relatively recently that behavioral and social scientists have focused attention on the area (Espinoza & Newman, 1979). As recently as 1979, it was reported in a review of research on stepchildren and their families that only 11 studies had been published (Espinoza & Newman, 1979). Early empirical work tended to focus on stressful and negative aspects of remarriage and stepfamilies (Bowerman & Irish, 1962). These studies, coupled with a larger body of clinical literature, led to the conclusion that parental remarriage had negative effects on children (Espinoza & Newman, 1979; Ganong & Coleman, 1984).

The effect of remarriage on children is an important question. Nearly one-fifth of all children in the United States under 18 years of age currently reside in a stepfamily household (Glick, 1989). An unknown percentage of the approximately 24% of children under 18 who live with a single-parent also have a stepparent with whom they may reside or visit on a part-time basis. If current rates of marital dissolution and remarriage continue, over one-third of all U.S. children can expect to become stepchildren before they reach the age of 18 (Glick, 1989).

A number of reviews of literature examining the effects of parental remarriage on various aspects of children's development were conducted in the past decade. These qualitative reviews by Jolliff (1984), Skeen, Covi, and Robinson (1985), Ihinger-Tallman (1988), Hetherington (1989), and Hetherington, Stanley-Hagan, and Anderson (1989) did not yield definitive conclusions, however. For example, Hetherington (1989) indicated that children in the long run may be survivors, losers, or winners of their parents' remarriage.

In a 1984 integrative review of research on the effects of remarriage on children, it was concluded that parental remarriage was not related to problem behavior or negative attitudes toward self and others in stepchildren (Ganong & Coleman, 1984). Drawing conclusions was hindered, however, because the research was plagued with conceptual and methodological problems, such as: the use of a deficit-comparison model, limited conceptualization of family structural variables, a failure to account for the complexity of stepfamilies, small or nonrandom samples, reliance on self-report questionnaires, and the use of data gathered from only one family member (Ganong & Coleman, 1984).

The purpose of this review is to apply meta-analytic techniques to the body of literature examining the effects of remarriage on stepchildren. Because of the inconsistency of findings in previous reviews, and because inconsistent findings prevail in current literature, meta-analytic techniques seem particularly well suited (Glass et al., 1981). By employing meta-analytic techniques, both the presence and magnitude of any differences can be determined. In addition, meta-analysis allows for the assessment of whether differences in study outcomes can be explained by variation in study characteristics such as sampling procedure or measurement.

One of the major underlying assumptions of the increasing concern over the divorce and remarriage rate is that, "the new forms of living arrangements that develop after the dissolution of the nuclear family are unhealthy for the society as well as the individuals involved" (Baydar, 1988, p. 967). Of particular concern is the effect of marital transitions on children, the "innocent victims" of these transactions. Although there is a widespread belief that two adults in a household provide more stability for children, regardless of the adults' relationship to the child, there is also the perception that stepchildren have a more difficult time. The problem areas most frequently explored in relation to stability in stepchildren have been the general areas of self-esteem and behavioral problems. These two areas are, therefore, the focus of the meta-analyses reported here.

SELF-ESTEEM

In an earlier review (Ganong & Coleman, 1984) it was concluded that, although there is some conflicting evidence, children in stepfamilies do not appear to differ significantly in self-esteem from children in nuclear or single parent households. It was noted that earlier studies found self-esteem to be lower in stepchildren (Kaplan & Pokorny, 1971; Rosenberg, 1965) while more recent studies found no differences (e.g., Raschke & Raschke, 1979; Wilson et al., 1975). However, conflicting evidence regarding stepchildren's self-esteem continues to be reported. For example, Hetherington et al. (1985) reported that children in stepfather families had lower self-esteem than those in nuclear families, but Bray (1988) found that children in stepfamilies did *not* suffer from self-esteem problems relative to children from nondivorced families.

BEHAVIORAL PROBLEMS

Family disruption has long been considered to be related to child behavioral problems (Bitterman, 1968; Burchinal, 1964). However, little support for this was found in the small sample of studies previously reviewed (Ganong & Coleman, 1984). Unfortunately, the evidence that stepchildren showed no more problem behaviors than children in single-parent and nuclear families was based on comparisons of studies with substantial flaws in design. Drawing meaningful conclusions was further hampered by the conceptual difficulties in comparing studies that included a wide diversity of behaviors (e.g., drug use, psychosomatic complaints, school behaviors).

METHOD

Sample of Studies

Studies were retrieved from earlier reviews (Ganong & Coleman, 1984; 1986; 1987; Hetherington, 1989; Ihinger-Tallman, 1988), and more recent studies were added via computer searches of the following data bases: Psychological Abstracts, 1970-1989; Sociological Abstracts, 1970-1989; and ERIC, 1970-1989. Key words used were stepchild, stepmother, stepfather, stepfamily, and remarriage. In addition, a bibliography compiled by the Remarriage and Stepparenting Focus Group of the National Council on Family Relations was examined (Pasley et al., 1988).

The following criteria were used in selecting studies for this review: (a) the main focus of the study was the comparison of self-esteem or behavior problems of stepchildren to children from nuclear and/or single-parent households; (b) the report was of empirical research; and (c) the study was published in a book or journal. The final sample was 24 studies that produced 57 effect sizes.

Variables Coded from Each Study

The following information was recorded from each study: geographic location in which the study was conducted, date of publication, source of publication (book, journal), independent variables, dependent variables, total sample size, number of stepchildren in the sample, sampling procedure, characteristics of the sample (e.g., race, SES, number of siblings), ages of stepchildren in the sample, methods used (observation, self-report, ratings by others, interviews), measurements used for the dependent variables, and quality of the study. Study quality was evaluated with an adaptation of a coding scheme devised by Berlinsky and Biller (1982). Each study was coded initially by one of the authors. The other author or a graduate assistant then independently coded the studies. Inter-rater agreement was .85.

Meta-Analyses Performed

Separate meta-analyses were conducted for comparisons of: (a) the self-esteem of stepchildren and children from nuclear families; (b) the self-esteem of stepchildren and children in single-parent households; (c) the internalizing behavior problems of stepchildren and children in nuclear families; (d) the externalizing behavior problems of stepchildren and children in nuclear families; (e) the internalizing behavior problems (e.g., depression, anxiety) of stepchildren and children from single-parent households; and (f) the externalizing behavior problems (e.g., fighting) of stepchildren and children from single-parent households. A total of six separate meta-analyses were conducted.

Effect Size Estimates

The effect size estimate used in this review is *d*, the difference between the means of two groups, divided by the pooled within group standard deviation. In studies with more than one effect size, an average effect size was computed for each study. The effect sizes were corrected for sample size biases using the weighted integration method developed by Hedges and Olkin (1985). The study outcomes were combined by averaging the effect sizes. In addition, homogeneity analyses were performed to see whether the individual effect sizes in each meta-analysis varied around the mean effect size; chi square was calculated to test whether the variability in the effect size was significantly different from what would have occurred by sampling error alone (Hedges & Olkin, 1985).

Since it was not possible to calculate an effect size for a sizeable percentage of the studies, two other methods of combining study results were employed. One was a method of counting test results in which the proportion of significant differences in an expected direction was calculated, and this proportion was compared to the proportion that would have been expected by chance (Rosenthal, 1978). The other method consisted of combining p values. For each comparison the one-tailed probability levels and the associated standard normal deviate (z) were recorded. The combined p value was calculated by summing the z scores and dividing the total by the square root of the number of studies in the comparison (Rosenthal, 1984). The z score was then converted back to the associated p level. This p value indicates the probability that the results of this group of studies could have been produced by chance.

RESULTS

Self-Esteem Differences

Characteristics of studies. A total of 24 studies examined the self-esteem of stepchildren. The meta-analysis consists of the 16 studies that compared the self-esteem of stepchildren to children from other family structures. The excluded reports included an intervention study, 5 studies that correlated children's views of themselves with their perceptions of their parents and stepparents, and 2 that compared children who had stepfathers with those who had stepmothers.

The earliest study was published in 1965, and the most recent was reported in 1989. Four appeared as book chapters, and the rest were published in journals. Five studies included children from stepfather households only, 4 were from both stepmother and stepfather households, 1 was from stepmother households only, and 5 failed to identify the type of stepfamily situation in which the child resided. Only 9 studies included sex of the child as an independent variable. A wide variety of ages were represented in these studies: 8 included grade school children in their samples, 10 included children in secondary schools, 2 had college student samples, and 1 assessed the self-esteem of adult stepchildren.

Self-esteem was measured with several different instruments: the Rosenberg Self-Esteem Scale (Kaplan & Pokorny, 1971; Pasley & Healow, 1988; Rosenberg, 1965), the Piers-Harris Self-Concept Scale (Amato & Ochiltree, 1987; Bray, 1988; Raschke & Raschke, 1976), and the Personality Attribute Inventory (Johnson & Hutchinson, 1989; Parish & Taylor, 1979; Parish & Dostal, 1980; Parish, 1981; Parish & Parish, 1983; Boyd et al., 1983; Nunn et al., 1983; Parish, 1987). One study used a behavioral observation to assess self-esteem (Santrock et al., 1982), and one assessed self-esteem using a single item from a large national survey (Wilson et al., 1975).

Stepchildren vs. Children from Nuclear Families

The 15 studies comparing the self-esteem of stepchildren and nuclear family children had a total sample of 9279 (see Table 1 for summary statistics). The effect sizes were coded so that positive values represented higher self-esteem for nuclear family children. The unweighted effect size was +.12 and the weighted effect size was +.11. The 95% confidence interval ranged from +.05 to +.18, indicating that children in nuclear families had slightly higher self-esteem than stepchildren did. This analysis included 4 studies whose effect sizes were estimated rather than calculated. When insufficient data were provided to derive an effect size and results were described as nonsignificant, a conservative estimate of .00 was made for the effect (Cooper, 1984). With those 4 investigations removed, the weighted effect size ($d+$) increased to +.14, with the 95% confidence interval ranging from +.07 to +.22 (see Table 2 for results on effects).

It should be noted that in only two studies were there more than one effect size value. For these two studies, the effect size used in the meta-analyses was the average of the study effects. Since the

Table 1. Summary of Meta-Analytic Statistics of Research Comparing the Self-Esteem of Children in Stepfamilies and Nuclear Families

Study	Sample Size	Weighted Effect Size	95% Confidence Limits for d Lower	Upper	Z	Tests[a]
Rosenberg (1965)	3759	.1400	.1019	.1801	2.79	1-1
Kaplan & Pokorny (1971)	388	.1465	.0270	.1728	0	0-1
Wilson et al (1975)	1652	.0535	-.0048	.1012	0	0-1
Parish & Taylor (1979)	362	.4055	-.1558	.9668	1.65	1-1
Raschke & Raschke (1979)	201	.0002	-.1392	.1396	0	0-1
Parish & Dostal (1980)	606	.0520	-.1824	.2864	1.28	0-1
Parish (1981)	279	.0000	-.0599	.0599	0	0-1
Santrock et al (1982)	36	.1231	-.2362	.4824	0	0-1
Parish & Parish (1983)	328	.0269	-.0813	.1351	0	0-1
Nunn et al (1983)	374	.3527	.0548	.6506	1.75	1-1
Amato & Ochildtree (1987)	256	.2400	-1.0095	1.4895	1.28	0-1
Parish (1987)	268	.0000	-.3493	.3493	0	0-1
Pasley & Healow (1988)	499	---	---	---	---	0-1
Bray (1988)	60	.3296	---	---	0	0-1
Johnson & Hutchinson (1989)	167	---	---	---	---	0-1

[a]Numbers in this column refer to the number of statistically significant tests and the total number of tests.

number of effect sizes within these studies was small (both had 2), and since so few studies had multiple effect sizes to calculate, it is unlikely that this seriously influenced the results (Hunter et al., 1982).

The homogeneity analysis indicated that 100% of the variance could be attributed to sampling error (chi square = 7.65, $df = 10$, $p = .66$). Therefore, it can be assumed that differences are not due to study characteristics but are due to differences between the two groups.

Table 2. Magnitude of Effect for Comparisons of Stepchildren and Children in Nuclear Families

	Self-Esteem	Internalizing Behavior	Externalizing Behavior
N of Studies	11 (15)[a]	3 (6)	4 (7)
M Effect Size	.14[b]	-.30[c]	-.10
95% Confidence Interval	.07 to .22	-.40 to -.20	-.20 to -.10
Total N of Subjects	8066 (9279)[d]	3292 (16,190)	3417 (16,315)
Chi Square Based on Step vs. Nuclear	.11 (11/15)[e]	.56 (13/32)	.73 (18/44)
Chi Square Based on Significant Differences	14.45[f] (3/15)	87.86 (9/31)	10.80 (12/44)
Mean P value	.015	.0001	.001

[a]Numbers in parentheses are total number of studies

[b]Positive values mean children in nuclear families scored higher

[c]Negative values mean stepchildren scored higher

[d]Numbers in parentheses are total number of subjects for all studies

[e]First number in parentheses are total number of subjects for all studies

[f]First number is number of tests with statistically significant results in favor of nuclear family children.

The proportion of the 15 tests found in these studies that reported significantly higher self-esteem for children in nuclear families was .20, a value that differed significantly from the proportion expected by chance. This is consistent with the results of the combined probability test that indicated the self-esteem of stepchildren was significantly lower than the self-esteem of children in nuclear families ($p < .02$).

Stepchildren vs. Children from Single-Parent Households

Thirteen studies looked at self-esteem differences between stepchildren and those in single-parent households (see Table 3 for summary statistics). The effect sizes were coded so that positive values represented higher self-esteem for stepchildren than children living with single parents. The weighted effect size for all studies, including those in which null findings that could not be calculated

Table 3. Summary of Meta-Analytic Statistics of Research Comparing the Self-Esteem of Children in Stepfamilies and Single-Parent Families

Study	Sample Size	Weighted Effect Size (d)	95% Confidence Limits for d Lower	Upper	Z	Tests[a]
Rosenberg (1965)	577	.2500	.08749	.4126	2.3269	1-1
Kaplan & Pokorny (1971)	146	.0593	-.3242	.4428	0	0-1
Parish & Taylor (1979)	69	-.0176	-.6032	.5680	0	0-1
Raschke & Raschke (1979)	107	.1807	-.2330	.5944	0	0-1
Parish & Dostal (1980)	265	-.0791	-.3213	.1631	1.282	0-1
Parish (1981)	122	---	---	---	---	0-1
Santrock, et al (1982)	36	.5424	-.1614	1.2462	1.645	1-1
Parish & Parish (1983)	179	.0000	.0000	.0000	0	0-1
Nunn et al (1983)	140	.1006	-.2627	.4639	0	0-1
Amato & Ochiltree (1987)	144	-.2079	-.5444	.1286	1.282	0-1
Parish (1987)	117	---	---	---	---	0-1
Pasley & Healow (1988)	143	---	---	---	---	0-1
Johnson & Hutchinson (1989)	56	---	---	---	---	0-1

[a]Numbers in this column refer to the number of statistically significant tests and the total number of tests.

were given a value of 0.00, was +.07. The effect size for the 9 studies in which effect sizes were calculated was +.09. These results indicate that the self-esteem of stepchildren is slightly higher. The confidence interval for the weighted *d* was −.01 to +.20. Since this confidence interval contains both negative and positive effect sizes, it is possible that there is no difference in self-esteem between these two groups. The homogeneity analysis showed that 100% of the variance could be explained by sampling error (11.51, $df = 1$, $p = .22$); therefore differences are not an artifact of study characteristics.

The proportion of the tests that found significantly higher self-esteem in stepchildren was .15, a proportion that did not differ significantly from the proportion expected by chance. The combined probability method, however, indicated a significant difference between the two groups of children ($p < .05$), with stepchildren having higher self-esteem (see Table 2).

In general, the results show that children in nuclear families report higher self-esteem than stepchildren, although the magnitude of differences is extremely small. Stepchildren do not differ, in general, from children in single-parent households.

Behavior Problems

Over 40 studies examined differences in the behavior problems reported for stepchildren and children from other family structures. These investigations included a wide range of problem behaviors, such as reported drug use, premarital pregnancy, and school absences. Meta-analytic studies often have been criticized for comparing "apples and oranges" (Cooper, 1984). After carefully considering this extreme variety of behavioral problems, we decided to take a conservative approach and only meta-analyze studies with conceptually similar definitions of behavior. The only clustering of studies large enough to consider for this analysis was a group of investigations in which the dependent variables were ratings of the child's behavior. It is this group that is reported here.

Characteristics of studies. Fifteen studies, all published since 1980, contained ratings of children's behavior problems. Ten of these studies are included in this meta-analysis. Four of these studies appeared as book chapters and the rest were published in journals. The excluded studies were comparisons of children from stepmother and stepfather households.

Ratings of children's behaviors tended to be made by only one person, usually a parent ($n = 7$), but one study sampled teachers (Touliatos & Lindholm, 1980) and one included ratings from parents, stepparents, and teachers (Hetherington et al., 1985).

A variety of ratings scales were used in these studies. The Achenbach Child Behavior Checklist was used most often ($n = 6$), followed by the Louisville Child Behavior Checklist ($n = 2$), and several scales that were used once (Conners Parent Questionnaire, Quay Behavior Problem Checklist, the Behavior Rating Inventory for Children). In addition, some nonstandardized measures ($n = 3$) and a psychiatric screening were used ($n = 1$).

Sample sizes ranged from 60 to 7000. Most of the studies were based on relatively small nonprobability samples, but three studies contained large probability samples (Peterson & Zill, 1986; Wadsworth et al., 1985; Zill, 1988). Two longitudinal investigations were represented; the Peterson and Zill (1986) and Zill (1988) reports are based on the National Survey of Children data set and the Hetherington, Cox and Cox (1985) report is partially based on a longitudinal study of children whose parents divorced when they were preschoolers. Of these reports, only the Zill (1988) study contained sufficient information about the data to calculate an effect size. The other studies were included in the combined probability and the vote counting calculations.

Stepchildren vs. Children from Nuclear Families

Ten studies compared the behavior problems of stepchildren and children from nuclear families. Effect sizes could be calculated from 5 of these (see Table 4). Effects were coded so that negative values mean that stepchildren have more behavior problems. A common way of conceptualizing children's problem behavior is to categorize it as either internalizing (e.g., depression, anxiety) or externalizing (e.g., fighting). Separate analyses were run to see if stepchildren differ from children in nuclear families on internalizing or externalizing (antisocial) behaviors.

Three studies reported data on internalizing behavior in enough detail to conduct a meta-analysis (see Table 2). The weighted d was equal to $-.30$. The 95% confidence interval was $-.40$ to $-.20$, indicating that the studies were consistent in reporting more internalizing behavior problems for stepchildren.

The counting method for this comparison resulted in 13 differences from 32 reported tests. Unfortunately, 5 of the 8 studies in this comparison contained multiple tests of significance (ranging from 2 to 12), so nonindependence of results is a problem. However, the findings are still informative; the proportion of tests with significant differences (29%), all of which were in the direction of indicating more behavior problems for stepchildren, was significantly different from what would be expected by chance (chi square = 87.85, $p <$

Table 4. Summary of Meta-Analytic Statistics of Research Comparing the Behavior Problems of Children in Nuclear Families and Stepfamilies

Study	Sample Size	Weighted Effect Size	95% Confidence Limits for d Lower	Upper	Z	Tests[a]
Touliotos & Lindholm (1980)	3289	--- (---)	--- (---)	--- (---)	1.645 (0)	3-4 (0-6)
Garbarino, et al (1984)	62	--- (---)	--- (---)	--- (---)	--- (---)	1-1 1-1
Hetherington, Cox & Cox (1985)	60	---	---	---	1.645 (1.645)	13-24 (1-12)
Wadsworth, et al (1985)	2806	-.1300 (-.0400)	-.0140 (-.0516)	-.2460 (-.0284)	3.25	1-1
Brady, Bray & Zeeb (1986)	426	-.0382 (-.043)	-.2352 (-.2400)	+.1588 (+.1540)	3.25 (3.25)	1-1 1-1
Peterson & Zill (1986)	877	--- (---)	--- (---)	--- (---)	1.645 (1.645)	2-4 (2-2)
Amato & Ochiltree (1987)	125	+.0003 (---)	-.4316 (---)	.4322 (---)	1.645	0-2
Bray (1988)	60	-.1125 (-.0425)	-.7498 (-.1468)	.5248 (+.0618)	1.645 (1.645)	2-2 1-1
Zill (1988)	8600	---	---	---	1.645 (1.645)	1-1

Note. Statistics for Internalizing Behaviors are shown in parantheses.

[a]Numbers in this column refer to the number of statistically significant tests and the total number of tests.

.0001). Five of the 8 studies reported generally more internalizing behavior problems for stepchildren. The combined p was less than .001, providing further evidence that stepchildren were rated as having more internalizing behavior problems (see Table 5).

Four studies contributed effect sizes to the comparison of externalizing behaviors between stepchildren and children in nuclear families. The weighted mean effect size was equal to −.10, with a 95% confidence interval of −.20 to −.01. Once again, stepchildren are consistently seen to exhibit more behavioral difficulties than children in nuclear families, although the differences between the two groups are small. Both the vote counting method and the combined p level indicated that stepchildren were seen as having more antisocial behavior (see Table 5).

Table 5. Magnitude of Effect for Comparisons of Stepchildren and Children in Single Parent Households

	Self-Esteem	Internalizing Behavior	Externalizing Behavior
N of Studies Studies	9 (13)[a]	2 (6)	4 (7)
M Effect Size	.09[b]	.07[b]	-.08[c]
95% Confidence Interval	-.01 to .20	-.04 to .18	-.19 to .03
Total N of Subjects	1653 (2091)[d]	3114 (7137)	3286 (7252)
Chi Square Based on Step vs. Single parents	3.12 (2/13)[ef]	4.00 (3/18)[f]	4.89 (4/23)[ef]
Chi Square Based on Significant Differences	8.63 (2/13)[eg]	14.45 (3/18)[g]	20.40 (4/23)[eg]
Mean p Value	.05	.15	.09

[a]Numbers in parentheses are total number of studies

[b]Positive values mean stepchildren scored higher

[c]Negative values means stepchildren scored lower

[d]Numbers in parentheses are total number of subjects in all studies

[e]Three studies found difference in favor of children in single-parent households

[f]First number in parentheses indicates tests with differences in the stepchild direction. Second number is total number of tests in that comparison.

[g]First number is number of tests with statistically significant results in favor of stepchildren.

Stepchildren vs. Children in Single-Parent Households

In the comparison of stepchildren to children in single-parent households, effects were coded so that positive values meant stepchildren have more behavioral problems. Nine studies examined these differences and five studies contained enough data to be used in this meta-analytic comparison (see Table 6).

Only 2 studies looked at internalizing behaviors. The mean effect size was +.07 and the confidence interval was −.04 to +.18. Therefore, even though the mean effect size indicates that stepchildren have more internalizing problems than children living with one parent, the inclusion of 0.0 within the confidence interval leads to the conclusion that there are no differences between the two groups.

Table 6. Summary of Meta-Analytic Statistics of Research Comparing the Behavior Problems of Children in Stepfamilies and Single-Parent Families

Study	Sample Size	Weighted Effect Size	95% Confidence Limits for d Lower	Upper	Z	Tests[a]
Wadsworth et al (1985)	2806	-.1299 (-.0799)	-.2441 (-.1941)	-.0157 (+.0343)	1.645 (1.645)	1-1 (1-1)
Brady, et al (1986)	308	+.0311 (+.0337)	-.1913 (-.1887)	.2535 (+.2261)	0 (1.645)	0-5 (2-7)
Amato & Ochiltree (1987)	115	+.0141	-.4223	.4505	0	0-4
Isaacs & Leon (1988)	57	-.0125	-.5185	.4935	0	0-1

Note. Statistics for Internalizing Behaviors are in parentheses.

[a]Numbers in this column refer to the number of statistically significant tests and the total number of tests.

The vote counting method showed a difference in the proportion of tests ($p < .05$) with significant results in the direction of stepchildren having fewer problems, but the combined probability method indicated that the overall probability of stepchildren having fewer internalizing behavior problems than children in single-parent households was not different from chance ($p = .12$).

For externalizing behaviors, the weighted mean was −.08, with a confidence interval ranging from −.19 to +.03. Since the confidence interval includes the value of zero, it should not be concluded that these two groups differ in exhibiting externalizing behavior problems. The proportion of tests that found stepchildren having significantly fewer problems than children in single-parent households was .23, a statistically significant difference from what would be expected by chance (chi square = 6.05, $p = .02$). However, the combined p level did not reach .05.

DISCUSSION

Stepchildren and Nuclear Family Children

The self-esteem of stepchildren was lower than that of children in nuclear families. The effect sizes for the studies comparing stepchildren to children in nuclear families were consistent in indicating higher self-esteem for those in nuclear families. However, the magnitude of differences in self-esteem between stepchildren and children in nuclear families were small. The majority of effect size estimates were less than .20, and many were much smaller. According to Cohen's (1977) criteria for evaluating the magnitude of effects, these effect sizes are not large enough to be considered very meaningful, representing a difference of less than one-sixth of a standard deviation.

Stepchildren also were consistently rated as having more behavior problems than children in nuclear families. The magnitude of effects were generally small, particularly for externalizing behaviors (−.10), but the differences in internalizing behaviors were large enough to be meaningful (−.30). These findings indicate that stepchildren may be more at risk for emotional problems such as guilt, depression, and anxiety, than children who live with both of their parents. It should be noted that these estimates are based on a small number of studies, and more studies need to be done that involve more sophisticated designs.

Stepchildren and Children with Single Parents

Stepchildren did not differ substantially from children in single-parent households in self-esteem or behavior problems. Stepchildren had slightly higher self-esteem and fewer externalizing behavior problems, but they also had slightly more internalizing behavior problems. Again, it should be noted that effect and size are not large and the number of studies are small.

Even had the effect sizes been much larger, however, important questions would remain unanswered. For example, we could not, based on the extant body of research, have determined if differences in the self-esteem of children in different family structures, particularly those in single-parent and stepfamily households, is ameliorated over time. It could be that children's self-esteem is lowered during the divorce process and improves over time. We also could not make judgements about sex differences in self-esteem, nor could we identify the correlates of high self-esteem for children in different family structures.

CONCLUSIONS

First, since the effect sizes in the studies reviewed were consistently small, it can be concluded that stepchildren generally do not differ greatly from children in other family structures. In fact, it could be argued that family structure per se has relatively little influence on children's self-esteem and reported behavior problems, although it may be that other variables related to family structure do wield important influences. Furthermore, given these small effect sizes, an argument can be made that additional studies comparing stepchildren to children from other families, similar to the ones reviewed here, would add little enlightment to an understanding of the effects of parental remarriage on children.

Therefore, another conclusion that can be drawn is that further studies in which simple comparisons of children from different family structures are made are generally not needed. This is not to suggest that no more comparison studies are needed, however. Exceptions would include examinations of interactive hypotheses, such as "gender by family structure" effects. For example, if stepdaughters exhibit more of a certain behavior than stepsons (e.g., truancy), comparison groups of children from other family structures are needed so that we can know whether this outcome is true only in stepfamilies or if this behavior is more characteristic of girls in general.

Researchers who plan to do comparative studies should address a number of design problems that occurred in the studies reviewed here. For example, explanations of how target children in families were selected was seldom mentioned. Reporting of family structure variables also was often incomplete; information such as the precursor to remarriage (i.e., were the adults previously never married, divorced, or did a previous relationship end in death) and the length of time the child resided in a single-parent household were either not gathered or were omitted from published reports. In addition to structural variables, data also need to be reported about the quality of the family relationships, such as the relationship between the child's biological parents (i.e., nonexistent, hostile, friendly), parent-child relations, or the quality of parental remarriage. These and other potentially important variables that could be related to stepchildren's behavior and self-esteem were frequently ignored. The quality of the remarriage and stepfamily dynamics should not be ignored in studying these variables. The self-esteem of some children may be greatly enhanced by living in a high-quality, stable stepfamily environment. It is naive to assume that remarriage has a universal, uniform effect on children's self-esteem and behavior.

What is needed rather than simple comparative studies are investigations that focus on why some stepchildren fare better than others. For example, researchers interested in self-esteem might best invest their time exploring the factors that contribute to high self-esteem in stepchildren. This would necessitate correlational designs, longitudinal studies, careful attention to family structure and family relationship variables, and large samples. Recently, designs incorporating all or part of these components have been employed. For example, represented in the body of recent research are longitudinal investigations (Bray, 1988; Isaacs & Leon, 1988), large samples or samples limited to specific types of stepfamilies so that differences in types of stepfamilies can be compared (Zill, 1988), and studies using multiple methods of data collection (Hetherington, Cox & Cox, 1985). Clearly, some progress is being made in the sophistication of research designs.

Still lacking, however, are designs more clearly connected to theory. Although limited attempts have been made to utilize theory, the literature related to stepchildren's self-esteem and behavior remains primarily atheoretical or, at best, the theories are implicit. Although some studies previously collected data prospectively, retrospective data could also enhance our understanding of stepchildren depending on the question or theory being questioned. More specificity in the conceptualization of outcome variables is also needed. For example, if boundary and hierarchy issues in a stepfamily are problems, as is suggested in the clinical literature (Visher & Visher, 1988), behaviors such as running away from home may be more common among stepchildren. This kind of specific information about the behavior of stepchildren is more valuable than knowing how they compare to other children on some global assessment of behavioral problems.

The question of the effects of remarriage on children's self-esteem and behavior is not yet satisfactorily answered. Although better designed studies are beginning to be conducted, stepfamilies are very complex, and complex methods need to be utilized in examining them. An enhanced understanding of stepchildren can only come about through advancements in our ability to study them.

REFERENCES

Amato, P. R. & Ochiltree, G. (1987). Child and adolescent competence in intact, one-parent, and step-families: An Australian study. *Journal of Divorce, 10*(3-4), 205-217.

Baydar, N. (1988). Effects of parental separation and reentry into union on the emotional well-being of children. *Journal of Marriage and the Family, 50*, 967-981.

Berlinsky, E., & Biller, H. (1982). *Parental death and psychological development.* Lexington, MA: Heath.

Bitterman, C. (1968). The multimarriage family. *Social Casework, 49*, 218-221.

Bowerman, C. E., & Irish, D. (1962). Some relationships of step-children to their parents. *Marriage and Family Living, 24*, 113-121.

Boyd, D.A., Nunn, G.D., & Parish, T.S. (1983). Effects of marital status and parents' marital status on evaluation of self and parents. *Journal of Social Psychology, 119*, 229-234.

Burchinal, L. G. (1964). Characteristics of adolescents for unbroken, broken and reconstituted families. *Journal of Marriage and the Family, 24*, 44-51.

Brady, C. P., Bray, J. H., & Zeeb, L. (1986). Behavior problems of clinic children: Relation to parental marital status, age and sex of child. *American Journal of Orthopsychiatry, 56*, 399-412.

Bray, J. (1988). Children's development during early remarriage. In M. Hetherington & J. Arasteh (Eds.), *Impact of Divorce, Single Parenting and Stepparenting on Children* (pp. 279-298). New York: Erlbaum.

Brody, G.H., Newbaum, E., & Forehand, R. (1988). Serial marriage: A heuristic analysis of an emerging family form. *Psychological Bulletin, 103*(2), 211-222.

Cohen, J. (1977). *Statistical power analysis for the behavioral sciences.* New York: Academic.

Coleman, M., & Ganong, L. (1990). Remarriage and stepfamily research in the 1980s: Increased interest in an old family form. *Journal of Marriage and the Family, 52*, 925-940.

Cooper, H. (1984). *The integrative research review.* Beverly Hills: Sage.

Espinoza, R., & Newman, Y. (1979). *Stepparenting* (DHEW Publication #48-579). Rockville, MD: U.S. Department of Health, Education, & Welfare.

Ganong, L., & Coleman, M. (1984). Effects of remarriage on children: A review of the empirical literature. *Family Relations, 33*, 389-406.

Ganong, L., & Coleman, M. (1986). A comparison of clinical and empirical literature on children in stepfamilies. *Journal of Marriage and the Family, 48*, 309-318.

Ganong, L. & Coleman, M. (1987). Effects of parental remarriage on children: An updated comparison of theories, methods, and findings from clinical and empirical research. In K. Pasley & M. Ihinger-Tallman (Eds.), *Remarriage and stepparenting: today: Current research and theory* (pp. 94-140). New York: Guilford.

Garbarino, J., Sebes, J., & Schellenbach, C. (1984). Families at risk for destructive parent-child relations in adolescence. *Child Development, 55*, 174-183.

Glass, G., McGaw, B., & Smith, M. (1981). *Meta-analysis in social research.* Beverly Hills, CA: Sage.

Glick, P. (1989). Remarried families, stepfamilies, and stepchildren: A brief demographic analysis. *Family Relations, 38*, 24-27.

Hetherington, E. M. (1989). Coping with family transitions: Winners, losers, and survivors. *Child Development, 60*(1), 1-14.

Hedges, L., & Olkin, I. (1985). *Statistical methods for meta-analysis.* Orlando, FL: Academic.

Hetherington, E. M., Cox, M., & Cox, R. (1985). Long-term effects of divorce and remarriage on the adjustment of children. *Journal of the American Academy of Child Psychiatry, 24*, 518-530.

Hetherington, E. M., Hagan, M., & Anderson, E. (1989). Marital transitions: A child's perspective. *American Psychologist, 44*, 303-312.

Ihinger-Tallman, M. (1988). Research on stepfamilies. *Annual Reviews of Sociology, 14*, 25-48.

Isaacs, M. & Leon, G. (1988). Marriage and its alternatives following divorce: Mother and child adjustment. *Journal of Marital and Family Therapy, 14*, 163-173.

Johnson, M. & Hutchinson, R. (1989). Effects of family structure on children's self-concepts. *Journal of Divorce, 12*, 129-138.

Jolliff, D. (1984). The effects of parental remarriage on the development of the young child. *Early Child Development and Care, 13*, 321-333.

Kaplan, H. B., & Pokorny, A. (1971). Self-derogation and childhood broken home. *Journal of Marriage and the Family, 33*, 328-337.

Nunn, G., Parish, T., & Worthing, R. J. (1983). Perceptions of personal and familial adjustment by children from intact, single-parent and reconstituted families. *Psychology in the Schools, 20*, 166-174.

Parish, J. G., & Parish, T. S. (1983). Children's self-concepts as related to family structure and family concept. *Adolescence, 18*, 649-658.

Parish, T. S. (1981). Young adults evaluations of themselves and their parents as a function of family structure and disposition. *Journal of Youth and Adolescence, 10*, 173-178.

Parish, T. S. (1987). The effects of family structure and birth order on college students' rating of sex and parents. *College Student Journal, 21*, 266-269.

Parish, T. S., & Dostal, J. (1980). Evaluations of self and parent figures by children from intact, divorced, and reconstituted families. *Journal of Youth and Adolescence, 9*, 347-351.

Parish, T. S., & Taylor, J. (1979). The impact of divorce and subsequent father absence on children's and adolescent's self-concept. *Journal of Youth and Adolescence*, *8*, 427-432.

Pasley, K. & Healow, C. (1988). Adolescent self-esteem: A focus on children in stepfamilies. In Mavis Hetherington & J. Arasteh (Eds.), *Impact of Divorce, Single-parenting and Stepparenting on Children* (pp.263-277). New York: Erlbaum.

Pasley, K., Ihinger-Tallman, M., Ganong, L., Coleman, M., Rodgers, R., Crosbie-Burnett, M., & Giles-Sims, J. (1988). *Bibliography on remarriage and stepfamily.* Madison, WI: NCFR Focus Group on Remarriage and Stepparenting.

Peterson, J. & Zill, N. (1986). Marital disruption, parent-child relationships, and behavior problems in children. *Journal of Marriage and the Family, 48*, 295-307.

Raschke, H. J., & Raschke, V. J. (1979). Family conflict and children self-concepts: A comparison of intact and single-parent families. *Journal of Marriage and the Family, 41*, 367-374.

Rosenberg, M. (1965). *Society and the adolescent self-image.* Princeton, NJ: Princeton University Press.

Rosenthal, R. (1978). Combining effects of independent studies. *Psychological Bulletin*, *85*, 185-193.

Rosenthal, R. (1984). *Meta-analytic procedures for social research.* Beverly Hills, CA: Sage.

Santrock, J. W., Warshak, R., & Elliott, G. (1982). Social development and parent-child interaction in father-custody and stepmother families. In M.E. Lamb (Ed.), *Non-traditional families: Parenting and child development* (pp. 289-314). Hillsdale, NJ: Erlbaum.

Skeen, P., Covi, R. B., & Robinson, B. E. (1985). Stepfamilies: A review of the literature with suggestions for practitioners. *Journal of Counseling and Development*, *64*, 121-125.

Sweetser, D. A. (1985). Broken homes: Stable risk, changing reasons, changing forms. *Journal of Marriage and the Family, 47*, 709-715.

Touliatos, J., & Lindholm, B. (1980). Teachers' perceptions of behavior problems in children from intact, single-parent, and stepparent families. *Psychology in the Schools*, *17*, 264-269.

Visher, E., & Visher, J. (1988). *Old loyalties, new ties.* New York: Brunner/Mazel.

Wadsworth, J., Burnell, I., Taylor, B., & Butler, N. (1985). The influence of family type on children's behaviour and development at five years. *Journal of Child Psychology and Psychiatry and Allied Disciplines*, *26*, 245-254.

Wilson, K. L., Zucher, L. A., McAdams, D. C., & Curtis, R. (1975). Stepfather and stepchildren: An exploratory analysis from two national surveys. *Journal of Marriage and the Family, 37*, 526-536.

Zill, N. (1988). Behavior, achievement, and health problems among children in stepfamilies: Findings from a national survey of child health. In M. Hetherington & J. Arasteh (Eds.), *Impact of Divorce, Single-Parenting and Stepparenting on Children* (pp. 325-368). New York: Erlbaum.

Social Support Received by Children in Stepmother, Stepfather, and Intact Families

Cheryl L. Pruett
Robert J. Calsyn
Fred M. Jensen

SUMMARY. This study compared the (step)mother-(step)child relationship among college students using social support concepts in three family types: stepmother, stepfather, and intact. As predicted, when compared to the relationship between children and their biological mothers in other family types, children in stepmother families perceived less relationship quality, less support and more conflict with their stepmother. However, children in stepmother families did not perceive more overall family conflict or less family cohesion than children in the other family types. Similarly, children in the stepmother families were no less satisfied with the overall social support they received from their entire social network than children in the other family types.

Over nine million children currently have a stepparent (Cherlin & McCarthy, 1985). Glick (1980) estimated that by 1990 approximately 30% of all children in the United States will be living in a

Cheryl L. Pruett, PhD, is on the faculty at the University of Missouri-St. Louis; Robert J. Calsyn, PhD, is Director of the Gerontology Program; Fred M. Jensen, PhD, is also on the faculty at University of Missouri-St. Louis, 8001 Natural Bridge Road, St. Louis, MO 63121-4499.

[Haworth co-indexing entry note]: "Social Support Received by Children in Stepmother, Stepfather, and Intact Families," Pruett, Cheryl L., Robert J. Calsyn and Fred M. Jensen. Co-published simultaneously in the *Journal of Divorce & Remarriage* (The Haworth Press, Inc.) Vol. 19, No. 3/4, 1993, pp. 165-179; and: *The Stepfamily Puzzle: Intergenerational Influences* (ed: Craig A. Everett), The Haworth Press, Inc., 1993, pp. 165-179. Multiple copies of this article/chapter may be purchased from The Haworth Document Delivery Center [1-800-3-HAWORTH; 9:00 a.m. - 5:00 p.m. (EST)].

stepfamily. Although stepfamilies are increasingly prevalent, remarriages involving stepchildren are more likely to end in divorce than remarriages not involving stepchildren (Furstenberg & Spanier, 1984; White & Booth, 1985). Moreover, previous research suggests that stepmother families (i.e., families with a biological father and a stepmother) experience even more relationship problems than stepfather families (i.e., families with a biological mother and a stepfather) or intact families (Furstenberg, 1987). The stepmother-stepchild relationship may be considered a fundamental dyad in the stepfamily as women are typically ascribed responsibility for child-rearing and family cohesion. Stepmothers may be an important source of support, and perceptions of support likely influence the quality of this important stepfamily relationship.

The present study compares the (step)mother-(step)child relationship using social support concepts in three types of families: stepmother, stepfather, and intact. We chose social support dimensions to describe the (step)child-(step)mother relationship because previous research has found that social support is correlated with psychological well-being and the reduction of stress in other populations (Cohen & Wills, 1985).

Social support researchers distinguish between functional measures of social support and network measures of social support (Cohen & Wills, 1985). Functional measures describe the types of social support received (i.e., tangible assistance, information, esteem, and belongingness). Tangible assistance includes things such as financial or physical assistance. Esteem support provides information to the individual that s/he is valued for who they are as a person. Informational support is the provision of advice or information that may be helpful in coping with a stressful situation. Belongingness support provides social companionship and inter-connectedness with a social group.

Network measures of social support include size of the social support network, proximity of the supporters, density (i.e., how many supporters know each other), reciprocity, and dimensionality (i.e., how many support functions does a given supporter provide). Researchers also distinguish between *perceived support* (i.e., the perception that support would be available if needed) and *enacted support* (i.e., support actually received).

Although the stepfamily literature has not used social support concepts in examining the relationship between stepmothers and their stepchildren, the sparse research literature does suggest some hypotheses.

Hypothesis 1: In describing the (step)mother-(step)child relationship, stepchildren will rate quality of the relationship with their stepmother lower and perceive the stepmother as less supportive than children in the other groups. Several authors (Bowerman & Irish, 1962; Ganong & Coleman, 1987) have reported that stepchildren perceive their stepmother as more detached and distant.

Hypothesis 2: Children in stepmother families will receive less functional social support in all categories than children who live with their biological mothers. Santrock and Sitterle (1987) found that stepchildren reported that their biological mothers were more sensitive and understanding (esteem support) than their stepmothers. Similarly, Santrock and Sitterle (1987) and Furstenberg (1987) found that stepmothers were less involved in the activities of their stepchildren, including school activities and recreational activities, suggesting that stepmothers provide less tangible and belongingness support. Furstenberg (1987) provides indirect support that stepchildren experience less belongingness support as they frequently omitted various step relations in describing their family network.

Hypothesis 3: Children in stepfamilies (both stepmother and stepfather) will perceive the family as more conflicted and less cohesive than children in intact families. As indicated earlier, remarriages involving children are more likely to end in divorce than remarriages not involving children, suggesting family conflict (White & Booth, 1985; Cherlin, 1978). Similarly, stepchildren are more likely to be moved out of the remarried family (White & Booth, 1985), again suggesting less cohesion and more conflict. Finally, remarried couples report more family conflict than first married couples (Waldren, Bell, Peek & Sorrell, 1990).

Hypothesis 4: Stepmothers will be listed as a source of conflict more frequently in stepmother families than biological mothers will be listed as a source of conflict in the other two types of families. Although both Bernard (1956) and Ferri (1984) conclude that stepmother-stepchild relations are generally satisfactory, a sizeable minority of their subjects described their relationships with their stepmothers as hostile. Similarly, subjects in other studies (Bowerman & Irish, 1962 and Ganong & Coleman, 1987) reported feeling that their stepmothers preferred other family members and were discriminatory.

Hypothesis 5: Stepchildren will report larger social networks, with each network member providing fewer support dimensions (i.e., lower dimensionality) when compared to children in intact families. This hypothesis is based on the simple fact that the stepfamily situation provides for an additional set of step kin relationships not available in intact families; however, we expect that these relationships may be more limited in terms of the supportive functions provided by each relationship.

Hypothesis 6: A 2 $\times$ 3 gender by family structure (stepmother vs. stepfather vs. intact) interaction is expected on social support, such that stepdaughters will perceive the least support and biological daughters the most support. Sons and stepsons are predicted to receive intermediate levels of support. This hypothesis is based on normative child rearing practices which encourage greater attachment between mothers and daughters than between mothers and sons. As a consequence, the introduction of a stepmother is hypothesized to cause feelings of divided loyalties and other conflicts more salient for daughters than sons. Previous research has provided conflicting evidence regarding this hypothesis. Clingempeel, Brand, and Ievoli (1984) reported that stepdaughters had more difficulty with their stepmothers than stepsons, whereas Santrock, Warshak, and Elliott (1982) reached the opposite conclusion.

METHOD

Subjects

Subjects were 104 undergraduate students (mean age = 19.5 years); 39 resided with their biological parents (intact family); 35 resided with their biological mother and stepfather (stepfather family); and 30 resided with their biological father and stepmother (stepmother family). The subjects were recruited from undergraduate psychology classes and received extra credit for their participation. A special effort was made to recruit students in stepmother families, as the percentage of the population living in this type of family is much less than the other two family types. Phone calls were made to students known to live in this type of family based on responses from a previous questionnaire.

Relationship Quality

To determine relationship quality, all subjects were asked to rate on seven-point Likert scales: how well they got along with their (step)mother, closeness to their (step)mother, and the level of satisfaction with this relationship. Cronbach's alpha computed on this three-item scale equaled .93, suggesting that this measure has adequate internal consistency. Higher scores on the scale indicated a more positive relationship.

Social Network Measures

A modified version of the Arizona Social Support Interview Schedule (Barrera, 1981) was used to measure social network dimensions. Rather than an interview format, subjects were asked on a questionnaire to identify the people who "are important in a number of different ways," eliciting information about who provides supportive functions. Four supportive functions (esteem, tangible assistance, information, and belongingness) were described to elicit the names of network members. Up to five individuals could be identified. Additionally, subjects rated their level of satisfaction with their network in relation to each of the four supportive functions. Ratings were provided in a seven-point Likert format, ranging from "very dissatisfied" to "very satisfied," with a higher score indicating greater satisfaction. Finally, subjects were asked to identify those individuals who are a source of upset or conflict. This instrument provides a measure of total network size (the total number of people providing at least one supportive function), dimensionality (the number of functions served by each individual network member), and conflicted network size (the number of network members who were also a source of interpersonal conflict).

Perceived Social Support

The *Interpersonal Support Evaluation List* (ISEL) student scale was modified for the current study. The ISEL (Cohen & Hoberman, 1983) was designed to measure the *perceived availability* of four support functions–esteem, tangible assistance, appraisal (information), and belongingness. A confirmatory factor analysis of the ISEL indicates that this instrument provides a measure of each of the four support functions, as well as a general, second-order social support factor (Brookings & Bolton, 1988). The ISEL has been shown to possess adequate internal reliability (alpha coefficients ranging from .77 to .86) and test-retest reliability (correlations ranging from .71 to .87) for a one-month period (Cohen, Mermelstein, Kamarck, & Hoberman, 1985).

The revised measure (ISEL-R) consists of 44 items, 11 items measuring each function. All items were modified to focus specifically on the subject's perception of support provided by the mother/stepmother. Six of the original statements designed to measure belongingness support were inappropriate for the current study, and were replaced with statements more appropriate to the current investigation. A four-alternative response format was utilized, ranging from "definitely true" to "definitely false." Subscale items were summed to provide a total support score (range 44-176). A higher score is indicative of higher levels of perceived support.

A pilot study was conducted to explore the internal consistency of the revised measure. Reliability coefficients ranged from .74 to .86 for the ISEL-R suggesting that the measure was sufficiently reliable. Coefficient alphas for the current sample on the ISEL-R were as follows: tangible assistance, .85; appraisal, .90; esteem, .78; belongingness, .92; and, overall, .88.

Enacted Support

The *Inventory of Socially Supportive Behaviors* (ISSB) (Barrera, Sandler, & Ramsay, 1981), was modified for the current investigation and test items were altered to reflect support provided exclusively by the mother/stepmother. Rather than forty items, the modified ISSB-R scale consists of 31 items; nine items measuring directive guidance (information), 10 items measuring non-directive support (esteem), seven items measuring positive social interaction (belongingness), and five items measuring tangible assistance. Items were eliminated based on the factor analysis of Barrera and Ainlay (1983) or because they were not appropriate for the (step)mother-child relationship. Three new items were developed.

Reliability coefficients computed on the pilot sample for the ISSB-R ranged from .75 to .91. Similar analyses of the current sample revealed comparable reliability. Coefficient alphas for the ISSB-R on the current sample were as follows: tangible assistance, .79; information, .90; esteem, .91; belongingness, .85; and, overall, .88.

Family Environment

Two subscales of the *Family Environment Scale* (Moos, 1974) were administered. The cohesion subscale is a measure of the degree of support, help, and commitment of family members. The conflict subscale is a measure of openly expressed anger and conflict in the family. Each subscale consists of nine statements and the subject must indicate whether the statement is "True" or "False" of his/her family. Scores may range from 0-9, with higher scores indicating higher levels of each domain. The FES has been widely used and has been shown to possess adequate reliability and internal consistency (Moos & Moos, 1986).

RESULTS

Check on Internal Validity

Selection poses the greatest threat to the internal validity (Cook and Campbell, 1979) of a study like the present one in which research participants were not randomly assigned to the various levels of the independent variable (i.e., family structure in this study). To determine whether research participants were equivalent on variables other than family type, a number of between group analyses were run on various demographic variables. The results of those analyses are reported below and indicated that the groups were equivalent on those variables, indicating no selection threat to internal validity.

Of the 104 subjects, 38 were male and 66 were female, and the proportion of males and females was generally equivalent in each group: 14 males and 25 females in the intact family group; 12 males and 23 females in the stepfather family group; and, 12 males and 18 females in the stepmother group. Chi square analysis reveals that the groups did not differ on the gender dimension (χ^2 = .23, df = 2, p = .88). Twenty subjects identified themselves as African-American, seventy-eight as Caucasian, and six as 'other.' The groups did not differ significantly by race (χ^2 = 4,45 , df = 4, p = .61).

The sample may be characterized as generally middle-class. Using Hollingshead's Two-Factor Index of Social Position (1957), which weights occupation and education, the sample as a whole is middle-class (Level III). Chi square analysis (χ^2 = 13.7, df = 8, p = .08) indicates that the groups were not significantly different in regard to socio-economic status.

Participants in the stepfather group had lived with their family for an average of 8.9 years compared to participants in the stepmother group who averaged 5.6 years. Length of step-family membership was significantly different across groups (F = 6.44, df = 1,62, p = .01). However, because length of family membership did not significantly correlate with the dependent measures, it was not controlled for in subsequent analyses.

Chi square analyses of cause of separation (χ^2 = 2.02, df = 2, p = .36), rate of adoption by the custodial stepparent (χ^2 = .10, df = 1, p = .74), and custody arrangements (χ^2 = .88, df = 11, p = .34) indicate that the stepfamily groups did not differ significantly on these dimensions.

Hypotheses Testing

Subjects' mean scores on relationship quality, functional social support, and social network measures appear in Table 1. Means are provided for subscales as well as overall scale scores.

Hypothesis 1. A MANOVA was conducted to explore the differences between relationship quality, ISEL-R total, and ISSB-R total scores for the three groups. The overall MANOVA was significant (F = 4.86, df = 6,188, p < .001) as were the univariate F tests. The quality of the stepmother-stepchild relationship was rated as significantly poorer (F = 13.51, df = 2,96, p = .01) than the quality of the

Table 1

Means and standard deviation on relationship quality, functional support, and social network variables.

	1 Stepmother family		2 Stepfather family		3 Intact family	
Measure	Mean	SD	Mean	SD	Mean	SD
Relationship Quality (RQ)	13.3	5.3	19.0	2.9	16.7	3.9
Family Environment Scale						
Cohesion (CFCH)	5.5	2.8	6.2	2.3	6.2	2.1
Conflict (CFCN)	3.9	2.5	3.0	1.9	3.5	2.1
ISEL-R						
Tangible	31.6	7.8	38.3	5.3	37.4	4.9
Esteem	33.7	4.0	38.3	3.5	37.1	4.0
Information	26.7	9.0	33.8	7.3	30.5	8.2
Belonging	27.8	9.8	36.8	5.2	35.9	6.2
TOTAL	120.8	28.6	147.4	17.3	141.1	20.2
ISSB-R						
Tangible	9.2	4.1	12.7	4.9	11.7	3.6
Esteem	20.5	9.3	30.1	9.5	28.4	10.0
Information	17.3	7.1	22.5	8.0	21.8	7.2
Belonging	13.8	5.6	20.2	5.6	19.4	6.3
TOTAL	61.0	24.0	85.2	24.8	81.4	23.4
Network Satisfaction						
Tangible assistance	5.9	0.8	6.1	0.9	6.1	0.9
Informational	5.9	0.9	5.9	1.1	5.7	1.4
Esteem	5.9	0.8	5.9	0.8	5.7	1.2
Belongingness	6.2	0.9	5.9	1.2	6.0	1.3
Total Network Size	6.8	2.4	6.5	1.7	6.9	2.0
Number of functions per 'average supporter'	2.2	0.5	2.3	0.4	2.4	0.5

mother-child relationship in the other two family types. Similarly, children in stepmother families reported less total support, both perceived ($F = 12.18$, $df = 2,96$, $p < .01$) and enacted ($F = 7.96$, $df = 2,96$, $p < .01$), than children in the other groups as predicted. Post-hoc comparisons using Tukey's HSD revealed that the stepmother group's total relationship, total ISSB-R, and total ISEL-R, were significantly different at the .05 level from the scores for the other two groups.

Hypothesis 2. To explore specific social support functions, four subscale scores were calculated for the ISEL-R and ISSB-R. The significant MANOVA ($F = 2.72$, $df = 18,176$, $p < .001$) indicated differences between groups and individual ANOVAs were examined to determine the nature of these differences.

Across all support functions, stepchildren reported receiving less support (perceived and enacted) from their stepmother than subjects in other groups. Stepchildren *perceived* less tangible ($F = 10.73$, $df = 2,96$, $p < .01$), informational ($F = 5.37$, $df = 2,96$, $p < .01$), esteem, ($F = 11.54$, $df = 2,96$, $p = .01$), and belongingness support ($F = 13.33$, $df = 2,96$, $p < .01$), and reported *receiving* less tangible ($F = 5.11$, $df = 2,96$, $p < .01$), informational, ($F = 4.07$, $df = 2,96$, $p < .01$), esteem ($F = 7.03$, $df = 2,96$, $p < .01$), and belongingness support ($F = 8.98$, $df = 2,96$, $p < .01$). Post hoc comparisons using Tukey's HSD procedure indicated that on all variables the stepmother group was significantly different at the .05 level from the other two groups. On the perceived informational support variable, all three groups were significantly different from each other with the children from intact families perceiving more informational support available than children from stepmother families, but less than stepfather families.

Hypothesis 3: A MANOVA comparing Family Environment Scale subscale scores across groups was computed and the overall F was not significant ($F = .83$, $df = 4,194$, $p = .50$). Contrary to the prediction, children in stepfamilies did not perceive the current family as significantly more conflicted or less cohesive than children in intact families.

Hypothesis 4: Consistent with our hypothesis, children in stepmother families listed their stepmother as a source of upset and conflict more frequently than children in the other groups listed their mother as a source of upset and conflict ($\chi^2 = 6.87$, $df = 2$, $p = .03$). Two-thirds (20 out of 30) of the children in the stepmother family identified their stepmother as a source of conflict, whereas less than half (18 out of 39) in intact families and only a third (12 out of 35) of children in stepfather families listed their mother as a source of conflict.

Hypothesis 5: Contrary to our prediction, children in step-families did not have larger support networks (F = .23, df = 2, 101, p = .79). There were also no between group differences (F = .38, df = 2, 101, p = .56) in dimensionality (i.e., the number of support dimensions provided by the average supporter); we had predicted that the average supporter of children in stepfamilies would provide fewer support dimensions.

Hypothesis 6: A 2 × 3 MANOVA (gender × family structure) was computed to explore differences in total perceived and enacted support and relationship quality by gender. The interaction between gender and family structure was not significant (F = .53, df = 6, 182, p = .77). Thus, contrary to our prediction, a child's gender did not affect the amount of perceived or enacted social support received in the various family structures.

Other Findings. On the general social support network measure we asked respondents how satisfied they were with the support they received from all sources for each of the support functions. Using MANOVA there were no significant differences between family types in support satisfaction (F = .37, df = 10,182, p = .95) for any of the support functions. Thus, even though the children in stepmother families reported receiving less support from their stepmothers than the other children received from their biological mothers, children in stepmother families were no less satisfied with the overall level of support that they received. Similar to the findings of Santrock and Sitterle (1987) fathers of children in stepmother families were listed more frequently as supporters than in the other two family types, suggesting that fathers are able to compensate for some of the support not provided by the stepmother.

DISCUSSION

In general, the present study supported the proposition that children in stepmother families receive less support from their stepmothers than children in other family structures receive from their biological mothers. It would appear that perceived deficits in supportive behavior detracts from the quality of the stepmother-stepchild relationship. Children in stepmother families describe their relationship with their stepmother as less close than children in other family types describe their relationship with their biological mothers. Additionally, children in stepmother families have more conflict with their stepmothers than children in the other family types have with their biological mothers. These findings are consistent with the assumption that perceived deficits in supportive behavior negatively impact this important stepfamily relationship.

Our research is consistent with the findings of most previous research on step-families (Bowerman & Irish, 1962; Ganong & Coleman, 1987; Sanstrock & Sitterle, 1987; Furstenberg, 1987), and suggests that social support is an important factor influencing stepfamily relationships. Other research has shown that stepmothers agree with the perceptions of their stepchildren, namely that the relationship is less close, more distant, and more conflicted than the relationships between biological parents and their children (Ambert, 1986; Hobart, 1987; Hobart & Brown, 1987).

It is important to emphasize that it was not stepfamily living in general that was a negative experience for stepchildren in our study. The children in stepfather families had the most positive relationship with their mothers of all three family types. Rather, it was the specific stepmother relationship that was evaluated less positively than the relationship between children and their biological mothers.

Does social support work differently in (step)mother-child relationships for the three groups? We did examine the correlations between the various social support functions and overall relationship quality for each of the family types separately. As one would expect, nearly all of these correlations are moderately high (.50 or above). There was one notable exception, however. The correlation between tangible assistance received and relationship quality was only .17 and .12 for the two groups living with their biological mothers; however, the same correlation in the stepmother group was .52. This pattern of findings suggests that the quality of the child-(step)mother relationship depends in part on specific tangible assistance that the stepmother provides her stepchild, whereas the relationship between adolescent children and their biological mothers has become more symbolic and no longer dependent on the concrete dispersal of rewards. Given the small sample size and the large number of correlations that were calculated, these results must be viewed cautiously. However, future research should concentrate on determining what variables, including the provision of tangible rewards, mediates the quality of the relationship between stepmothers and stepchildren. Visher and Visher (1990) offer additional hypotheses regarding how successful step-relationships develop.

Contrary to the findings of previous researchers (Bernard, 1956; Bowerman & Irish, 1962; Clingempeel, Brand, and Ievoli, 1984) we found no support for the hypothesis that females would have more difficulty relating to stepmothers than males. The age of our subjects and the greater time elapsed since the stepmother was introduced into the family of our subjects may explain the discrepancy from previous research.

Although the relationship between stepmothers and their children is not perceived as positively as the relationship between children and their biological mothers, most stepchild-stepmother relationships are described neutrally, not negatively. Moreover, children in stepmother families do not perceive any more family conflict than children in stepfather or intact families. It is also important to note that children in stepmother families are no less satisfied than other children with the level of social support that they receive from their social network as a whole. Our results conflict with studies using younger children who have lived in step families for less time than our sample had (generally, less than two years). Most of these other studies (Cherlin, 1978; White & Booth, 1985; Guisinger, Cowan, & Schuldberg, 1989) have reported more problems in stepfamilies than in intact families or remarriages not involving children. It is generally assumed that the first two years of stepfamily reconstitution are the most difficult as relationships are being forged. Although our particular sample of stepfamilies may over-represent "successful stepfamilies," (i.e., families who have stayed together an average of 5-9 years and have children attending college) the current sample does provide some insight into the quality of these 'stable' relationships. Future research with more representative sampling with different age children is needed to better determine what percentage of stepfamilies are coping successfully as compared to intact families.

Despite the possible limits in the generalizeability of our findings, it is important to remember that the internal validity of our design is quite strong, because our stepfamily samples did not differ from our intact families across a number of demographic variables.

REFERENCES

Ambert, A. (1986). Being a stepparent: Live-in and visiting stepchildren. *Journal of Marriage and the Family*, 48, 795-804.

Barrera, M. (1981). Social support in the adjustment of pregnant adolescents. In B.H. Gottlieb (Ed.), *Social Support and Social Support Networks*, (pp.69-96). Beverly Hills, CA: Sage Publications.

Barrera, M., & Ainlay, S.L. (1983). The structure of social support: A conceptual analysis. *Journal of Community Psychology*, 11, 133-143.

Barrera, M., Sandler, I.N., & Ramsay, T.B. (1981). Preliminary Development of a Scale of Social Support: Studies on College Students. *American Journal of Community Psychology*, 9, 435-447.

Bernard, J. (1956). *Remarriage*. New York: Dryden Press.

Bowerman, C.E., & Irish, D.P. (1962). Some Relationships of Stepchildren to Their Parents. *Journal of Marriage and Family Living*, 24, 113-121.

Brookings, J.B., & Bolton, B. (1988). Confirmatory Factor Analysis of the Interpersonal Support Evaluation List. *American Journal of Community Psychology*, 16, 137-147.

Cherlin, A. (1978). Remarriage as an Incomplete Institution. *American Journal of Sociology*, 84, 634-650.

Cherlin A., & McCarthy, J., (1985). Remarried Couple Households: Data from the June 1990 Current Population Survey. *Journal of Marriage and the Family*, 47, 23-30.

Clingempeel, W.G., Brand, E., & Ievoli, R. (1984). Stepparent-Stepchild Relationships in Stepmother and Stepfather Families: A Multi-method Study. *Family Relations*, 33, 465-473.

Cohen, S. & Hoberman, H.M. (1983). Positive Events and Social Supports as Buffers of Life Change Stress. *Journal of Applied Social Psychology*, 13, 99-125.

Cohen, S., Mermelstein, R., Kamarck, & Hoberman, H.M. (1985). Measuring the Functional Components of Social Support. In I.G. Sarason & B.R. Sarason (Eds.), *Social support: Theory, research, and applications*, (pp.73-94). Boston: Martinus Nijhoff Publishers.

Cohen, S. & Wills, T.A. (1985). Stress, Social Support, and the Buffering Hypothesis. *Psychological Bulletin*, 98, 310-357.

Cook, T.D. & Campbell, D.T. (1979). *Quasi-experimentation: Design & Analysis Issues for Field Settings*. Chicago: Rand McNally.

Ferri, E. (1984). *Stepchildren: A national study*. Windsor, UK: Nfer-Nelson.

Furstenbuerg, F.F. (1988). Child Care After Divorce and Remarriage. In E.M.

Hetherington & J. Arasteh (Eds.), *Impact of Divorce, Single-parenting, and Stepparenting on Children*, (pp. 245-261). Hillsdale, NJ: Erlbaum.

Furstenberg, F., & Spanier, G. (1984). The Risk of Dissolution in Remarriage: An Examination of Cherlin's Hypothesis of Incomplete Institutionalization. *Family Relations*, 33, 433-441.

Ganong, L.H., & Coleman, M.M., (1987b). Stepchildren's Perceptions of Their Parents. *Journal of Genetic Psychology*, 148, 5-17.

Glick, P. (1980). Remarriage: Some Recent Changes and Variations. *Journal of Family Issues*, 1, 455-478.

Guisinger, S., Cowan, P.A., & Schuldberg, D. (1989). Changing Parent and Spouse Relations in the First Years of Remarriage of Divorced Fathers. *Journal of Marriage and the Family*, 51, 445-456.

Hobart, C. (1987). Parent-child Relations in Remarried Families. *Journal of Family Issues*, 8, 259-277.

Hobart, C., & Brown, D. (1988). Effects of Prior Marriage Children on Adjustment in Remarriage: A Canadian Study. *Journal of Comparative Family Studies*, 19, 381-396.

Moos, R.H. (1974). Family Environment Scale. Palo Alto, CA: Consulting Psychologists Press.

Moos, R.H., & Moos, B.H. (1986). Family Environment Scale. Palo Alto, CA: Consulting Psychologists Press.

Santrock, J.W., & Sitterle, K.A. (1987). Parent-child Relationships in Stepmothers Families. In K. Pasley & M. Ihinger-Tallman (Eds.), *Remarriage and Stepparenting*, pp. 273-299. New York: Guilford Press.

Santrock, J.W., Warshak, R.A., & Elliott, G.L. (1982). Social Development and Parent-Child Interaction in Father-Custody and Stepmother Families. In M.E. Lamb (Ed.), *Nontraditional Families: Parenting and Child Development*, pp. 289-314. Hillsdale, NJ: Lawrence Erlbaum Associates.

Visher, E.B., & Visher, J.S. (1990). Dynamics of Successful Stepfamilies. *Journal of Divorce & Remarriage*, 14, 3-12.

Waldren, T., Bell, N.J., Peek, C.W., & Sorrell, G. (1990). Cohesion and Adaptability in Post-divorce Remarried and First Married Families: Relationships with Family Stress and Coping Styles. *Journal of Divorce & Remarriage*, 14, 13-28.

White, L.K., & Booth, A. (1985). The Quality and Stability of Remarriages: The Role of Stepchildren. *American Sociological Review*, 50, 689-698.

Influences on the Quality of Stepfather-Adolescent Relationships: Views of Both Family Members

Ann R. Skopin
Barbara M. Newman
Patrick C. McKenry

SUMMARY. Using dyadic responses, this study of 50 middle to upper-to-middle class stepfather families examined factors that influence the quality of the stepfather-adolescent relationship. Correlational analysis indicated that agreement between the stepfather and mother regarding the raising of the adolescent (from the perspective of both the stepfather and the adolescent) was the most significant predictor of relationship quality. Other predictors were stepfather's satisfaction with his marriage and the adolescent's perception of family income. The importance of a family systems perspective is addressed.

Ann R. Skopin, PhD, is Professor of Gerontology Technology at Columbus State Community College, Columbus, OH 43215. Barbara M. Newman, PhD, is Associate Provost and Professor in the Department of Family Relations and Human Development at The Ohio State University, Columbus, OH 43210. Patrick C. McKenry, PhD, is Professor in the Department of Family Relations and Human Development and Black Studies at The Ohio State University, Columbus, OH 43210.

This study is part of a larger research project entitled "Divorce and the Transition to Remarriage: A Study of Stepfamilies with Adolescent Children" funded by the Ohio Agricultural Research and Development Center (H-839).

[Haworth co-indexing entry note]: "Influences on the Quality of Stepfather-Adolescent Relationships: Views of Both Family Members," Skopin, Ann R., Barbara M. Newman and Patrick C. McKenry. Co-published simultaneously in the *Journal of Divorce & Remarriage* (The Haworth Press, Inc.) Vol. 19, No. 3/4, 1993, pp. 181-196; and: *The Stepfamily Puzzle: Intergenerational Influences* (ed: Craig A. Everett), The Haworth Press, Inc., 1993, pp. 181-196. Multiple copies of this article/chapter may be purchased from The Haworth Document Delivery Center [1-800-3-HAWORTH; 9:00 a.m. - 5:00 p.m. (EST)].

INTRODUCTION

As of 1987, there were an estimated 11 million remarried families, constituting 21.4% of all married-couple families in the United States. Of these remarried families, 4.3 million are stepfamilies (Glick, 1989). A stepfamily is generally defined as a family created by remarriage with at least one partner's child from a previous marriage (Fillinson, 1986; Giles-Sims, 1984). In 1987, 12% of children under age 18 in two-parent families, or 5.85 million minor children, were stepchildren (Glick, 1989). Approximately one in every ten children under age 18 (approximately seven million children) are living with their natural mother and a stepfather (Glick, 1979). This increasing number of stepfamilies has resulted in the role of stepfather becoming a rather common phenomena.

Although stepfamilies are becoming more common, these family forms are often complex and problematic, involving continuous relationships with a former spouse, in which child-sharing is a part. Cherlin (1978) hypothesizes that problems in stepfamilies are caused by the lack of "routinization of everyday behavior resulting in the incomplete institutionalization" (p. 334) of the roles for family members. Thus, role ambiguity is a particular problem in stepfamilies because expectations of stepparents have not been delineated by society. Similarly, society has not developed terms, customs, or behavioral norms to be used in coping with the complex interrelationships of stepfamilies. Without them, stepfamilies are forced to develop coping behaviors of their own for many of their daily encounters. Cherlin concludes that this lack of "habituated behavior" (p. 334) causes life to be more complicated and stressful than that of the traditional family.

The role of stepfather is far more common than that of stepmother because children more frequently reside with their mothers (Cherlin & McCarthy, 1985; Spanier & Glick, 1981). Several authors have summarized the problematic areas of the stepfather role. Johnson (1980) delineated the following concerns: complex roles and relationships between past and present families; individual variability in the lives of "children, the natural parents, the stepparent, and external environmental conditions" (p. 306); and conflict over territory and different lifestyles. Robinson (1984), reviewing clinical studies of stepfathering, listed the following general problem areas most often reported: authority and discipline with stepchildren; demonstration of affection; concern regarding inappropriate sexual attraction across generations; money; loyalty; and surname conflicts. Keshet (1980), using a systems approach to analyze the problems of the stepfather role, suggests that after the separation of the natural parents, the parent-child subsystem becomes companionable, supportive, and intense, and develops strong outer boundaries. The reorganization of family "power, authority, and nurturing strategies" (p. 522) makes it possible for the families to continue functioning as a unit. It is into this self-sufficient unit that the stepfather enters.

Nelson and Nelson (1982), using social exchange theory, outline the following problem areas within the stepfather role: "discipline, kinship terms, family loyalty, and monetary conflicts" (p. 227). Visher and Visher (1978) suggest that if the stepfather has children, the effects of guilt concerning the abandonment of his own children may result in (a) resentment and possible abuse of stepchildren, (b) problems dealing with the competition between his new wife and his own children, and (c) excessive pacification of his own children as well as his first wife. Various studies have examined the stepparent-child adjustment process by age group.

The age of the child, particularly adolescence, has been identified by some as an important factor in the formation of the stepfather relationship. Bernard (1956) found "the general consensus among remarried parents seems to be the very young or quite grown-up children tend to assimilate a new parent more easily than do adolescents" (p. 216). The findings of Wallerstein and Kelly (1980) from their longitudinal study of children of divorced parents support the conclusion that older children have more difficulty with a stepfather than do younger children. They found adolescents generally resisted their stepfathers and did not develop a close relationship with their stepfathers.

Additionally, Hetherington (1987), in her five-year follow-up of divorced and remarried mothers, found that stepfathers and stepdaughters experienced increased negative interaction as the length of a positive remarriage increased; an opposite pattern existed within the first married families.

A ROLE THEORY PERSPECTIVE

Nye and McLaughlin (1976) state "family roles encompass the essential activities of family life . . . it follows that the more competently one spouse enacts these roles, the more rewards he or she provides for the other spouse" (p. 192). Role performance is a central part of marital and family happiness; thus, the enactment of the stepfather role affects the quality of family relationships. Role theory contends that the ease with which roles are entered is determined, in part, by anticipatory socialization and lack of role conflict (Burr, 1973). Another factor that determines role performance is role reciprocity (Newman & Newman, 1980). These three concepts from role theory–anticipatory socialization, role conflict, and role reciprocity–appear salient in the enactment of stepfather role.

Anticipatory socialization refers to opportunities for rehearsing a role according to societal norms. Cherlin (1978) contends that because there are no behavioral norms for the role of stepfather, the stepfather not only lacks the opportunity to practice the role, but experiences confusion and uncertainty about the appropriate role behaviors. This lack of social norms for the stepfather-adolescent relationship results in "more opportunity for disagreements and divisions among family members" (Lutz, 1983, p. 335). The independent variables suggested by this concept of anticipatory socialization include: *the closeness of the stepfather to his natural children* and *the length of courtship time between the stepfather and the natural mother.*

Role conflict is defined as "the presence of incompatible expectations for a social role" (Cherlin, 1978, p. 129). Predictable examples of parent-adolescent conflict as discussed by Peterson (1986) include the "conflicting expectations of peer and parents" (p. 25). Parents may react to the adolescent's need for independence by becoming more rigid and strict and, in this way, extend the adolescent's dependency. Cherlin (1978) discussed role conflict for stepfathers by examining the incompatibility of expected behaviors held by the stepfather himself, his wife, and the natural father. Frequent contractual issues are discipline, financial support, and guilt occurring because of divided loyalties between previous and present families.

The concept of role conflict suggests examination of the amount of conflict between the natural parent and stepparent over raising the adolescent. The stepfather may be perceived by the mother as an outsider or an intruder, and consequently too harsh or, at the other extreme, non-involved because the adolescent isn't really his child. Additionally, the stepfather may experience conflict within himself in regard to the amount of discipline, authority, and financial support expected of him. The concept of role conflict also suggests examining the adolescent's divided loyalties between the natural father and the stepfather as a factor that may limit the ability of the adolescent to invest himself in the stepfather relationship without causing feelings of betrayal to his natural father.

The gender of the adolescent is another variable that may be associated with the concept of role conflict as it affects the quality of the adolescent-stepfather relationship. Sexual norms in families have been clearly established for "blood" relatives; however, a female adolescent and a stepfather are sexually mature people living in the same house in close proximity. The roles of adolescent and stepfather which are expected to be enacted as child and parent may conflict with male-female attraction. This may cause discomfort with the family nudity, display of physical affection, and even intimate communication. The independent variables suggested by this concept of role conflict are *the amount of agreement between the mother and stepfather regarding the raising of the adolescent* and *the adolescent's relationships with the noncustodial parent* and *gender of the adolescent.*

Role reciprocity is defined as the extent to which "each role is . . . linked to one or more related roles . . . each role is partly defined by the other roles that support it" (Newman & Newman, 1980, p. 64). The role behaviors of stepparents and adolescent are interdependent, each can only function in part as well as the other performs the reciprocal role. Thus, the poorly defined roles within the stepfamily may detract from role reciprocity. The quality of the stepfather-adolescent relationships may be a product of unclear and poorly linked roles.

Role reciprocity can be examined by exploring the amount of *time the natural parent and the adolescent spent as a single parent family.* Because the stepfather's role is determined to a great extent by the role the adolescent plays as stepchild, a longer period of time may be associated with a stronger bond, thus indicating a greater resentment of the intrusion of the stepfather. This might be especially true if the adolescent has taken on the role of adult companion to the mother. Role reciprocity also suggests examining the relationship between *the stepfather's satisfaction with the remarriage* and the quality of the stepfather-adolescent relationship. Perhaps dissatisfaction with one relationship is a good indicator of dissatisfaction with the other. If the stepfather cares very deeply for the mother, and the mother supports his parenting efforts, then he might be willing to work harder to improve his relationship with the adolescent.

HYPOTHESIS

Using role theory as a framework for this study, several factors were identified as possible predictors of the quality of the stepfather-adolescent relationship. The variables delineated included: *the closeness of the stepfather to his natural children, length of courtship time between the stepfather and the natural mother, the amount of agreement between the mother and the stepfather regarding the raising of the adolescent, the adolescent's relationship with his/her noncustodial parent, the gender of the adolescent, the years the adolescent lived in a single parent home,* and the *stepfather's satisfaction in the remarriage.* Because of the well established relationship between family income, age of adolescent, and length of time living in the stepfamily to adjustment to stepfamily living, the variables were controlled prior to examining these hypothesized predictors.

Relationship Quality. The dependent variables of relationship quality were the adolescent's and stepfather's scores on the Parent-Adolescent Communication Scale (Olson, 1982). The first subscale, Open Family Communication, measures the more positive aspects of parent-adolescent communication, and the second subscale, Problems in Family Communication, measures the negative aspects of communication. The scale consists of a total of 20 items, 10 in each subscale. The items are of the Likert type, moderately agree, neither agree nor disagree, moderately disagree, strongly disagree. These items are scored with a single sum score with a possible range of 20-200. Cronbach's alpha on both scales was established at .88 (Olson, 1982). Only the total score was used in this study.

Anticipatory socialization. The closeness of the stepfather to his natural children was measured by a five-item rating scale (1 = "very close" and 5 = "distant"). *The length of courtship time between the stepfather and the natural mother* was the self-reported raw number of years the stepfather dated his current spouse.

Role Conflict. The amount of agreement between the mother and the stepfather regarding the raising of the adolescent was self-reported by the stepfather using a five-item rating scale (1 = "always agree" and 5 = "never agree"). *The adolescent's relationship with his/her noncustodial parent* was assessed with a five-item rating scale (1 = "very close" and 5 = "distant"). *The gender of the adolescent* was an assigned characteristic.

Role Reciprocity. The years the adolescent lived in a single parent home was the raw number of years reported by the adolescent. *The stepfather's satisfaction in the remarriage* was the total score on the Marital-Comparison Index (Sabatelli, 1984), measuring the extent to which his marital expectations have been met. The instrument consists of 36 items that measure equity and commitment within a relationship. Sabatelli (1984) reports a Cronbach alpha coefficient for internal consistency of .93.

Confounding Variables. The age of the adolescent was self-reported chronological age on the last birthday. *The family income* was self-reported total family income by the stepfather. *The adolescent's time in present family* was the self-reported number of years according to the adolescent.

METHODS

Sample

The data used to address the study hypotheses were derived from a larger study of 100 stepfamilies–50 stepfather and 50 stepmother families–who resided in a large midwestern and a large southeastern city. Only the 50 stepfather families were used in this phase of the study. For inclusion in this study, the stepfather had to have been remarried for at least a year to a woman who was divorced. The mother must have an adolescent child between the ages of 12 and 18 who lived with the family. There could be no mutual children between them. (Only two of the stepfathers had their own children living with them.) The average family income fell within the interval of $50,000 to $74,999. Sixty-six percent of the stepfathers and 54% of the mothers had completed four years of college. Forty-eight percent of the stepfathers and 14% of the mothers had graduate degrees. Thus, the sample was largely middle to upper-middle class. The number of years the stepfathers had been married to their spouses ranged from one year to thirteen years, with a mean of 4.8 years. The majority of the families were Protestant (60%).

Data Collection

Data were collected through the administration of paper and pencil questionnaires. The independent completion of the questionnaires by each family member (stepfather, natural mother, and adolescent child) was assured by the presence of project personnel. The reputational sample of families was obtained through support groups, colleagues, and their referrals, resulting in a homogeneous, all-white, middle- to upper-middle-class sample. Subjects were mailed a letter of introduction inviting them to participate in the study. The letter was followed by a phone call to determine interest in participation and for administration of the questionnaire.

Instrumentation

The questionnaire consisted of demographic and family background questions as well as standardized instrumentation selected for its relevance to role theory and psychometric properties. Standardized measures used in this phase of the study included Olson's (1982) Parent-Adolescent Communication Scale, and Sabatelli's (1984) Marital Comparison Level Index. The letter was followed by a phone call to set up an appointment.

Data Analysis

The relationship between the dependent and independent variables was investigated by correlation analysis–Pearson's *r* and stepwise multiple regression. Two stepwise multiple regressions were performed–one using the stepfather's score as the dependent variable and the second using the adolescent's score as a dependent variable. The technique of casewise deletion was included in the correlation process because the variables were not interdependent and also to maximize use of the data. The three confounding variables were controlled by partialing out their effects on the correlation between the independent and dependent variables.

Additional analyses included a *t* test to determine the differences between the stepfather's and adolescent's scores on the perceived quality of their relationship; also because gender is a categorical variable, a *chi square* was performed to determine the effect of the adolescent's gender on the quality of the stepfather-adolescent relationship.

RESULTS

Correlations between the independent and dependent variables are presented in Table 1. Of the seven variables used to examine predictors of quality in stepfather-adolescent relationship, the frequency of agreement between the stepfather and mother regarding the raising of the adolescent was significantly and positively related to both the stepfather's and adolescent's perception of the quality of their relationship. The stepfather's satisfaction with his remarriage was also significantly related to his perception of the quality of the stepfather-adolescent relationship. However, his satisfaction with the marriage was not related to the adolescent's perception of the quality of their relationship. The remaining five variables were not significantly related to the measure of relationship quality.

Multiple regression was used to confirm the predictive power of the two independent variables. In the first stepwise multiple regression, using the stepfather's score as the dependent variable, only one predictor was selected. This predictor was *frequency of agreement between the stepfather and the mother regarding the raising of the adolescent* (see Table 2).

In the second stepwise multiple regression, using the adolescent's score as the dependent variable, two predictors were found to be statistically significant. These were *family income* and *frequency*

TABLE 1. Correlations Among Dependent and Independent Variables Controlling for Income, Adolescent's Age and Time in Current Family

	Stepfather's Score on Communication Scale	Adolescent's Score on Communication Scale
Stepfather's Relationship with Own Children	-.15 n = 36	.13 n = 36
Courtship Time	-.09 n = 27	-.01 n = 45
Frequency of Agreement	***.42 n = 45	**.32 n = 44
Adolescent's Relationship with Natural Father	.11 n = 45	-.04 n = 45
Time Spent in a Single-Parent Home	.07 n = 45	.07 n = 45
Stepfather's Satisfaction with Remarriage	**.30 n = 45	.10 n = 45
Income	.01 n = 48	*.33 n = 48
Adolescent's Age	-.06 n = 48	.00 n = 48
Time in Current Stepfamily	.22 n = 48	.10 n = 48

* p = .01
** p = <.05
*** p = <.005

of agreement between the stepfather and mother regarding the raising of the adolescent (see Table 3).

A *t* test was conducted to determine the differences between the stepfather's and adolescent's scores on the communication scales; the difference was significant, $t = 2.19$, df = 49, $p < .05$. The study mean scores on the dependent measures were slightly lower than

TABLE 2. Summary Table for Regression of F Score on Frequency of Agreement

Source	df	b	Adjusted Multiple R^2	F	p
Regression	1				
Frequency of Agreement		-8.25	0.17	8.97	.005
Residual	38				

TABLE 3. Summary Table for Regression of A Score on Income and Frequency of Agreement

Source	df	b	Adjusted Multiple R^2	F	p
Regression	2				
Income		4.35			
Frequency of Agreement		-5.78	0.33	10.45	.000
Residual	37				

the norms established for the instrument. The mean of the stepfather's scores was 62.6 (S.D. 14.72) compared to Olson's reported mean of 72.55 (S.D. 10.74). The mean of the adolescent's scores was 57.58 (S.D. 14.34) compared to Olson's reported mean of 63.74 (S.D. 12.02).

Chi square analysis was used to determine the relationship between the gender of the adolescent and the quality of the stepfather-adolescent relationship as perceived by the stepfather and the adolescent. The results were nonsignificant–from the perspective of both stepfather and adolescent.

DISCUSSION AND CONCLUSIONS

This study found that the frequency of agreement between the stepfather and the mother regarding the rearing of the adolescent was most positively related to the quality of the stepfather-adolescent relationship from the perspective of both stepfather and adolescent. Seventy percent of the stepfathers reported they "usually agreed with the child's mother." Bohannan (1979) emphasized that disagreements regarding the raising of children that align children with their mother against "that man" (p. 353) may, in turn, put the marriage at risk. Mowatt (1972) reported disagreement over discipline and the punishment of children as common problems. Robinson (1984), in his review of clinical studies of stepfathering, also listed authority and discipline among areas of conflict. It appears that agreement between parents about raising the adolescent was related to both the stepfathers' and the adolescents' perceptions of the quality of stepfamily life.

This study also revealed that the stepfather's relationship with the adolescent was positively related to his marital satisfaction. The roles of husband and stepfather seem to be reciprocal. Stepfathers who reported more happiness with their marriages perceived a higher quality stepfather-adolescent relationship. However, the adolescent's perception of the quality of the stepfather-adolescent relationship was not related to the stepfather's view of the marriage. The adolescent was perhaps too far emotionally removed to assess this relationship accurately. Brand and Clingempeel (1987) suggest that "a more positive marital relationship may encroach even more on special roles" (p. 141) which the children have acquired while living in a single-parent home such as independence or an "egalitarian relationship with the custodial parent" (p. 141).

Stepfathers appeared to be more satisfied with the new family structure than the adolescent. The mean scores on the measure of communication of the adolescent and the stepfather indicated a significant difference between their perceptions of the stepfather-adolescent relationship. Lutz (1983), in her study of adolescent's perceptions of stepfamily life, reported that adolescents' responses suggest that "the more they care for a stepparent, the worse they feel" (p. 371), and that caring for the stepfather was very stressful. Bowerman and Irish (1962) reported that "the level of affection toward stepfathers is usually markedly lower than toward real fathers" (p. 116).

These differing patterns among family members about what is salient would indicate the importance of examining whole family data and thus taking a family systems perspective when studying stepfamilies. These findings suggest that the stepfather's parental and marital roles are very much interrelated. Satisfaction with one is related to satisfaction with the other. Also, the stepfather's ability to arrive at satisfactory agreements with his wife in regard to child-rearing was related to satisfaction in the parental role with the adolescent.

This small-scale survey of 50 stepfather families has emphasized the interrelationship of the parental and marital roles in predicting stepfather-adolescent role adjustment. Yet, many questions remain to be addressed in our understanding of the dynamics of this relationship.

Further research using whole family data is needed to determine other variables that might affect relationships. The small sample size used in this study limited the number of questions that could be asked. Other role-related variables that might be examined would include sibling relationships, family support for the stepfamily, and family perceptions of stepfamilies in general.

The families studied here appeared to be relatively well adjusted. It may be that this sample represented well-functioning, stable, upper-middle class stepfamilies whose level of satisfaction in the relationship was unusually high. The generalization of these findings to those families that are problematic for whatever reason is thus questionable.

The limitations of pencil and paper questionnaires also should be considered in future study in this area. Using an interview in addition to the questionnaire would allow for more probing questions as well as more confirmatory questions. The ambiguity of the stepfamily roles may well be reflected in responses reflecting a high degree of social conventionality. Further research might also include video-taped observations as well as qualitative accounts to more accurately assess family interaction patterns.

In terms of deriving implications for intervention, this study would suggest that the marital relationship itself is a salient factor related to the stepfather-adolescent relationship. The two variables that were identified as significant were components of the interpersonal relationship between the stepfather and the mother. An emphasis on developing a strong, well-functioning, marital relationship as the basis for the stepfamily would thus appear important. Pill (1990) in her study of non-clinical families, suggests that a "psychoeducational focus" (p. 192) may help stepfamilies set realistic expectations for stepfamily functioning. This "reframing" contributes to better adaptation to stepfamily life. Therefore, in addition to developing interpersonal communication skills, the importance of openly discussing unresolved issues from the previous marriages, as well as recognizing the influence of those on the remarriage, must be addressed.

Consistent with the findings of this study, Orleans and colleagues (1989) in their analysis of factors positively affecting the stepfather's satisfaction with their remarriage, found the "husband's self-perceived significance in decision making" (p. 376) and "decision agreement between husband and wife" to be the most important factors. Thus, stepfather involvement as opposed to exclusion would seem to be important in strengthening these families. Too often it is falsely assumed that stepfathers desire minimal involvement in the childrearing process.

REFERENCES

Bernard, J. (1956). Remarriage: A study of marriage, New York: Russell and Russell.

Bohannan, P., & Yahraes, H. (1979). Stepfathers as parents. In E. Corfamn (Ed.), *Families today: A research sampler on families and children* (pp. 347-362). NIMH Science Monograph. Washington, D.C.: U.S. Government Printing Office.

Bowerman, C.E., & Irish, D.P. (1962). Some relationships of children to their parents. *Journal of Marriage and Family Living*, *24*, 113-131.

Brand, E., & Clingempeel (1987). Interdependence of marital and stepparent-stepchild relationships and children's psychological adjustment: Research findings and clinical implications. *Family Relations*, *36*, 140-145.

Burr, W.R. (1973). *Theory construction and the sociology of the family.* Wiley & Sons: New York.

Cherlin, A., & McCarthy, J. (1985). Remarried couple households: Data from the June 1980 current population survey. *Journal of Marriage and the Family*, 47(1), 23-30.

Cherlin, A. (1978). Remarriage as an incomplete institution. *American Journal of Sociology, 84*, 634-650.

Filison, R. (1986). Relationship in stepfamilies: an examination of alliances. *Journal of Comparative Family Studies, 17*, 43-61.

Giles-Sims, J. (1984). The stepparent role, expectations, behavior and sanctions. *Journal of Family Issues, 5*, 116-130.

Glick, Paul C. (1979). Children of divorced parents in demographic perspective. *Journal of Social Issues, 35*, 170-182.

Glick, Paul C. (1989). Remarried families, stepfamilies, and stepchildren: A brief demographic profile. *Family Relations, 1989, 38*, 24-27.

Hetherington, M. (1987). Family relations six years after divorce. In K. Pasley & M. Ihinger-Tallman (Eds.), *Remarriage and Stepparenting, current research and theory*. New York: Guilford Press.

Johnson, H.C. (1980). Working with Stepfamilies: Principles of practice. *Journal of Social Work*, 50, 304-308.

Keshet, J.K. (1980). From separation to stepfamily. *Journal of Family Issues, 1*, 455-478.

Lutz, E.P. (1983). The stepfamily: An adolescent perspective. *Family Relations, 32*, 367-375.

Mowatt, M. (1972). Group psychotherapy for stepfathers and their wives. *Psychotherapy: Theory, Research and Practice, 9*, 328-331.

Nelson, M., & Nelson, G.K. (1982). Problems of equity in the reconstructed family: A social exchange analysis. *Family Relations, 31*, 223-231.

Newman, B.M. & Newman, P.R. (1980). *Personality Development Through the Life Span*, California: Brooks Cole.

Nye, F.I. & McLaughlin, S. (1976). Role competence and marital satisfaction. In F. I. Nye & S. McLaughlin (Eds.) *Role structure and analysis of the family* (pp. 191-206). California: Sage.

Olson, D.H., (Ed.) (1980) (Available from Dr. David H. Olson, Family Social Science, University of Minnesota, 290 McNeal Hall, St. Paul, MN 55108).

Orleans, M., Palisi, B. J. & Caddell, D. (1989). Marriage adjustment and satisfaction of stepfathers: their feelings and perceptions of decision-making and stepchildren relations. *Family Relations, 1989, 38*, 371-377.

Peterson, G.W. (1986). Family conceptual frameworks and adolescent development. In G.K. Leigh and G.W. Peterson (Eds.), *Adolescents in families*, 12-37. Cincinnati: South-Western Publishing Company.

Pill, Cynthia (1990). Stepfamilies: Redefining the family. *Family Relations, 1990, 39*, 186-193.

Robinson, B.E. (1984). The contemporary American stepfather. *Family Relations, 33*, 381-388.

Sabatelli, R.M. (1984). Marital Comparison Level Index. Available from Ronald M. Sabatelli, University of Connecticut, U-117, Storrs, CT 06268.

Spanier, G.B., & Glick, P.C. (1981). Marital instability in the United States: Some correlates and recent changes. *Family Relations, 30*, 329-338.

Visher, E., & Visher, J. (1978). Common problems of stepparents and their spouses. *American Journal of Orthopsychiatry*, *48*, 252-262.

Wallerstein, J. & Kelly, J.B. (1980). *Surviving the breakup*, New York: Basic Books.

Whiteside, Mary F. (1989). Family rituals as a key to kinship connections in remarried families. *Family Relations*, *38*, 34-39.

The Effects of Child Support Receipt and Payment on Stepfamily Satisfaction: An Exploratory Study

Amy Benson
Kay Pasley

SUMMARY. The purpose of the present study was to examine how the payment or receipt of child support affected stepfamily adjustment. Other information about changes in child support and child support compliance after remarriage was obtained. Data from 74 remarried individuals who were either paying or receiving child support were used. The results indicated that for those that reported changes in child support, payers reported paying more while receivers reported receiving less child support. Very few variables differentiated those who received child support from those whose ex-spouse was noncompliant. Findings further showed that child support had no significant effect on stepfamily adjustment.

Accompanying the rising divorce rate of the past 20 years has been an increase in remarriage and stepfamily formation (Robinson, 1984). In the existing research literature on remarriages and stepfamilies one theme is evident: remarriages face unique problems and complexities in comparison to first marriages (Ihinger-Tallman &

Amy Benson, MS, is a doctoral student and Kay Pasley, EdD, is Associate Professor in the Department of Human Development and Family Studies, University of North Carolina at Greensboro, 1104 Stone Building, Greensboro, NC 27412-5001.

[Haworth co-indexing entry note]: "The Effects of Child Support Receipt and Payment on Stepfamily Satisfaction: An Exploratory Study," Benson, Amy, and Kay Pasley. Co-published simultaneously in the *Journal of Divorce & Remarriage* (The Haworth Press, Inc.) Vol. 19, No. 3/4, 1993, pp. 197-220; and: *The Stepfamily Puzzle: Intergenerational Influences* (ed: Craig A. Everett), The Haworth Press, Inc., 1993, pp. 197-220. Multiple copies of this article/chapter may be purchased from The Haworth Document Delivery Center [1-800-3-HAWORTH; 9:00 a.m. - 5:00 p.m. (EST)].

Pasley, 1987; Messinger, 1976; Roberts & Price, 1985; Visher & Visher, 1988).

When two people enter a remarriage the structural organization is different than that of first marriage due to the interaction of different family systems (Ganong & Coleman, 1989; Messinger, 1976). Consequently, members are often surprised at the adjustments required in remarriage around children, ex-spouses, and finances (Ganong & Coleman, 1989; Goetting, 1982; Messinger, 1976).

While much of the literature has addressed the adjustment process and problems when children are a part of remarriage, few have addressed financial issues in remarriage. Highlighting the likely strain caused by financial issues, Messinger (1976) reported that remarried couples ranked difficulty with finances second only to children in a list of problem areas.

For many remarried families, child support reflects the combined problematic nature of children and finances. A divorced person who has children typically has some financial obligation or tie to them, regardless of whether they live in the same household. Generally, remarriage does not legally terminate those financial responsibilities. In the remarried family not only is parental authority often shared between two households, but financial maintenance also may be divided between the nonresidential and residential parent.

Where the stepparent fits into the financial maintenance of stepchildren is unclear, and couples may have different and conflicting perceptions on how to manage their complex financial responsibilities and resources. Consequently, several issues in regard to child support are likely to arise with remarriage. It may be that conflict arises over the lack of consistent child support payments, or it may be that conflict arises over feelings of pressure and resentment generated by the financial demands of two families (Ramsey, 1986; Robinson, 1984). Furthermore, remarriage by either parent may act to mediate the equity considerations around child support payments. The result may be changes in the nature of payment or payment may cease altogether.

The child support literature has focused on the lack of payment compliance and the subsequent impact of noncompliance on female-headed households and AFDC (Christensen, Dahl, & Rettig, 1990; Teachman, 1990; Weitzman, 1985). The establishment and enforcement of child-support obligations is a difficult problem for state and federal governments, and concerns about who should be financially obligated to support stepchildren can be a source of disagreement for remarried couples (Giles-Sims & Urwin, 1989). Child support links two former households, increasing the complexity of the remarried family structure and possibly creating role conflict (Clingempeel & Brand, 1985).

Realizing that a substantial number of people live in stepfamilies (Glick, 1989) and the challenges facing remarried families, the study of the impact of child support on the remarried family is warranted. The study reported here examined the effect of child support receipt and payment on stepfamily adjustment. The study also sought to answer three questions: (a) Do child support payments change with remarriage? (b) What is the nature of change? (c) What other variables (e.g., education, number of children, income) are related to child support compliance?

RELEVANT LITERATURE

Families operate as systems; they have rules, role functions, and boundaries which keep them functioning. The stepfamily is different from first families in that different interacting family systems and subsystems are created with remarriage at the same time when the need to establish new family rules and role functions occurs. For the stepfamily there may be financial obligations to others outside the new couple system and ties to nonresidential children. Hence, child support is likely to create continued interaction between systems and potentially confused, overlapping roles, rules, and boundaries in the new family. If confusion is prolonged, family stress, conflict, and dysfunction can occur; thus, the family must work to successfully integrate the two units (Boss & Greenberg, 1984; Weston & Macklin, 1991).

Key Problems in Stepfamilies: Children and Money

Nearly 60% of remarried couples have custody of a child from a previous marriage of one spouse, and 20% generally have nonresidential children (Glick, 1991). When there are children present, the chance for marital dissolution is slightly increased (Ganong & Coleman, 1989). Children act as a link between the former, ex-spouse household and the remarried household (Jacobson, 1987). Movement between households can result in unclear boundaries and lead to confusion regarding the rights and duties of family members.

In addition to children, research has confirmed that remarried couples are challenged by financial issues and economic problems (Albrecht, Bahr, & Goodman, 1983; Ganong & Coleman, 1989). While evidence shows that financial issues are a major source of marital discord, little is known about the financial practices of remarried couples and the effects of these practices on the quality of familial relationships. It has been suggested that problems stemming from financial issues may be a result of attempting to combine two households, demands imposed by ties to a previous family, and needing to find suitable ways to handle two economies (Albrecht, 1979; Dahl, Cowgill, & Asmundsson, 1987; Ihinger-Tallman & Pasley, 1987; Lown & Dolan, 1988; Messinger, 1976). For the remarried family, it is possible that the perception of being a self-sufficient unit has been altered by the need to confer with the ex-spouse regarding visitation, holidays, and child support (Walker & Messinger, 1979). This is compounded when both spouses in the remarried family have children from previous marriages, requiring both affection and economic resources to flow to another family unit.

Child support subsumes issues regarding children and money. As such, child support can represent fertile ground for conflict in remarriage. No clear guidelines exist for dealing with the financial problems remarried couples may face, such as balancing responsibilities between financial support of the current and former family (Ramsey, 1986). Given the likelihood of a stepparent simultaneously having to support two households, guilt feelings over divided loyalties may be common, and greater opportunities for disagreement and strain among family members can result (Nelson & Nelson, 1982).

In an early examination of the legal responsibilities of stepparents, Kargman (1983) noted that many stepfathers voluntarily contribute to the support of stepchildren during marriage while discontinuing support for their biological children. Often stepparents contribute support because child support from the nonresidential parent is absent or unreliable. As a result, economic strain on the remarried couple can occur (Goetting, 1982; Lown, 1984).

Family law does not provide clear rules that specify the rights and responsibilities of the stepparent-child relationship (Mahoney, 1984). As such, a stepparent may be ambivalent about occupying the family provider role without having other typical parental rights.

A primary question in much of the child support literature is: Should the stepparent be considered a legal resource for stepchildren? In interviews with 101 divorced fathers, Tropf (1984) found that 35% of his sample believed that the stepfather should be the primary financial provider to the stepchildren, and 18% felt they should share the provider role. Yet, in the view of The Child Support Enforcement Program, financial support should be provided by the biological father/parent (Ramsey, 1986). The available literature on child support and remarriage reveals contradictory evidence regarding the effects of remarriage on such payments. While the marital status of the father has been found to have no effect on payment, the mother's remarriage has been found to negatively affect her receipt of child support (Cassetty, 1978; Hill, 1988; Peterson & Nord, 1990).

Several interpretations for this finding have been offered. First, Cassetty (1978) suggested that the father's remarriage may reflect the level of importance he places on family life and a greater sense of family responsibility. On the other hand, ceased or reduced payments with the residential mother's remarriage was suggested as an indicator of the reduced sense of family obligations by another man replacing him in the provider role (Hill, 1984). Hill also proposed that equitable treatment becomes a factor when either parent remarries. For example, each dollar given to former family means a dollar less for the new family. As well, remarriage of the residential parent raises equity considerations regarding increased financial resources from a new spouse and how continued support will be allocated to the children. Lastly, Tropf (1984) suggested that pressure from the ex-wife to reduce or abandon his parental obligations upon her remarriage may be a reason for the decrease in payment.

Emphasizing the many inconsistencies and opinions regarding this issue, Haskins (1988) examined fathers' view of child support. He found that fathers denied (a) having a new family or believed that (b) the ex-wife did not need money as reasons for delinquent child support payments. However, others have found that many fathers are delinquent in paying (Teachman, 1990), particularly when children are present in a father's remarriage (Wallerstein & Huntington, 1983). A new wife may resent support being given to an ex-spouse and nonresidential children, especially if *her* ex-spouse fails to pay child support or if she was not previously married (Dahl et al., 1987; Lown & Dolan, 1988). Thus, it is probable that support payments decline with the father's remarriage due to his assuming responsibilities for a second family (Furstenberg, Nord, Peterson, & Zill, 1983). In fact Buehler, Hogan, Robinson, and Levy (1986) found that remarried women whose ex-spouse had not remarried reported higher economic well-being than those whose ex-spouse had remarried. They concluded that this finding highlights the complexity of linked families and raises the difficult question of to whom the remarried man owed the majority of his resources–his former spouse or his newly formed family.

Factors Affecting Compliance. Besides the remarriage of ex-spouses, many other factors are believed to be related to child support compliance. Demographic variables such as race, educational level, employment status, and income have all been examined, yielding mixed results (Braver, Fitzpatrick, & Bay, 1991; Hill, 1984; Peterson & Nord, 1990; Teachman, 1990; U.S. Census, 1986). As well, family/marital factors have been studied in relation to child support compliance. Examples of these variables include number of children, length of prior marriage, and parental contact with nonresidential children (Chambers, 1979; Dudley, 1991; Furstenberg et al., 1983; Grief, 1986; Teachman, 1990). It also has been noted that not knowing how or what the monetary support was being spent on was a factor in fathers' delinquent payment (Nuta, 1986; Wright & Price, 1986). While these findings are limited to divorced families, little evidence is available regarding how these same variables affect compliance following remarriage.

Stepfamily Adjustment

Assuming Turkel (1988) and Nuta (1986) were correct in suggesting a couples' financial arrangement serves as a symbol or reflection of the marital state, it is likely that the incoming/outgoing child support arrangement also may influence family and/or marital adjustment. In one of the few studies to examine this hypothesis, Giles-Sims (1984) assessed the relationship between parental role sharing, feelings of affect between households, and the stepfamily environment. She classified 35 stepfamilies into one of four developed typologies: cooperative, hostile, indifferent, and resentful. She found that those cooperative couples had the most optimal family environment, characterized by the highest levels of cohesion and the lowest level of conflict. These families reported a high degree of contact with the nonresidential parent, *few problems with visitation and child support*, and positive feelings and appreciation toward the nonresidential parent. Those families who had the most negative stepfamily environment, the hostile group, were defined by a high degree of contact with the ex-spouse, problems with child support/visitation, and negative feelings toward the ex-spouse. The remaining stepfamilies were independent of the outside parent. These couples reported being relieved or indifferent to lack of contact and child support and fell between the high and low scores on cohesion and conflict. Because child support was included within the larger measure of parental contact and only 16 wives received child support in the study, it was impossible to ascertain the degree to which child support alone influenced the stepfamily environment.

METHOD

Subjects

Data for this study were from a larger project on remarried couples (Edmundson & Pasley, 1985). Participants for the study were obtained from the Fayette County, Kentucky, marriage license records. To be considered eligible for participation, remarried couples had to meet three criteria: (1) At least one spouse had to have been remarried, (2) The marriage was intact at the time of contact and had occurred between 1980 and 1985, (3) The couple resided in Fayette County and their name appeared in the 1985 telephone directory.

From the list of potential subjects, a random list of 698 households was generated. An introductory letter was mailed to each household, explaining the study along with two copies of the questionnaire and return envelopes. The procedure followed an adapted form of Dillman's Total Design Method (Dillman, 1978). The adaptation was that the final contact consisted of a telephone call rather than contact through registered mail. Of the 698 couples solicited for participation, 336 did not satisfy the criteria (e.g., they were separated, divorced, or had remarried their prior spouse, or they could not be reached by mail or telephone). Information on nonrespondents was not available. The final response rate was 46.8% or 294 individuals. For the present study the responses from only those who reported they received or paid child support were included in the analysis ($n = 74$) or 25% of the sample.

Description of Participants

The primarily white, protestant subsample consisted of 38 males and 36 females. For over 50% of both males and females in the sample the current marriage represented a remarriage for both spouses. Prior marriages were most likely to have ended by divorce rather than death of a spouse. The average age of participants was 39.5 years for men and 33.12 years for women. The length of current marriage for both groups was approximately equal, almost 4 years. However, the mean length of prior marriage for men was 10.5 years (range: 12-396 months) compared to only 6.7 years (range: 2-168 months) for women. Both groups averaged slightly over 3 years between marriages.

All of the men and slightly less than half the women (47.1%) were employed full time. The remainder of the women worked part time (29.4%), were homemakers (17.6%), or were unemployed (5.9%). Regarding highest level of education, about 68% of the women compared to 58% of the males reported having completed some high school or less. In addition, 32.3% of the females and 30.6% of the males completed some or all of college. For males the mean income was $40,000 to $49,999 and for females it was $30,000 to 39,999.[1]

Measures

The measures used were general items regarding child support and compliance. To determine child support compliance, two questions were asked: "What is the total amount you are supposed to receive/pay each month? How much do you actually receive/pay?" The dollar amount the subjects reported paying or receiving as child support was subtracted from the amount they reported they were supposed to pay or receive. If the dollar amount was calculated to be 0 or greater, then subjects were considered to be in compliance. Noncompliance occurred if the result was a negative amount. Additional items provided information about court orders for receipt and payment of child support and asked, "Are you under court order to pay/receive child support? How many children have court orders for support? About how many months do you receive/pay support? About how many months each year do you receive/pay the *full* amount due?" Those who received their awarded child support are referred to as *compliant receivers,* while those who did not receive their court awarded child support are identified as *noncompliant receivers.*

To assess whether child support had changed with remarriage, subjects were asked: "Have there been any changes in the court order since your marriage to your current spouse? Have there been any changes in the child support you actually receive? Have there been any changes in the child support payments you make since your marriage to your current spouse?" In addition, to ascertain the nature of such changes, another question asked, "What changes have occurred?" Responses included "more support," "less support," "more/less consistent," "terminated."

Other questions of interest asked about purchases made with the child support and the frequency of non-residential children's visitation. Also, certain information regarding demographic characteristics was obtained. This information included: length of marriage to current spouse, length of marriage to ex-spouse, current employment status, total family income in 1985, children's age, number of children in the family, level of education, and ethnic orientation.

Stepfamily adjustment, the dependent variable, was conceptualized as one's satisfaction with family functioning. Two items were included to assess this variable. The Family Satisfaction Scale (Olson & Wilson, 1985) assessed satisfaction with family cohesion and adaptability as conceptualized by the Circumplex Model (Olson & McCubbin, 1983). Respondents' responses range from extremely dissatisfied (1) to extremely satisfied (5), with higher scores indicating greater satisfaction.

Test-retest reliability reported $r = .75$. In addition, the Cronbach alpha coefficients were reported as .85 for the cohesion and .84 for the adaptability subscales, with the total scale having a Cronbach alpha of .92 (Olson & Wilson, 1985).

A second assessment of satisfaction was obtained from the single, subjective item which asked, "Overall which of the following words best describes how happy you are with your family right now?" Responses range from "extremely unhappy" to "perfect"; again high scores indicated more happiness.

Data Analysis

Because some respondents were married couples, all analyses controlled for gender. Based on the individual answers from the respondents, males and females were categorized as representing stepfamilies which paid child support and stepfamilies which received child support. Responses were first analyzed with frequency counts to describe the following: (a) those who received and paid child support, (b) those whose receipt, payment, and/or court order had changed since remarriage, and (c) the nature of the change (e.g., more, less, terminated, etc.). Next, *t*-tests were used to examine differences between level of adjustment for respondents who reported paying and receiving child support and those who received at least what they were ordered to (compliant receivers) with those who received less than what was ordered (noncompliant receivers). Chi-square analyses and *t*-tests also were used to test for significant differences between payers and receivers and compliant and noncompliant receivers of child support on certain variables (e.g., education, ethnicity, length of prior marriage, child's age, income, frequency of visitation, etc.).

RESULTS

Frequency counts suggested that of the 38 men and 28 women who responded, 87% of the men and 25% of the women were court ordered to *pay* child support. Of the 26 men and 36 women who responded to the question regarding receipt of child support, 21% of the men and 81% of the women were under court order to *receive* child support. None of the subjects were found to be both paying and receiving child support.

Those Who Paid Child Support

When asked how many children they were responsible for paying support toward, the majority of the males (69%) and all females owed child support for only one child. The average amount of child support the fathers and mothers were ordered to pay was $261.55 and $252.63, respectively. The mean amount the men in this sample reported to actually be paying was $284, with the women payers reporting slightly more ($288.57). Over 90% of both males and females reported paying child support all 12 months in the full amount.

Those Who Received Child Support

Similarly, for the majority of males and females who received child support, support was ordered for only one child. The average amount the males were supposed to receive was $214.38, while the actual amount they reported receiving was $150.71. The females reported they were supposed to receive an average amount of $230.39, but the average they reported actually receiving was $166.08. The consistency of receipt of child support for both men and women ranged from receipt all 12 months in the full amount to never receiving their child support or never receiving it in the full amount.

Changes in Child Support After Remarriage

Payments Made. As Table 1 indicates, approximately one third of the 33 paying males in the sample responded that changes occurred in the child support they paid following remarriage. Of the 10

Table 1

Changes in Child Support Since Remarriage and Nature of Change

Group		Payment Changed	Nature of Change			
			More	Less	Less Consistent	More
Payers						
Men	n = 33	11 (33.0%)	7	3	--	
Women	n = 10*	3 (30.0%)	2	--	--	
Receivers						
Men	n = 11*	3 (27.3%)	1	2	--	
Women	n = 29	10 (34.5%)*	3	3	2	
Court Order						
Men	n = 19*	5 (26.3%)	--	2	--	
Women	n = 31*	9 (29.0%)	6	2	--	

* Denotes inconsistent n's.

women who answered, slightly fewer (30%) indicated changes in their payments.

Payments Received. Results from the question asking about changes in the child support received showed that of the 11 men who answered, the majority (73%) reported no changes had occurred. Of the 29 women who reported receiving child support, approximately one half said there had been no change and 34% reported change occurred.

Changes in the Court Order. Of the men in this sample, 37% reported no change had occurred in their court order following remarriage while 13% reported some change. For women, 61% reported no change while 25% reported some change since remarriage.

The Nature of the Change. Frequencies counts indicated payment had increased and decreased among those who reported change in child support. These results also appear in Table 1. Looking at both men and women, the majority of those who responded reported paying more child support after their remarriage.

Of those receiving child support and who reported changes in the amount they received, only one man received more and two men received less. For the 10 responding females, 30% received more,

30% received less, 20% reported less consistent payments, 10% received more consistent payment since remarriage. Regarding changes in the court order, two of the five men who responded were ordered to receive less support. Of the nine women who reported a change in their court order, most (67%) were ordered to receive more support.

Variables Differentiated Child Support Compliance or Paying/Receiving

The data suggested that for about 41% of the 29 women who had an award for child support, the ex-spouses were reported to be noncompliant in paying. The remaining women (48%) indicated they received what they were supposed to receive. For males, data were available on only seven men who reported receiving child support. Approximately 43% reported receiving what they were supposed to, and 57% received less than was court ordered.

Because analyses revealed no subjects to be noncompliant in paying child support, only those who received child support were used in further analyses. *T*-tests and chi-square analyses were performed to determine significant differences between those who received what they were supposed to and those who did not (their prior spouse was designated as noncompliant). These two groups were compared on the following variables: frequency of visitation, income, education, number of children, length of current marriage, length of marriage to ex-spouse, time between marriages, employment status, how child support was used, and occupational title.

Three of the 10 variables significantly differentiated between the compliant and noncompliant groups for women: frequency of child's visitation (t-test $= -7.00$, df $= 2.00$, $p = .020$), family income (t-test $= -2.30$, df $= 18.67$, $p = .033$), and length of marriage to ex-spouse (t-test $= -3.06$, df $= 12.29$, $p = .010$). Women who were receiving at least what was court ordered reported more frequent visitation by children living outside the home, having higher income, and being married almost 5 years longer in their prior marriage than did those women whose ex-spouse was noncompliant in paying child support. Analyses on the same 10 variables showed no significant differences between men whose ex-spouse was compliant and those whose ex-spouse was noncompliant in paying child support.

In asking this question the intention was to determine which of the variables differentiated the two groups: compliant receivers and noncompliant receivers. However, since few significant differences were found between groups, further analysis was not pursued.

Child Support and Stepfamily Adjustment

Comparisons of stepfamily adjustment were made between the payers and receivers of child support. Also, comparisons were made between the compliant and noncompliant receivers of child support. Interestingly, when comparing the mean scores from this sample with the reported norms for the satisfaction scale, the majority of this sample scored below the 10th percentile. The norm was a score of 47.0 (Olson & Wilson, 1985). The participants in the present study had a mean satisfaction score of 34.66 for men and 33.53 for women, suggesting very low family satisfaction with the cohesion and adaptability of their current family for both payers and receivers.

Analyses of both males and females revealed no significant differences between the payers and receivers on family satisfaction or happiness (Satisfaction: males, t-test = .63, df = 12.30, p = .54; females, t-test = .89, df = 32, p = .378. Happiness: males, t-test = 9.40, df = 35, p = .695; females, t-test = .19, df = 34, p = .85). However, mean scores on the single-item happiness measure indicated that subjects were generally "happy" to "very happy" with their family situation at the time of the data collection. As expected, satisfaction and happiness scores were positively correlated (men r = .7054, women r = .5533).

In addition, the results of the analyses comparing the child support receivers who received what was ordered (compliant receivers) and those whose ex-spouse was reported to be *noncompliant* indicated no significant differences on satisfaction and happiness for either the men or women in this sample. Comparing mean scores of the two groups, both men and women who received what they were supposed to had slightly higher family satisfaction although not significantly higher.

DISCUSSION

Recall that for the majority child support payments reported did not change following remarriage. This finding is consistent with that of prior studies (Furstenberg & Nord, 1985; Seltzer, Schaeffer & Charng, 1989). This may suggest that for persons who elect to remarry the pattern of financial responsibility develops during the single-parent phase and remains stable.

The majority of those who paid child support and reported the payments changed following remarriage, typically reported paying more. For males, this finding is consistent with that of other research. It has been suggested that when nonresidential fathers remarry, payment tends to improve possibly due to the greater importance placed on family life and responsibilities to prior family (Cassetty, 1978). Payment by remarried nonresidential mothers has not been the focus of past research, but the same reasoning might apply. In fact, for women remarriage often provides greater economic resources on which to draw.

For the few who did report paying less, it could be that child support payments were reduced because of simultaneously providing support to two families (Furstenberg et al., 1983; Wallerstein & Huntington, 1983). Also, it may be that a new spouse resents the ties to a prior family and consciously or unconsciously pressures the parent to discontinue his/her payment as an indicator of commitment to the new marriage.

Despite some subjects reporting paying less child support, no subjects reported paying below what was ordered. Thus, for this sample reductions in payment did not result in what was categorized as noncompliant behavior. In addition, the payers of child support in this study had higher incomes than did the receivers. Perhaps for those paying child support having an adequate income for both families was not problematic.

For the receivers, slightly over half reported receiving less or less consistent payments since their remarriage. U.S Census data (1985, 1986) indicated that of those receiving child support, only about half receive the full amount due them. In addition, several studies have indicated that the remarriage of women negatively affects the receipt of child support (Cassetty, 1978; Hill, 1988; Peterson & Nord, 1990). The current finding is congruent with earlier findings. It may be that when a woman remarries, the nonresidential father views the stepfather as replacing him in the provider role and/or feels it is the stepfather's responsibility to support the children (Hill, 1984; Tropf, 1984).

For the men who reported receiving less, reduced payments may represent resentment on the part of the ex-spouse toward the new wife. Child support may have been an expression of her power in the ex-spousal relationship and may have served as a means to punish an ex-spouse. Although this is speculative, it is in accordance with other scholars (Dolan & Lown 1985; Grief, 1986).

Regarding *changes in the court order for receiving child support,* an interesting point of difference was found. Females reported the court ordered more child support to be received. For those men who responded, 40% reported they were ordered to receive less child support. Although the 40% represents very few cases, these results are interesting in the light of the fact that the husband's income was most often used to support children in the home. This may imply that, in addition to receiving less child support, the new wife's income also may be used in the support of children in the home. As such, the family economies in these cases may be strained.

Regarding the findings of court reductions in the amount males received, a new spouse's income may have been viewed as decreasing the need for payment by the nonresidential mother. On the other hand, a judge may conclude that if the male could assume the responsibility for a new family, he could be the sole financial provider for his residential children also. However, for women it may be that the nonresidential husband also was remarried. Assuming his spouse worked, the court may presume he could afford more child support due to dual-wage earners regardless of new family obligations.

Regarding the factors associated with support compliance for women, frequency of visitation was significantly related to receipt of child support. Women who received child support were more likely to have more frequent contact with children living outside the stepfamily household. Several interpretations are plausible. Some mothers may have split custody of biological children residing elsewhere while others reported the visitation of stepchildren. Under conditions of child support receipt, it may be that split custody or stepfamilies which have both residential and nonresidential children feel encouraged to continued contact with the nonresidential children. They also may represent coparental relationship characterized by greater cooperation between the biological parents which is evident in the frequent visitation and child support compliance. It also may indicate a greater emotional involvement with and orientation toward "family" in general or children elsewhere on the part of these participants. However, it is beyond these data to test such hypotheses.

Those women who received their court-ordered child support had a significantly higher income. This was not surprising given that other studies (Furstenberg & Nord, 1985; Teachman, 1990) and reports from the U.S Bureau of Census (1986) indicated child support awards and receipt are more likely for women with higher incomes. They may be more able to afford legal counsel to negotiate a better settlement, or with higher income these mothers are more likely to invest more in their children (Teachman, 1990). The latter is in line with fathers' feelings that inappropriate spending of child support by the mother is grounds for not paying (Wright & Price, 1986).

For women, length of prior marriage also was found to be significantly related to compliance in receiving child support. Those women who received child support were married significantly longer to their ex-spouse than were women who did not receive child support. Duration of first marriage may be one measure of the time and emotional investment fathers made in a marriage prior to divorce. Such investment may increase their motivation to provide child support (Teachman, 1990; Chambers, 1979).

Nonsignificant results were found for the other variables (education, number of children, length of current marriage, length of time between marriages, occupational status, employment status, and what was bought with child support). These findings only add to the inconclusive results of prior studies. It may be that these demographic characteristics are less salient indicators of those receiving child support than for those who pay child support. Characteristics of the payer, as well as his/her orientation to family, are known to influence child support compliance (Braver et al., 1991; Grief, 1986). However, no information on the ex-spouse was available.

For men, no significant differences on any of the 10 variables were found. The sample size (7 men) did not permit valid statistical comparisons. Although demographic and marital factors are considered the major correlates of child support receipt for women and payment for men (Dudley, 1991; Grief, 1986), it is not known whether these factors apply to males who reported receiving child support.

Regarding child support and stepfamily satisfaction, differences in level of satisfaction were found between (a) those who paid and those who received child support and (b) those who received and those who did not receive child support. This finding and the general low level of satisfaction for the sample were somewhat surprising. Several interpretations are possible. For example, the data indicated that the sample was somewhat over representative of those paying and receiving child support. According to the U.S Bureau of the Census (1987), the percentage of nonresidential fathers who paid child support was approximately 61%, as compared to 86.8% of the men in this sample. Estimates from prior studies revealed that anywhere from 14% to 59% of nonresidential mothers are ordered to pay child support, with 25% of the women in the present study paying. In addition, as reported earlier, it was estimated that 60% of residential mothers in the U.S. have a child support award (U.S. Bureau of Census, 1987). Of the mothers in this study approximately 80% reported awards. However, for men, the 31% receiving child support in the current study represents more than the estimated 13%. These differences could reflect some individuals reporting for their spouses rather than for themselves; the figures would indicate over-reporting. However, it is beyond the scope of these data to determine over-reporting.

A second interpretation stems from the findings regarding the demographic characteristics of the sample. The sample was a predominately white, protestant, middle-class group who generally had some high school or a college education. These characteristics alone suggest the sample is not representative.

A final interpretation stems from the self-report nature of the data. It may be inaccurate, as fathers are known to over-report and mothers under-report such figures (Braver et al., 1991).

Family satisfaction did not differ significantly between payers and receivers. In the present study, the majority of the payers were males and for about half of the subjects the second wife also had children. It could be that spouses emphasize the importance of child support. In such cases where new spouses encourage payment, that payment less likely affects family satisfaction, as it is viewed as a responsibility and obligation despite possible financial difficulties.

Several explanations can be offered for the finding of no significant differences between those who were compliant and noncompliant receivers. The literature has suggested that couples may feel differently or have mixed feelings about child support. Some couples are indifferent to the lack of contact and child support from an ex-spouse, while others appreciate or exert pressure on ex-spouses to reduce their parental obligations when remarriage occurs (Giles-Sims, 1984; Tropf, 1984). Individuals who received child support may include (a) those who are indifferent to their receipt of child support, (b) those who wish or prefer no involvement with the ex-spouse in terms of child support and/or contact, and (c) those who are bothered by their ex-spouse's noncompliant payment of child support. Inability to discriminate these groups might mask differences in the groups in this study.

In addition, it may be that the particular outcome measure here (satisfaction) is not affected by the receipt or payment of child support. Other outcomes might be more readily affected, such as family stress or financial well-being. In the present study, perception of economic adequacy was significantly affected by the receipt of child support. The inconsistent or absent child support likely results in perceived economic strain (Goetting, 1982).

Another possibility is that child support in and of itself does not affect stepfamily functioning. Rather it may interact with other variables to negatively influence family satisfaction. For example, it may be the amount of contact with the ex-spouse around issues of child support and custodial/visitation agreements which affects family satisfaction. On the other hand, it may be that different variables than those examined here are responsible for the overall low family satisfaction found. Recall that remarried families face many complexities. It could be that problems with children, the number of members in the new family, other financial issues, or the general balancing of first and second family responsibilities work together or alone to create the low levels of satisfaction (Pasley & Ihinger-Tallman, 1982). It may be that financial and emotional issues around child support per se, rather than the paying or receiving of child support, contributes to low satisfaction. Given that over half of the total sample was found to be paying child support, it is possible that the financial responsibility to the previous family may have created competing demands for resources and mixed feelings over where primary responsibilities should lie (Nelson & Nelson, 1982).

On the average these couples were married less than 4 years. Research has indicated lower satisfaction, lower cohesion, and higher marital instability in the early years due to the structural complexity in remarriage and expectations of having an instant, close family (Weston & Macklin, 1990; Visher & Visher, 1988). As such, stepfamily members may need to work to clarify roles and patterns of interaction with first families around child support and economic responsibilities. Given more time, the stepfamily may work out and discover ways to operate and deal with child support issues which promote greater satisfaction.

CONCLUSIONS

The present study incorporated a number of suggestions which have been made in the literature regarding studies on child support. Despite the lack of significant findings, several points are important and worthy of attention. First, these families were not satisfied with the closeness of their family or how adaptable they perceived the family to be. Exploration of additional variables which may affect stepfamily adjustment is important as well as the consideration of the possible unconscious harboring of bad feelings regarding child support. This may be best untangled using a different research methodology such as interviews. In addition, since the findings suggest that the payment and receipt of child support do not directly influence satisfaction and happiness, it would be an important next step to examine how *perceptions* of child support affect family adjustment rather than reported behaviors. Increasingly perception is conceptualized as being an important factor affecting behavioral outcome (McCubbin & Thompson, 1987).

Given the limitations of the data, replication of the current study with a larger sample and additional questions on child support, reports from the nonresidential parent, and the ex-spouse relationship would help to clarify the present results. In addition, given that past research in the area of child support has been somewhat inconclusive, further research is warranted to determine whether and how various factors influence the receipt of child support as well as the direct affects child support has on family functioning. Finally, child support is most often viewed as one means to decrease welfare spending and poverty. These data suggest that child support policies also must be sensitive to their possible effects on the growing number of stepfamilies as well as on life of the nonresidential parent.

NOTE

1. This sample is similar to the general population of Fayette County in terms of level of education. The majority of the population (71.6%) reported having 12 years or more of education and 25.6% reported having 16 years or more in 1980 (U.S. Bureau of the Census, 1988). However, this sample is unique in its reported level of income. In 1985 the median household income was $28,673 (Center for Business and Economic Research, 1988) compared to the reported family income of this sample at $50,000-$59,000 for the same year.

REFERENCES

Albrecht, S. L. (1979). Correlates of marital happiness among the remarried. *Journal of Marriage and the Family, 41*, 857-867.

Albrecht, S., Bahr, H., & Goodman, K. (1983). *Divorce and remarriage: Problems, adaptations and adjustments.* Westport: Greenwood.

Braver, S., Fitzpatrick, P., & Bay, R. (1991). Noncustodial Parent's report of child support payments. *Journal of Family Relations, 40*, 180-185.

Boss, P., & Greenberg, J. (1984). Family boundary ambiguity: A new variable in family stress theory. *Family Process, 23*, 535-546.

Buehler, C., Hogan, J. M., Robinson, B., & Levy, R. J. (1986). Remarriage following divorce: Stressors and well-being of custodial and noncustodial parents. *Journal of Family Issues, 7*, 405-420.

Cassetty, J. (1978). *Child support and public policy.* Lexington Mass: Lexington Books. Center for Business and Economic Research. (1988). *1988 Kentucky statistical abstracts.* Lexington, KY: University of Kentucky.

Chambers, D. L. (1979). *Making fathers pay: The enforcement of child support.* Chicago, IL: University of Chicago Press.

Christensen, D. H., Dahl, C. M., & Rettig, K. D. (1990). Noncustodial mothers and child support: Examining the larger context. *Family Relations, 39*, 388-394.

Clingempeel, W. G., & Brand, E. (1985). Quasi-kin relationships, structural complexity, and marital quality in stepfamilies: A replication, extension, and clinical implications. *Family Relations, 34*, 401-409.

Dahl, A. S., Cowgill, K. M., & Asmundsson, R. (1987). Life in remarriage families. *Social Work, 32*, 40-44.

Dillman, D. A., (1978). *Mail and telephone survey: The total design method.* New York: John Wiley & Sons.

Dolan, E. M., & Lown, J. M. (1985). The remarried family: Challenges and opportunities. *Journal of Home Economics, 77*, 36-41.

Dudley, J. R. (1991). Exploring ways to get divorced fathers to comply willingly with child support agreements. *Journal of Divorce & Remarriage, 14*, 121-135.

Edmundson M.E., & Pasley, K. (1985). *The effects of financial management on adjustment.* Project funded by the University of Kentucky.

Furstenberg F., & Nord, C. (1985). Parenting apart. Patterns of childrearing after marital disruption. *Journal of Marriage and Family, 47*, 893-904.

Furstenberg, F. F., Jr., Nord, C. W., Peterson, J. L., & Zill, N. (1983). The life course of children of divorce: Marital disruption and parental contact. *American Sociological Review, 48*, 656-668.

Ganong L., & Coleman, M. (1989). Preparing for remarriage: Anticipating the issues, seeking solutions. *Family Relations, 38*, 28-33.

Giles-Sims, J. (1984). The stepparent role: Expectations, behavior, sanctions. *Journal of Family Issues, 5*, 116-130.

Giles-Sims, J., & Urwin, C. (1989). Parental custody and remarriage. *Journal of Divorce, 13*, 65-79.

Glick, P. C. (1989). Remarried families, stepfamilies, and stepchildren: A brief demographic profile. *Family Relations, 38*, 24-27.

Glick, P. C. (1991, October). *Parents with young stepchildren and with adult stepchildren: A demographic profile.* Paper presented at the annual meeting of the Stepfamily Association of America, Lincoln, NB.

Goetting, A. (1982). The six stations of remarriage: Developmental tasks of remarriage after divorce. *Family Relations, 31*, 213-222.

Grief, J. B. (1986). Mothers without custody and child support. *Family Relations, 35*, 87-93.

Haskins, R. (1988). Child support: The men's view. In S. Kamerman & A. Kahn (Eds.), *Child support: From debt collection to social policy* (pp. 306-327). Newbury Park: Sage.

Hill, M. (1984). *PSID analysis of matched pairs of ex-spouses: Relation of economic resources and new family obligations to child support payments.* Unpublished manuscript, Institute for Survey Research, University of Michigan.

Hill, M. (1988, April). *The role of economic resources and dual-family status in child support payments.* Paper presented at the Population Association of America Meetings.

Ihinger-Tallman, M., & Pasley, K. (1987). *Remarriage*. Newbury Park, CA: Sage.

Jacobson, D. S. (1987). Family type, visiting, and children's behavior in the stepfamily: A linked family system. In K. Pasley & M. Ihinger-Tallman (Eds.), *Remarriage and stepparenting: Current research and theory* (pp. 257-272). New York: Guilford Press.

Kargman, M. W. (1983). Stepchild support obligations of stepparents. *Family Relations, 32*, 231-238.

Keshet, H. K. (1980). From separation to stepfamily: A subsystem analysis. *Journal of Family Issues, 1*, 146-153.

Lown, J. M. (1984, November). *Financial management practices of remarried families*. Paper presented at the Western Regional Management Family Economics Educators Conference. Honolulu, HI.

Lown, J. M. & Dolan, E. M. (1988). Financial challenges in remarriage. *Lifestyles: Family and Economic Issues, 9*, 73-88.

Mahoney, M. M. (1984). Support and custody aspects of the stepparent-child relationship. *Cornell Law Review, 70*, 38-78.

Messinger, L. (1976). Remarriage between divorced people with children from previous marriages: A proposal for preparation for remarriage. *Journal of Marriage and Family Counseling, 2*, 193-200.

Nelson, M., & Nelson, G. K. (1982). Problems of equity in the reconstituted family: A social exchange analysis. *Family Relations, 31*, 223-231.

Nuta, V. R. (1986). Emotional aspects of child support enforcement. *Family Relations, 35*, 177-181.

Olson, D. H., & Wilson, M. (1985). Family Satisfaction. In D. H. Olson, H. I. McCubbin, H. Barnes, A. Larsen, M. Muxen, & M. Wilson, (Eds.), *Family inventories: Inventories used in a national survey of families across the family life cycle* (pp. 43-50). St. Paul: Family Social Science.

Pasley, K., & Ihinger-Tallman, M. (1982). Stress in remarried families. *Family Perspective, 16*, 181-186.

Peterson, J. L., & Nord, C. W. (1990). The regular receipt of child support: A multistep process. *Journal of Marriage and Family, 52*, 539-551.

Ramsey, S. H. (1986). Stepparent support of stepchildren: The changing legal context and the need for empirical policy research. *Family Relations, 35*, 363-369.

Robinson, B. (1984). The contemporary American stepfather. *Family Relations, 33*, 381-388.

Roberts, T. W., & Price, S. J. (1985). A systems analysis of the remarriage process: Implications for the clinician. *Journal of Divorce, 9*, 1-25.

Seltzer, J. A., Schaeffer, N. C, & Charng, H. W. (1989). Family ties after divorce: The relationship between visiting and paying child support. *Journal of Marriage and the Family, 51*, 1013-1032.

Teachman, J. D. (1990). Socioeconomic resources of parents and award of child support in the United States: Some exploratory models. *Journal of Marriage and the Family, 52*, 689-699.

Tropf, W. D. (1984). An exploratory examination of the effect of remarriage on child support and personal contacts. *Journal of Divorce*, *7*, 57-73.

Turkel, A. K. (1988). Money as a mirror of marriage. *Journal of the American Academy of Psychoanalysis*, *16*, 525-535.

U.S. Bureau of the Census. (1985). *Child support and alimony: 1983* (Current Population Reports, Special Studies, Series P.23, No. 141). Washington D.C.: U.S. Government Printing Office.

U.S. Bureau of the Census. (1986). *Child support and alimony: 1983 supplemental report.* (Current Population Reports, Series P-23, No. 148). Washington D.C.: U.S. Government Printing Office.

U.S. Bureau of the Census. (1987). *Statistical Abstracts of the United States.* Washington D.C.: U.S. Government Printing Office.

U.S. Bureau of the Census. (1988). *County and cities databook, 1988.* Washington, DC: U.S. Government Printing Office.

Visher, E.B., & Visher, J.S. (1988). Treating families and problems associated with remarriage and step relationships. In C.S. Chillman, E.W., Nunnally, F.M. Cox (Eds.), *Variant family forms*, (Vol. 5, pp. 525-535). Beverly Hills, CA: Sage.

Wallerstein, J. S., & Huntington, D. S. (1983). Bread and roses: Nonfinancial issues related to fathers' economic support of their children following divorce. In J. Cassetty (Ed.), *The parental child support obligation* (pp. 135-155). Lexington MA: Lexington Books.

Walker, K. N., & Messinger, L. (1979). Remarriage after divorce: Dissolution and reconstruction of family boundaries. *Family Process*, *18*, 185-192.

Weitzman, L. (1985). *The divorce revolution: The unexpected social and economic consequences for women and children in America.* New York: Free Press.

Weston, C. A. & Macklin, E. D. (1991). The relationship between former spousal contact and remarital satisfaction in stepfather families. *Journal of Divorce & Remarriage*, *14*, 25-47.

Wright, D. W., & Price, S. J. (1986). Court-Ordered child support payment: The effect on the former-spouse relationship on compliance. *Journal of Marriage and the Family*, *48*, 869-874.

What's Fair? Concepts of Financial Management in Stepfamily Households

David Jacobson

SUMMARY. This paper describes sources of confusion and conflict in the practice and analysis of financial management in stepfamily households. Drawing on published reports and recent research, it examines divergent meanings of the concept of fairness. Understanding the beliefs and values about household finances and inheritance that guide remarried couples sheds light on the decisions they make and on the stresses they experience.

INTRODUCTION

The task of merging and managing finances in stepfamily households poses problems for both participants and observers. Financial issues are a major source of stress and strain in stepfamily households (Messinger, 1976, 1984; Espinoza and Newman, 1979: Visher and Visher, 1979; Goetting, 1982; Pasley and Ihinger-Tallman, 1982; Fishman, 1983; Keshet, 1987, 1988; Lown and Dolan, 1988; Cole-

David Jacobson, PhD, is Associate Professor in the Department of Anthropology, Brandeis University, Waltham, MA 02254.

The author expresses his appreciation to Lois Jacobson, Robert Hunt, and Robert Manners for their assistance in the preparation of this paper.

[Haworth co-indexing entry note]: "What's Fair? Concepts of Financial Management in Stepfamily Households," Jacobson, David. Co-published simultaneously in the *Journal of Divorce & Remarriage* (The Haworth Press, Inc.) Vol. 19, No. 3/4, 1993, pp. 221-238; and: *The Stepfamily Puzzle: Intergenerational Influences* (ed: Craig A. Everett), The Haworth Press, Inc., 1993, pp. 221-238. Multiple copies of this article/chapter may be purchased from The Haworth Document Delivery Center [1-800-3-HAWORTH; 9:00 a.m. - 5:00 p.m. (EST)].

man and Ganong, 1989), yet little is known about how such households manage their finances (see Fishman, 1983:361; Furstenberg, 1987:48-49; Coleman and Ganong, 1989:218).

Models of "common pot" or "two pot" strategies (Fishman, 1983) do not adequately describe the complicated financial arrangements found among couples living in stepfamily households. Although laudable as a pioneering study, Fishman's research has certain limitations. For example, the cross-sectional design of her research makes attributions of causality unwarranted, yet she asserts that different ways of managing household finances "foster" or "encourage" different degrees of "household unity" (1983:359). It is conceivable that the opposite relationship holds: that is, differences in household unity, or in spousal commitment to the marriage, foster or encourage different ways of managing household finances, as Fishman's example of a two pot stepfamily suggests. Longitudinal research is required in order to support such causal claims.

More importantly, studies of common pot and two pot strategies do not analyze the concepts and norms that underlie these patterns, ignoring, for example, differences between principles of allocation such as equality, need, and equity and the ways in which these are understood and utilized by different household members under different circumstances. Drawing on published reports and on data from recent fieldwork, this paper begins to remedy this deficiency by analyzing stepfamily members' beliefs about household finances and the ways in which contextual factors influence their application. Examining the meanings of the ideas people use in choosing between alternative courses of action sheds further light on the decisions they make and on the stresses they experience.

POOLING AND SHARING

Pooling and sharing of financial resources are reported to be primary patterns in American middle class households (Blumstein and Schwartz, 1983; Zelizer, 1989; Whyte, 1990; Millman, 1991). For example, Blumstein and Schwartz (1983:95) found that a majority (between 65% and 75%) of their sample of married couples favored pooling. The researchers do not indicate how many of their respondents were in first marriages or remarried. However, Coleman and Ganong (1989:225) found that a similar percentage (76%) of the stepfamily households they studied were "one pot families," pooling their financial resources. In these research reports, pooling generally refers to a couple's combining their money (and/or other assets) into a common fund, although few studies adequately analyze or present the relevant behavioral evidence. For example, Blumstein and Schwartz report attitudes towards pooling, rather than actual practices. They note (1983:558):

> We prefer to use an item about people's attitudes, rather than whether they do indeed pool, for two reasons: It is very difficult to measure the actualities of pooling, since its mechanics can be very complex. But more important, we feel that couple's actual pooling may be caused by many factors, some of which are not within the partners' control. Some may pool because one partner wants to, even though the other may not.

Just as pooling is not explicitly or systematically analyzed, the meaning of sharing is also problematic. For example, Wilson states that research on the topic of money in the family has focused primarily on the question of whether family resources are "shared" or are something for which there is "competition," yet she observes that little attention has been given to the meaning of the term "sharing" or to what constitutes a "fair share" (1987:19, 20). Lazear and Michael (1988) also note the problematic interpretation of sharing in the allocation of household resources. They state that "Government policies dealing with issues of poverty and family assume the *equal* distribution of family [i.e., household] resources among its members (or at least its adult members)" (1988:13, emphasis added), yet question the basis for that assumption (1988:14). Zelizer, too, emphasizes the unexamined nature of the distribution of household finances:

> . . . questions about how money is divided between family members are seldom even asked. Once money enters the family, it is assumed to be somehow *equitably* distributed among family members, serving to maximize their collective welfare. How much money each person gets, how he or she obtains it, from whom and for what, are rarely considered. And yet . . . the

> distribution of money among family members is often as lopsided and arbitrary as the distribution of national income among families. (1989:353, emphasis added)

In the stepfamily literature, too, the concept of sharing is unexplicated. For example, Fishman implies that equity is the operative principle in a Two Pot economy. That is, under this arrangement, each household member gets "his or her fair share," which is "dependent" upon contributions (1983:359). By contrast, in the common pot pattern, still another principle appears to govern the allocation of resources. In this type of relationship, according to Fishman, "both marital partners contribute all their resources to the household for all family requirements, with an accent on the word all. Distribution of money, goods and services is based on *need,* not on the origin of the resources" (1983:360, emphasis added). And Coleman and Ganong (1989:221) classified their respondents as a one pot marriage if they answered affirmatively to the question "Do you pool your incomes and share all expenses?" and as a two pot marriage if they answered negatively. The researchers did not determine what respondents meant by "sharing" nor their reasons for choosing one or another principle.

EQUALITY, NEED AND EQUITY

In these commentaries, researchers variously describe the allocation of household resources in terms of equality, need, and equity, without specifying the meanings of these concepts. This may cause confusion, especially when these concepts are used loosely and/or interchangeably, since, analytically, they represent different norms or principles of distribution. For example, in describing the feminism of the 1960s and the push of the feminist movement for gender equality, Skolnick quotes the NOW manifesto of 1966: "We do not accept that a woman has to choose between marriage and motherhood on the one hand, and serious participation in industry and/or the professions on the other. . . . We believe that a true partnership between the sexes demands a different concept of marriage, an *equitable* sharing of the responsibilities of home and children and of the economic burdens of their support" (1991:103, emphasis added).

If women earn less than men (which is generally the case) and share the economic responsibilities of domestic life equally, then they are contributing a disproportionally larger share of their incomes; if they contribute in proportion to their incomes, then the partnership is not an equal one. Which of these alternatives is considered to be "fair" depends on the normative principle invoked.

To understand these different rules and how they are applied, it is critical to differentiate between them, especially when people use the same idiom, that of "fairness," to describe different beliefs and/or practices. (The following discussion of the principles and problems of resource allocation draws heavily upon the work of Walster et al., 1978; Hochschild, 1981; and Deutsch, 1985.) Equality is typically defined as the equal distribution of shares among those who receive them. That is, shares are allocated in proportion to the number of recipients, regardless of their contribution to the pool of resources to be distributed. Need, as a principle of allocation, refers to the distribution of shares on the basis of necessity, without regard to contribution. If individuals have (or claim to have) different needs (differing by number, kind, or intensity), or if their needs are defined (by those with power and/or authority) as being different, then satisfying such needs must entail the unequal distribution of resources. Equity is defined as the relative distribution of resources, where each recipient's share is proportional to his or her contribution to them.

The meaning and application of each of these principles may be complicated in several ways. In the case of equality, the distribution of shares will be influenced by the criteria used for defining the shareholding unit and its boundaries and for determining inclusion in it. Each of these may be and usually is culturally variable and socially manipulable. For need, the issues are how it is determined and who determines it, again matters that are socially defined and culturally variable. For equity, too, the valuation of inputs and outcomes is variable and dependent on cultural standards. For example, age, gender, and/or other personal characteristics may be evaluated differently, or given different weights, as inputs and/or outcomes.

Still another source of complexity is that equality, need, and equity are also applied to the contributions to a common fund, not only to distributions from it. For example, people may pool their resources without regard to differences in income (as is usually implied in statements about pooling) or they may contribute equitably, that is, in proportion to income differences. In the latter case, for example, a person who earned twice as much as his or her spouse would contribute twice as much to a common fund, which could then be distributed on the basis of equality, need, or equity. In pooling, the criterion of ability is analogous to that of need, when the latter is defined as a principle of distribution, reflecting neither equality nor equity. As in the case of distribution, the application of these principles with regard to contributions is subject to culturally variable standards of evaluation.

In addition to the complexity and potential confusion caused by the various ways in which contributions and distributions can be determined and assessed, household financial management can be complicated when marital partners embrace different norms. Goetting notes this type of difficulty in her discussion of the tasks faced by those who remarry. She argues (1982:221) that "remarriage unites individuals from two different family systems and two different generations who have learned different and possibly opposing earning and spending habits. The problems involved in integrating such persons into a smooth functioning economic unit may provide a true challenge for all involved" (cf. Lown and Dolan, 1988:79). Of course, the problem of merging people with different beliefs, norms, and values, who come from different family cultures, is not peculiar to remarriage, although it is often exacerbated in stepfamily households.

PROBLEMATICS OF FINANCIAL MANAGEMENT IN STEPFAMILY HOUSEHOLDS

Although holding different norms and/or interpreting the same principle in different ways may cause problems for the members of any household, there are two factors that render financial management in stepfamily households particularly problematic. One is that in remarriages, husband and wife have different interests in and responsibilities to children from previous marriages. That is, in most states, stepparents have no legal obligations to support their stepchildren financially, and, correspondingly, stepchildren have no financial claims on their stepparents (Ramsey, 1986; Fine and Fine, 1992). Thus, partners in a remarriage have different rights and duties with respect to co-resident children, a difference that is often linked to their attitudes towards the issues of financial management.

The other factor that complicates financial management in stepfamily households is the context in which they are located. That is, people may use (or deem appropriate) different principles of distribution depending on their point of reference, whether, for example, they are thinking about the resources of their own household or those of a network of households. Thus, if a single household is taken as the relevant context, and equality as the principle of distribution, then the resources members receive from outside the household (i.e., from other households) are irrelevant, even if consequently the level or amount of resources available to members of the household is unequal. If a network of households is taken as the relevant context, and equality is the desired goal for members of a specific household, then resources received from other households are relevant, even though the principle of equality of distribution from within the household pool may be disregarded, making the operative principle, in effect, one of need and/or equity.

Goetting refers to a situation of this sort (see also Fishman, 1983:365). She writes:

> The problem of resource distribution refers to the issue of how the money should be spent: who should get how much of what is available? For example, if *his* daughter is given ballet lessons, should not *her* son be allowed tennis lessons, even though the sources of support for the two children are quite different? If the resources available to her son from her ex-spouse preclude such tennis lessons, should the stepfather finance such lessons for the sake of equity? (1982:221)

Actually, in this example, it is inaccurate to describe the stepfather's compensating for the differences between the resources available to his daughter and to his stepson as a matter of equity; rather, the relevant principle would be one of equality, that is, the equal treatment of children, without regard to their contributions or to those of their fathers.

This issue is not limited to the relationships between spouses and ex-spouses and children and stepchildren. It also is raised by grandparents who provide different (i.e., unequal) contributions to their grandchildren and stepgrandchildren, who are co-resident stepsiblings (cf. Cherlin and Furstenberg, 1986; Furstenberg, 1987:49).

The problem also applies to household contributions. A couple's contributions to their household expenses may be evaluated quite differently, depending on the way in which context is defined. Take, for example, the situation of a man who is supporting children in two households, from previous and current marriages. If he and his wife have the same incomes, and he puts a lesser amount into their common fund (because he is contributing to another household's pool), their arrangement may seem fair, according to the principle of equity, or unfair, according to one of equality. Of course, it may seem fair to him and unfair to her, since she is in effect supporting his children (her stepchildren) who live in another household (cf. Lown and Dolan, 1988:76-77).

All of these considerations are raised not only in the current management of household resources but also in matters of inheritance, when individuals in a remarriage plan for the future distribution of their financial assets (and other resources). Goody et al. (1976) have noted that the ways in which resources are distributed through inheritance will be connected to different relationships within a family, to different family structures, and to different modes of transmission, including whether or not resources are to be divided equally or unequally among various recipients. Thus, questions of what constitutes a "fair share" for spouses, children, stepchildren, as well as other friends and relatives, are complicated by beliefs about the distributive principle (equality, need, or equity) to be utilized and about the context (single household, network of households) in which it should be applied.

The difficulties that can develop from various combinations of different contributive and distributive principles, on the one hand, and differences in the units to which they are applied, on the other, are evident, although rarely analyzed, in examples found in the stepfamily literature. For instance, Fishman (1983) describes the case of the Becker/Robinsons, a "typical" common pot family (1983:362). At the time they were interviewed, the couple had been living in a stepfamily household for five years, with his two children and her three children. Both husband and wife work full time and they pool their earnings in a joint account, distributing financial resources according to the needs of individual household members (although Fishman does not indicate how such needs are determined or who determines them). Clearly, their contributions and distributions are not based on a principle of equity: the husband contributes 14% more income than does his wife (his salary represents 57% of their common pot), yet she and her children receive 14% more than he and his children, if the distribution of household resources is based on equality (i.e., per capita).

This case raises several unanswered questions about financial management in stepfamily households. For example, Fishman reports (1983:362) that for several months prior to being interviewed, this stepfamily had been living in a home "purchased jointly" by husband and wife, and presumably owned by them as joint tenants. It is unclear, however, which principle would govern the distribution of the house in the event of the death of either or both husband and wife. Under the present arrangement, should the husband die, his wife, as survivor, would own the house outright (if indeed they owned it as "joint tenants"). Should she then die, without remarrying or otherwise providing for his children, her children would inherit the property exclusively, which would be neither equal nor equitable for his children. On the other hand, if they owned the property as "tenants in common," then ownership could have been divided (equally or equitably) and each portion passed on to their respective children.

Alternatively, they could have established a trust (for example, a "Q-tip" or qualified terminable interest property trust) that would avoid this type of problem. This device would enable the surviving spouse to use the house, or the income from its sale, for the remainder of his or her life; when he or she subsequently died, the assets would then be distributed to the beneficiaries specified by the trust, including shares for both sets of children from their former marriages.

Fishman also describes the case of the Marshall/Lintons. Although she classifies this household as a two pot economy, it is essentially a three pot system. Husband and wife each have separate resources and checking accounts, although they both contribute to certain household and personal expenses. The household usually contains five people: husband, wife, and her three sons (ages 8-13). His two girls (a college student and a 16 year old) do not live with him, although the younger child visits every other weekend and on vacations. Her boys visit their father on vacations.

Although the data are incomplete, it seems that they manage their common finances by a combination of norms. Equity is the primary principle. For example, she puts all the child support she receives from her ex-husband into a common pot, drawing on it to buy clothes for herself and her children and food for the household. He puts a much smaller amount into the common pot (one-eighth the amount his wife contributes), "for his share of food and small expenses–drycleaning his clothes, things like that" (1983:364). On the other hand, he owns the house and pays all the "fixed expenses–mortgage, gas, and electric" (1983:364). Thus, it would appear that contributions are relative to available income (he pays child support to his ex-wife and provides tuitions and allowances for his children) and distributions are proportional to contributions. However, their arrangement must be more complicated than that, since Fishman reports that the wife "lamented the time wasted in detailed record-keeping to insure that expenses are *equally* shared" (1983:365, emphasis added). It is not clear which costs are so divided, other than that both are said to "contribute to ordinary entertainment expenses" (1983:365).

Fishman's account of this household also raises several questions. For example, it is not possible to determine which principles the couple are using, since data are not given on his income or his extra-household expenses or on the value attributed (by him and by her) to her contributions "in the form of time for housework and the preparation of meals" (1983:365). Similarly, it is not clear whether or not they take into account the fact that she does not expect to have to pay for her children's education, which she has been told will be paid for by their paternal grandparents. Nor is it certain what will happen when her boys go to college (other than that those costs will be paid for by their father's parents): when they leave the household, what will her contribution be, given that she will not be receiving child support? It is also unclear how he will divide his estate should he cancel their prenuptial agreement. What share of his estate will he assign to his wife and what proportion to his children? For example, if he lived in Massachusetts, and were to die intestate, his wife would get half of his assets and his daughters, the other half (*Massachusetts General Laws Annotated,* 1989), an outcome that would not necessarily be equitable or meet the needs of either spouse or children.

CASE STUDIES: PRINCIPLES AND PATTERNS OF HOUSEHOLD MANAGEMENT

Several case studies, based on ethnographic research in the Boston area, further depict the complexity of financial management in stepfamily households. Much of this information was provided by people who were participants in a stepfamily support group. I regularly observed discussions about financial issues (and other related matters) in this organization during its monthly meetings over a three year period (1986-1989). During that time and since then, I have also talked at greater length with thirty couples and conducted intensive interviews with ten others. All of these people are middle class, in terms of their educations, occupations, and incomes. For the interviews, husband and wife were questioned separately and the information they provided was kept confidential. I asked them about the ways in which they managed current household finances and about their plans for distributing their assets as bequests. More often than not, I was able to get only estimates of resources, incomes, and expenditures, although some informants provided detailed accounts.

The cases are selective in several ways. First, they involve people from a particular geographical, economic, and cultural context who volunteered to participate in discussions about the financial organization of stepfamily households. Second, they represent situations in which both husband and wife work and have incomes. Third, they focus on the problems posed in stepfamily households. In some instances, couples have resolved, or have moved towards resolving, these problems; however, attention is centered on the types of issues that have been or continue to be troublesome. These data do not warrant generalizations about stepfamily households, in

Boston or elsewhere. However, they do indicate how much more complex the issues are and permit a fuller analysis of them, including the beliefs that underlie diverse and not always consistent patterns of behavior.

Case #1

A prominent theme in stepfamily households is the question of what constitutes an equitable division of common expenses. This issue is particularly problematic when partners have unequal resources and/or unequal demands on them. For example, Amy and Alan have been married for two years. (I have changed the names and some other details of the domestic and personal lives of the people involved in order to protect the privacy of informants and to maintain the confidentiality of the fieldwork.) Their household also includes her two children from a previous marriage, who live with them full-time, except for brief visits with their father, and his two children, who live with them part-time, moving on alternate weeks to stay with their mother and stepfather. When they began to live together, Amy and Alan had agreed to contribute to household expenses "equitably," but each has a different view of what that concept means. Amy, who earns about two-thirds as much as her husband (and about 40% of their combined incomes), thinks that they should contribute to household expenses in proportion to their incomes, which is what they currently do.

However, Alan is upset at this arrangement, since his children live with them only half the time that hers do. Accordingly, he thinks that they should contribute to household expenses in proportion to their occupancy. That is, he thinks he should pay 40% of their joint monthly expenses. He bases his conclusion on a formula that reflects the number of people in the house and the amount of time they live there. Thus, he figures that Amy and her children represent 12 parts per month (3 people for 4 weeks) and he and his children represent 8 parts per month (1 person for 4 weeks plus two others for 2 weeks). For him, her children are clearly the point of contention; he says that he would have no problem contributing in proportion to incomes if it were only he and his wife or if his children also lived with them full-time. However, he argues that it is not fair that he provides a larger share of their resources and uses less of them. They do not see a solution to their problem and it is a source of tension between them.

Case #2

The case of Helen and Harry illustrates a variation on this theme. They have been married for six years and have been living in the house that she received as part of her divorce settlement. Her two children live with them full-time; his two children live with them every other weekend and on school vacations. This couple also contributes in proportion to their respective incomes; he earns slightly more than she does. Harry is not troubled by this arrangement. However, he is bothered by another aspect of it that is related to their future plans. When they married, husband and wife agreed that each would transfer their separate assets to their respective children and had wills drawn accordingly. (Each also has a separate insurance policy that designates the other as sole beneficiary.)

The problem is that Harry feels that he is subsidizing his stepchildren's legacy at the expense of that of his children. He thinks that as long as he is contributing to the mortgage payments that he should have a financial interest in the property: he suggests that he should be entitled to half of the house's appreciation since he began living there. Helen disagrees, arguing that Harry would have had to "pay rent" wherever he lived and, moreover, that he is getting "a lot of house" for the amount he contributes. He acknowledges that he would not have as much space if he were paying a like amount in the rental market, although he also points out that he would not need as much and that he would have a choice as to where he lived. He further contends that Helen would have had to pay the mortgage in any case and that his contribution to it benefits her children and not his. They are both distressed by this situation and have attempted to alleviate it by Helen's agreeing to pay for capital improvements and major repairs and maintenance. It is a solution that seems fair to both of them, although neither is particularly pleased by this compromise.

Case #3

In another case, similar to the preceding one, the couple's disagreement turns on the way in which husband and wife conceptualize their investment in the house in which they live. Fay and Frank have been married for almost twenty years. When her first husband died, Fay used the proceeds of his insurance policy as a downpayment on the house in which she now lives with her second husband. Frank has contributed to the mortgage since they married, paying more or less depending on whether or not Fay was earning an income. They have had a common pot economy since they were married and both state that this form of pooling and sharing has been fair. However, they disagree on the issue of who should inherit the house. Frank feels that some (unspecified) share in it should go to his children from his first marriage, since he has helped to pay off a major part of the mortgage. Fay does not accept Frank's premise, arguing, like Helen in the previous example, that his contribution was comparable to rent, but, more importantly, that the house is her children's legacy from their father. She does not describe the house as belonging to her; rather she describes herself as the "custodian" of her children's inheritance. It is an impasse for them: she does not agree with her husband's contention; her position aggravates him. (It is not clear whether he is more upset about the ultimate allocation of the property or about his wife's apparent disregard of his feelings and/or of his children's welfare.) It is not clear if or how they will resolve this issue or what difference it will make if they do not. They have lived with their disagreement on this point for a long time.

Case #4

Another case involves a couple who endorse an equitable sharing of current expenses, but who have disparate beliefs about the ultimate disposition of their assets. Wendy and Bill have been married for three years. She has two children from a previous marriage; he has none. Until recently, her younger child had lived with them. Bill's income is about 10% greater than Wendy's, and they divide common expenses equitably. Both say this is fair, although she describes herself as "vaguely uncomfortable about it" and would prefer to pool their resources. He is not willing to do that, and wants to maintain their current arrangement. However, he does not maintain this position when it comes to questions of inheritance. Aside from small bequests to his parents and siblings, Bill has drawn a will that leaves everything to Wendy. As he put it: "It's really simple when you don't have kids . . . and when you don't have many assets." His decision raises an interesting question: why insist on maintaining separate resources when he leaves practically all of his assets to his wife? The answer seems clear: his attitude towards household finances is based on the possibility of marital dissolution; his will assumes that the marriage will have endured. Wendy, on the other hand, leaves everything to her children, claiming that Bill is "self-sufficient." Neither Wendy nor Bill knows for certain the terms of the other's will.

Case #5

Matters of inheritance pose still other problems, particularly when both husband and wife have children from previous marriages. This is illustrated in the case of Jan and Jim, who have been married for twenty-three years. Jan has one child from her previous marriage and Jim has two children from his. In addition, they have a mutual child. From the beginning of their marriage, they have subscribed to a one pot strategy, pooling their resources and sharing them by need, if not equally. They also agree that the children should inherit equally. However, this does not mean that they plan to divide their assets evenly among the various children. Rather, the divisions they propose reflect their assumptions about the number of their legatees and about what the children are likely to inherit from others.

In what another informant described as the "new family math," Jan and Jim reckon their children differently. She counts their children according to the number each of them has produced. From her perspective, she has two children, one from each of her marriages, and he has three children, one from his current marriage and two from his previous marriage. She concludes that, in this sense, they have five children between them and that, by the principle of equality, each child should receive one fifth of their assets. By this method of calculation, their common child would receive 40%, because that child would be entitled to a one-fifth share from each of them; Jan's child from her first marriage would get 20% and Jim's children from his first marriage would get 40%, each receiving 20%. In contrast to his wife, Jim considers that they have four children between them, and, according to his view, each should receive one fourth of their assets. This would mean that the two children from his first marriage would get 50% of their estate, whereas the child of their current marriage would receive 25% of the pool, an amount equal to what would go to the child of her first marriage.

However, neither method of calculation will be the primary determinant of the bequests they will make to their children. Rather, their plan for distributing their assets is influenced by their appraisal of what their children will inherit from sources outside their household. Jim expects that his ex-spouse will have little to leave his children from that marriage and that he will be their sole or primary benefactor. Jan expects that her ex-spouse will provide a substantial legacy to her child from that marriage. These expectations have led Jan and Jim to propose that different shares of their assets be allocated to the various children. That is, they would like all of the children to have equal inheritances, a goal that can be obtained only if they treat them unequally, given the resources available to their other children (i.e., other than their mutual child) from the wider kinship networks in which they are embedded.

CONCLUSIONS

As is evident from the case studies, there are various reasons why a model of common or two pot strategies is not sufficient to analyze and understand the complexity of managing finances in stepfamily households. One is that people typically talk about "fairness" as an ideal of distributive justice, yet attach different meanings to that term. Another is that although husband and wife may contribute to a common fund, they may not draw from it in the same way, if they are guided by different norms of distribution. A third reason is that even when husband and wife endorse the same principle, they may interpret it differently (what is equal for one may be inequitable for the other), or disagree about its implementation, because they apply it to different units (i.e., a single household or a kinship network). A fourth reason is that either husband and/or wife may have one attitude towards meeting current household expenses and another regarding the future allocation of assets by way of inheritance. A fifth is that a couple who supports one principle in theory, may follow another (or others) in practice. Finally, it is not necessarily the case, as Fishman suggests, that spousal trust, or its absence, underlies the choice between the alternatives she describes. Instead, it may be a matter of meeting the obligations of supporting children from previous marriages and/or conserving assets that eventually will be passed on to them.

In short, these data suggest that more discriminating research is required about the financial strategies members of stepfamily households employ and that it include attention to the meanings people attach to ideas such as pooling, sharing, fairness, equality, need, and equity and to how these ideas shape (or are shaped by) practice.

They also raise questions about the relationship between the stress and strain engendered by financial issues and the stability of stepfamily households. It does not appear that such tensions necessarily lead to marital dissolution, since several of the stepfamily couples have been married for a long time. Rather, they may persist unresolved because individuals suppress them (cf. Wilson, 1987) or decide that other aspects of their marriages are more important to them. That is, as in other areas of married life (cf. Berger and Kellner, 1964:13-14; Hess and Handel, 1959:9-10; Keshet, 1988:34), couples may agree to disagree about the ways in which they manage their financial resources. Further research is needed to understand when and how this happens.

REFERENCES

Berger, P. and Kellner, H. (1964). Marriage and the construction of reality. *Diogenes*, *46*, 1-24.

Blumstein, P. and Schwartz, P. (1983). *American couples: Money, work, sex.* New York: William Morrow.

Cherlin, A. and Furstenberg, F. F., Jr. (1986). *The new American grandparent.* New York: Basic.

Coleman, M. and Ganong, L. H. (1989). Financial management in stepfamilies. *Lifestyles: Family and Economic Issues*, *10*, 217-232.

Deutsch, M. (1985). *Distributive justice: A social-psychological perspective.* New Haven: Yale University Press.

Espinoza, R. and Newman, Y. (1979). *Stepparenting.* Rockville, MD: DHEW Publication No. (ADM) 78-579.

Fine, M. A. and Fine, D. R. (1992). Recent changes in laws affecting stepfamilies: Suggestions for legal reform. *Family Relations*, *41*, 334-340.

Fishman, B. (1983). The economic behavior of stepfamilies. *Family Relations, 32*, 359-366.

Furstenberg, F. F. Jr. (1987). The new extended family: The experience of parents and children after remarriage. In K. Pasley and M. Ihinger-Tallman (Eds.), *Remarriage and stepparenting: Current research and theory.* (pp. 42-62).

Goetting, A. (1982). The six stations of remarriage: Developmental tasks of remarriage after divorce. *Family Relations, 31*, 213-222.

Goody, J., Thirsk, J. and Thompson, E. P. (1976). *Family and inheritance: Rural society in Western Europe, 1200-1800.* Cambridge: Cambridge University Press.

Hess, R. and Handel, G. (1959). *Family worlds: A psychosocial approach to family life.* Chicago: University of Chicago Press.

Hochschild, J. L. (1981). *What's fair? American beliefs about distributive justice.* Cambridge: Harvard University Press.

Keshet, J. K. (1987). *Love and power in the stepfamily.* New York: McGraw-Hill.

Keshet, J. K. (1988). The Remarried couple: stresses and successes. In W. R. Beer (Ed.), *Relative strangers: Studies of stepfamily processes* (pp. 29-53).

Lazear, E. P. and Michael, R. T. (1988). *Allocation of income within the household.* Chicago: University of Chicago Press.

Lown, J. M. and Dolan, E. M. (1988). Financial Challenges in Remarriage. *Lifestyles: Family and Economic Issues, 9*, 73-88.

Massachusetts General Laws Annotated. 1989. Volume 31, Chapter 190 (Descent and distribution of real and personal property).

Messinger, L. (1976). Remarriage between divorced people with children from previous marriages: A proposal for preparation for remarriage. *Journal of Marriage and Family Counseling, 2*, 2, 193-200.

Messinger, L. (1984). *Remarriage, a family affair.* New York: Plenum.

Millman, M. (1991). *Warm hearts and cold cash: The intimate dynamics of families and money.* New York: The Free Press.

Pasley, K. and Ihinger-Tallman, M. (1982). Stress in remarried families. *Family perspective, 16*, 181-190.

Ramsey, S.H. (1986). Stepparent support of stepchildren: The changing legal context and the need for empirical policy research. *Family Relations, 35*, 363-369.

Skolnick, Arlene. (1991). *Embattled paradise: The American family in an age of uncertainty.* New York: Basic.

Visher, E. B. and Mary J. (1979). *Stepfamilies: A guide to working with stepparents and stepchildren.* New York: Brunner/Mazel.

Walster, E., Walster, G. W., and Berscheid, E. (1978). *Equity: Theory and research.* Boston: Allyn and Bacon.

Whyte, M. K. (1990). *Dating, mating, and marriage.* New York: Aldine de Gruyter.

Wilson, G. (1987). *Money in the family: Financial organization and women's responsibility.* Brookfield, VT: Gower.

Zelizer, V. A. (1989). The social meaning of money: 'Special monies.' *American Journal of Sociology, 95*(2), 342-77.

(See other side for Costs and Payment Information)

COSTS: Please figure your cost to order quality copies of an article.

1. Set-up charge per article: $8.00
   ($8.00 × number of separate articles) ________
2. Photocopying charge for each article:
   - 1-10 pages: $1.00 ________
   - 11-19 pages: $3.00 ________
   - 20-29 pages: $5.00 ________
   - 30+ pages: $2.00/10 pages ________
3. Flexicover (optional): $2.00/article ________
4. Postage & Handling: US: $1.00 for the first article/
   $.50 each additional article ________
   Federal Express: $25.00 ________
   Outside US: $2.00 for first article/
   $.50 each additional article ________
5. Same-day FAX service: $.35 per page ________
6. Local Photocopying Royalty Payment: should you wish to copy the article yourself. Not intended for photocopies made for resale. $1.50 per article per copy
   (i.e. 10 articles x $1.50 each = $15.00) ________

GRAND TOTAL: ____________

METHOD OF PAYMENT: (please check one)

❑ Check enclosed ❑ Please ship and bill. PO # ____________

(sorry we can ship and bill to bookstores only! All others must pre-pay)

❑ Charge to my credit card: ❑ Visa; ❑ MasterCard; ❑ American Express;

Account Number: ____________ Expiration date: ____________

Signature: ✗ ____________ Name: ____________

Institution: ____________ Address: ____________

City: ____________ State: ____________ Zip: ____________

Phone Number: ____________ FAX Number: ____________

MAIL or *FAX* THIS ENTIRE ORDER FORM TO:

Attn: **Marianne Arnold**
Haworth Document Delivery Service
The Haworth Press, Inc.
10 Alice Street
Binghamton, NY 13904-1580

or FAX: (607) 722-1424
or CALL: 1-800-3-HAWORTH
(1-800-342-9678; 9am-5pm EST)